Judaism, Christianity, Islam,
Hinduism, and Buddhism on

MAKING AN HONEST LIVING

What Do We Owe the Community?

Edited by
JACOB NEUSNER
Bard College

D0206448

With essays by

BRUCE CHILTON
Bard College

CHARLES HALLISEY
Harvard University

BRIAN K. SMITH
University of California, Riverside

TAMARA SONN
College of William and Mary

WADSWORTH
™
THOMSON LEARNING

Australia • Canada • Mexico • Singapore • Spain • United Kingdom • United States

Religion Editor: Peter Adams
Assistant Editor: Kara Kindstrom
Editorial Assistant: Mark Andrews
Marketing Manager: Dave Garrison
Print Buyer: Robert King
Permissions Editor: Joohee Lee
Production Service: Matrix Productions

Text Designer: Karen Thomas
Copy Editor: Jan McDearmon
Cover Designer: Bill Stanton
Cover Image: PhotoDisc
Compositor: R&S Book Composition
Cover and Text Printer: Webcom, Limited

COPYRIGHT © 2001 Wadsworth, a division of Thomson Learning, Inc. Thomson Learning™ is a trademark used herein under license.

ALL RIGHTS RESERVED. No part of this work covered by the copyright hereon may be reproduced or used in any form or by any means—graphic, electronic, or mechanical, including photocopying, recording, taping, Web distribution, or information storage and retrieval systems—without the written permission of the publisher.

Printed in Canada

1 2 3 4 5 6 7 04 03 02 01

For permission to use material from this text, contact us by Web: www.thomsonrights.com
Fax: 1-800-730-2215   Phone: 1-800-730-2214

Wadsworth/Thomson Learning
10 Davis Drive
Belmont, CA 94002-3098
USA

For more information about our products, contact us:
Thomson Learning Academic
Resource Center
1-800-423-0563
http://www.wadsworth.com

International Headquarters
Thomson Learning
International Division
290 Harbor Drive, 2nd Floor
Stamford, CT 06902-7477
USA

UK/Europe/Middle East/
South Africa
Thomson Learning
Berkshire House
168-173 High Holborn
London WC1V 7AA
United Kingdom

Asia
Thomson Learning
60 Albert Street, #15-01
Albert Complex
Singapore 189969

Canada
Nelson Thomson Learning
1120 Birchmount Road
Toronto, Ontario M1K 5G4
Canada

Library of Congress Cataloging-in-Publication Data
Making an honest living: what do we owe the community?/edited by Jacob Neusner; with essays by Bruce Chilton . . . [et al.].
    p.   cm.—(Comparing religious traditions)
    ISBN 0-534-53056-7
    1. Religious ethics—Comparative studies. 2. Work—Moral and ethical aspects.
    I. Title: At head of title: Judaism, Christianity, Islam, Hinduism, and Buddhism on making an honest living.   II. Neusner, Jacob, [1932–]   III. Chilton, Bruce.   IV. Series.
BJ1188.M345 2000
291.5′64—dc21   00-042861

 This book is printed on acid-free recycled paper.

꩜

Contents

～❀～

Preface

Religions not only answer public questions about society, politics, and economics; they also guide individuals in their private lives, as people work their way through life from birth to death. So to make sense of the world in which we live, we compare and contrast the choices religions make. To understand the lives people lead, therefore, we study about the religions they profess and practice together. Here we experiment with what it takes to compare religions. That is because, in our view, to know only one religion is to understand no religion. Comparison alone affords perspective, a clear picture of the choices people make and the settings in which they make them. Each religion forms a coherent whole, the parts of which fit together within a particular rationality. When, as here, we compare the parts of one with the parts of another religious tradition, we gain perspective on the whole of each of those traditions. And since we take up what is to all of us a program of familiar human issues— family, work, and virtue—we deal with what is accessible to us all out of our life's experiences.

To identify the difficulty of comparing religious traditions, take the social order first of all. Religions shape economics, politics, and public policy. In economics, the science of the rational disposition of scarce resources, religions variously define what they mean by "scarce resources." Moreover, they form their own diverse definitions and distinctive conceptions of what we deem "rational," as a comparison between Christian and Buddhist philosophy makes clear. But even where religions concur, the agreement masks difference. Context is everything. Islam and Judaism and Christianity each impose its own prohibition upon usury. But each draws its own conclusions from that prohibition. When we look closely, we see that the comparison yields mostly contrasts.

So too, in politics each frames a doctrine of how religion relates to the state, that is, to the institutions that legitimately exercise violence. They may concur that the state should realize God's purpose. But they do not form a unified consensus upon the consequences of that conviction. For instance, Hinduism and Buddhism may appear to be in agreement in their uneasiness about the use of force by government, and both dream of a nonviolent state based on moral order. But they do not agree on what these dreams say about actual, less-than-perfect governments.

As to the requirements of the good and the just society formed by the faithful, all three frame a theory of "the mystical body of Christ," or "the Jewish People" (meaning the contemporary continuators of the Israel of which Scripture speaks), or "the ummah" or "community of Islam," a theory rich in implications for the social order. So even where religions appear to resemble one another, they turn out to differ.

The distinctions make a difference not only in intangible ways but to the everyday world, because religion shapes public affairs, not only personal proclivities. We may well form an intense, personal relationship with God. That begins in a private moment of encounter. But commonly, the personal preference spills over into public policy. That is why, when we study about religions, comparing and contrasting their positions on a common program, we deal with facts, not only feelings; culture, not only conscience. In two different traditions originating in India, for example, Hinduism and Buddhism, there is an apparent agreement that the ultimate religious goal consists of freedom or liberation from a world of repeated death and rebirth. But because of different conceptions of the true nature of the self in these two traditions, they have not only conceived of the religious goal differently but have also put forward different religious paths leading to the goal—paths that entail different social, economic, and even political consequences.

Whether religions concur or differ on matters of public policy, how we are to interpret their points of intersection is not always clear. People can say the same thing for different reasons, and they can mean different things by the same statement—and so is the case with religions. For understanding a given chapter in the story a religion tells depends on knowing what came before and what will happen next. Indeed, everything in the end makes sense only in the proper context. Hence, even at points of confluence, how are we to compare and contrast the social, political, and economic conceptions of the great religious traditions, when each body of thought focuses upon distinctive historical experience, a very particular context of public life? Therefore what looks alike—affirmations in common—may upon closer examination prove quite different, and difference may well obscure the meaning of points of concurrence.

That is because the work of comparing religions in their public dimensions involves many complications. When we wish to compare one religion with another, doctrines or practices concerning public life pertain to situations we may find alien or beyond all comprehending. What one religion deems weighty another ignores altogether. Church order preoccupies Christians, but structures that transcend the local circumstance of Judaism do not precipitate equivalent conflict. Judaism precipitates debates on "who is a Jew," or "who, and what, is Israel," meaning, we recall, the holy people of which Scripture speaks. But Catholics do not endlessly debate on who is a Catholic. Religions do not select their issues from a single menu; each frames its system in its own distinctive structure, and a common category formation does not accommodate them all. One may compare it to how they serve dim sum in a Chinese restaurant: different food comes on different carts.

So even if they say the same thing, the shared language does not yield the same consequences. That is why it is difficult for purposes of comparison and contrast to set side by side (to give one example) (1) Christian thinking about Church-state relations with (2) Islamic thinking about the same matter and (3) Judaic doctrines, beginning with the Hebrew Scriptures, about God's stake in holy Israel's public life. Christian doctrines of politics emerge from a long history of Western institutions of church and state and their relationships, and Islamic ones from a quite different history altogether, one of rapid expansion in a remarkably brief period. Judaic doctrines take account of political experiences, such as defeat and political disempowerment, that Islam in its formative age never knew. So if Judaism, Christianity, and Islam concur on valuing peace, as they do, or on assigning to the state responsibilities for the moral ordering of society, as they do, that does not mean they concur on much that matters. Even when religions talk about the same things and come to comparable conclusions, the differences in context make it difficult to find a level plane for the purposes of comparing and contrasting what different traditions say about the same matter. A negative example serves. Buddhist emphasis on monasticism and the rejection of family life prevents us from seeing how much South Asian Buddhists share with Hindus in the ethics of family life.

Given the variables and imponderables that religions draw in their wake, we may wonder whether the work of comparison and contrast in the end demands more than it is worth. Out of despair or sheer incredulity, some may retreat into a latitudinarian tolerance, dismissing religions as all right or all wrong—and who cares? For from such an attitude, all rationality fails. We may incline to give up trying to make sense of the world shaped by religions and the affect upon the world of religion. But these choices prove impractical. Religions make a large difference in their social settings, whether Islam in North Africa, the Middle East, India and Pakistan, and Indonesia and Malaysia; or Christianity in Europe and the Western hemisphere; or Hinduism in India; or Buddhism in Southeastern Asia, China, and Japan; or Judaism on its own in the State of Israel and in the Diaspora—and in its influence upon its continuators, Christianity and Islam. So however tentative our effort to understand the difference religion makes, we cannot desist from trying. For to make sense of the religiously and culturally diverse world in which we live, we need to find generalizations, traits of religion that emerge through the comparison and contrast of religions.

What makes comparison and contrast so urgent? The theory of the matter is simple. These form essential modes of thought when we try to generalize on the basis of a set of cases. If we need to make sense of many things, it is often by looking for what they have in common, the traits of the whole that govern the parts. In the present context, that means to try to generalize about *religion* out of the study of *religions*. Armed with such generalizations, we take up new cases and test them. That is to say, we ask, if I know this set of facts, what else do I know? And we answer that same question, the question of "what else," meaning at its foundation, "so what?"

For example, we may identify rituals important to Judaism and Islam and Buddhism. Can we then say what we mean by "ritual," defining the category out of data that we think belong in that category? Then we know something we may bring to new and unfamiliar data and try to make sense of them. Comparing religious traditions, then, opens the way to generalizing on some cases in quest of understanding about many more cases. Comparison and contrast open the way to answering the question, so what?

That quest for generalization about religion cannot be postponed, because religions—we cannot overstress—form a principal part of public life and culture in many, though not all, of the regions and nations of the world. And that also means, what people think about a given religion will shape the attitudes of nations toward one another. Even now, Western incomprehension of Islam spills over into fear of Muslims. And Islamic thinking about other religions also impedes Muslims' framing a comprehending attitude toward Christian minorities in Muslim countries and Christian, and secular, majorities in Western ones. Public policy in the coming century will encompass religions and our attitudes toward, our opinions of, various religious issues and entities. And because religion makes so vast a difference in so many parts of humanity, tolerance resting on indifference will not suffice. Conflicts loom. People make judgments. We can best confront difference in the benign setting of the academy, before we must face conflicts we cannot understand let alone avoid. To the work of sorting out difference, especially in religions, this labor of comparison and contrast therefore is essential. That means identifying what religions have in common, where they differ, and how to make sense of both. That is the work we undertake in this book and its companions. Where to begin?

We speak of practical things, urgent human questions to which all religions respond in one way or another. We have chosen three points to start with: religious traditions on family life, work, and personal virtue. We flatly claim that family, work, and virtue constitute categories of human existence that are close to universal. They constitute relationships and impose obligations to the others nearby, to the community at large, and to the self. "Family" pertains to relationships between me and those near at hand, "work" between me and those among whom I live, "virtue" between me and myself. Family, community, self—these take the measure of the lives we lead together, matters of public concern, not merely personal predeliction of no practical weight.

Accordingly, the scholars who join together in these pages concur that to study about religion, to seek generalizations that cases yield, one good starting point is to compare and contrast the views of the great religions on urgent and practical issues of everyday life. The reason is that, in our view, certain questions arise from experiences common to the bulk of humanity. That is why in this study religions meet on the neutral ground of what happens to every human being in the course of life.

Take death for example. If we ask Judaism, Islam, Buddhism, Christianity, and Hinduism to tell us what they have to say about what it means to live in the knowledge of the end to which life leads us all, the grave, we speak of what all must address. Not only so, but while diverse religions and cultures variously frame the issue of that shared experience, all take up precisely the same universal experience of humanity. Here our universal biology overrides our several, diverse cultures. When we speak of existential concerns common to the generality of humanity, that is what we mean. The case explains what we intend to do here. But here we choose practical issues of everyday life. That is because all religions take up the task of answering questions common to humanity in general. What are the universal human issues, the questions of shared and common existence, that we have chosen to take up in our exercise in comparing religious traditions?

1. Every person, whatever the particularities of circumstance, is born of a mother and father. The great world religions we examine here concur that special obligations link child to parent and parent to child. If, then, we wish to compare Judaism, Christianity, Islam, Hinduism, and Buddhism, we find a level plane in the common question: do I owe anything to my mother and father, and, if so, what do I owe my mother and my father, and what do they owe to me? In all five religions the family forms the building block of the social order. How does each define the family and the architecture of ethical obligations that family relationships entail?

2. Nearly every person lives in a community that accords to him or her its recognition and protection and assigns a position and a worthwhile task to participants in its shared life. So we reasonably set side by side the several world religions' answers to the question, what do I owe the community of which I am a part? For, once again, rising above the differences of context and circumstance, the human situation persists: we need guidance on the same matter, wherever we live. And that leads us to doctrines of work and rest, as religious theories of the social order.

3. Finally, and perhaps of greatest weight, everybody who lives at some point, in some way, must answer the question, who am I, and what is the meaning of my life? The language we have chosen is, what do I owe myself? The answers to these questions form a theory of personal virtue. And that makes us wonder how religions define the private person and transform him or her into the individual embodiment of public policy—as they surely do.

In framing these questions, then, we bring to the religious traditions an agenda of questions that pertain to the private lives of us all, wherever we are born and raised, whatever the religion we practice (if any). These questions of human existence, issues of private life, of home and family and the near-at-hand community—these prove relevant to all humanity, and, we claim, for all humanity in much the same way, in a shared and common context. For we think that birth to a mother and father, life in community, and the search for self-worth together form the great levelers of difference.

What does all this have to do with the comparison and contrast of religions in quest of generalization about religion? In learning from the five world religions described here, we address to them all one and the same question. That common question is uniformly divided up into the same parts, in the same language, for each of the religions examined in sequence. We see these questions as equally relevant, in proportion, in the same way, to all five religions. That is to say, Judaism, Christianity, Islam, Hinduism, and Buddhism all set forth doctrines of (1) family, (2) work, and (3) virtue. These doctrines provide clear and characteristic answers to the questions we have formulated. In other words, we have identified categories that, in our experience as scholars, fit well for the religions that we study, respectively.

Let us now turn to the categories we have chosen. How have we framed the questions? A few words of explanation are in order. In the several chapters, all of us follow a single outline. For the initial volumes of this exercise in comparing religious traditions, here are the outlines that dictate the presentation of each religion.

I. THE ETHICS OF FAMILY LIFE: WHAT DO WE OWE ONE ANOTHER?

  1. Conventional expectation versus this religious tradition: what do husbands and wives owe one another?

  2. What do parents owe their children?

  3. What do children owe their parents?

  4. When the family breaks down: what happens then?

  5. Unconventional families, supernatural families

II. MAKING AN HONEST LIVING: WHAT DO WE OWE THE COMMUNITY?

  1. Why must we work?

  2. How ought we to work? kinds of work to be preferred or avoided

  3. Why must we help others? private gain and public benefit

  4. When work does not work: unemployment, exploitation, and alternatives to proper work

  5. Unconventional work: working for God

III. THE LIFE OF VIRTUE: WHAT DO WE OWE OURSELVES?

  1. Conventional answers versus this religious tradition: who are we really? [conceptions of the person, or, in other words, theological anthropology]

  2. What are the social virtues? [for example, generosity, trust, gratitude]

  3. What is personal virtue? [for example, dignity, self-respect, hope]

  4. How does this religion define character, good and bad?

  5. Beyond the normal virtues: who is the extraordinary person? [for example, the saint]

So much for the common questions addressed to five religious traditions, questions that make possible the comparison and contrast of those traditions.

For all three topical expositions, a single pattern governs. We move from the conventional to the unconventional, and from the system when it works to the system when it breaks down. In each exposition we begin with the conventional issues of ordinary life. This means that through the first three sections we answer the question, what do people ordinarily mean by the matter under discussion, and what are the answers that this religion in everyday terms gives to the question? We then turn at the fourth section to how a given religion deals with failure. At the end, at the fifth section, we ask how a given religion altogether revises the conventional, this-worldly definition. Having laid out an account of matters that is uniform in structure for the religions portrayed here, we leave it to students to draw their own conclusions, frame their own judgments, in discussion beyond the pages of this book.

In the volume on family life, we begin with the family understood in a this-worldly framework, a conventional family, meaning husband, wife, and children, extending outward beyond the nuclear family to grandparents, uncles and aunts, dependents of various kinds, and castes. Then, second, we ask about how this religion deals with the breakdown of the norm, for example, with the family when it breaks down. Finally, we turn from the conventional to the unconventional definition of the same matter, for example, the supernatural family, the family defined in an other-than-this-worldly framework.

When it comes to work, we begin with the ordinary meaning of work, that is, what we do to support our families and ourselves, to earn our keep, and to contribute to the common good. Then we ask about doctrines that deal with the breakdown of the ordinary arrangements for everyday labor. Finally, we take up work in a different, unconventional context.

The same pattern governs the discussion of virtue, by which we mean, how we view ourselves. In this context we take for granted that people ordinarily aspire to think well of themselves, to live lives of virtue. That topic encompasses how this religious tradition defines a human being. Within that broad question are doctrines on public virtues, that is, admirable traits that make for a better society, as well as those on personal ones. The latter characterize individuals and point toward how a given religion defines a truly virtuous person. On the basis of doctrines of virtue we generalize in terms of character: what does this religion admire in the overall quality of a person; what marks a person as basically good or fundamentally evil? And, finally, we turn from the routine to the extraordinary: how does this religion identify the saint, the embodiment of virtue.

So we have undertaken an experiment in comparing religious traditions. Why have we done so? Once more: the payoff comes in the quest for generalizations, in the present instance, how religion shapes the traits of family, work, and virtue. We concentrate on practical questions of comparison, not only because we claim the issues addressed here face nearly all religions and the societies shaped by them, but also because these issues confront all of us as we make our way through life from birth to death. When we compare religions' patterns of belief and behavior, we may or may not cover topics of immediate relevance to our own circumstances. But when we ask about family, work, and virtue, we certainly inquire into what matters in the here and the now. That is the point at which generalization may take place.

For, as we shall see, religions really do concur on some practical matters, and they actually do make the same difference, each in its own context. That does not make them all alike, and it does not validate the ignorant dismissal of difference, "It doesn't matter what you believe as long as you're a good person." Nor does that concurrence permit us to reduce religions to religion, to define a generic religion. What we mean to show is the possibility of generalization, of moving from knowing this fact to explaining other facts, moving from the known to the unknown. That is how we meet our responsibility as academic scholars of religion and how we contribute to others outside of university life as well. All comes down to our sustained response to this simple question: if we know this, what else do we know?

Why the emphasis on practical matters? The academic study of religion maintains that we study about religions and religion and do not advocate the truth of one religion over another, and all of us in these pages affirm that conviction. But no one can imagine that the academic study of religion ought never present us with choices worthy of our consideration, ideas of other men and women that we may make our own. We represent the religions treated here as worthy of the close attention of inquiring minds, in quest, in the end, of insight into the human condition. No other single force in the social order, not politics, not economics, not psychology, not any of the other important elements in making the world what it is—none of them exceeds in power, or in pathos, the force of religion.

The partners in this project express thanks to Wadsworth Publishing Company for adopting the enterprise and guiding it from beginning to end. We benefited, especially, from the oversight and counsel of our editor, Peter Adams. We are also grateful for the helpful comments provided by the reviewers: Leslie Aldritt, Northland College; S. Daniel Breslauer, University of Kansas; Aminah Beverly McCloud, DePaul University; Preston McKever-Floyd, Coastal Carolina University.

The editor thanks the partners in this project for doing the work on time and with panache. He also expresses his personal gratitude to Bard College, for a research grant and for other support for his work as teacher and scholar.

Jacob Neusner
Editor
Bard College

Contributors

BRUCE CHILTON is Bernard Iddings Bell Professor of Religion at Bard College.

CHARLES HALLISEY is John L. Loeb Associate Professor of the Humanities at Harvard University, teaching on the Committee on the Study of Religion and in the Department of Sanskrit and Indian Studies.

JACOB NEUSNER is Research Professor of Religion and Theology at Bard College.

BRIAN K. SMITH is Professor of Religious Studies at the University of California at Riverside.

TAMARA SONN is Kenan Professor of Religious Studies at the College of William and Mary.

1

Judaism

BY JACOB NEUSNER

WHY MUST WE WORK?

In the Torah (a.k.a. Judaism) all questions find their answers within a cogent system, a statement of matters whole and complete, such that each part fits together with all others, the details recapitulating the main point. If we take a detail out of that context, we cannot make sense of that detail on its own. So it is when we address the matter of what we owe to the community, meaning our labor in the public interest. The sages of the Torah see Israel as a sacred society, "a kingdom of priests and a holy people," and quite logically, they also view work not as a mere secular necessity but as a sacred activity. But then they find a place for the definition of work within the larger statement of what it means to form holy Israel,[1] meaning God's first love on earth.

Why we must work finds its answer in the definition of labor. God in Creation is the model: in six days he made the world. So work is something that produces lasting results, accomplishes the purpose of the worker, and is done in the proper manner—all traits imputed to the acts of Creation that God performed in making the world. And, along these same lines, with the model of Creation in hand, the sages balance work against repose. On the seventh day God rested, the Creation having been perfected, blessed, and sanctified. So there is no considering the meaning of work without its complement, repose.

That is the supernatural context—the six days of labor, the seventh day of rest—in which we consider Judaism's view of work. Work is not merely something we are supposed to do in the interests of the community, so that the tasks of the world will be carried out, and each of us will earn a living. The Hebrew word for "work" is *abodah,* and it is the same word that is used for "divine service," or "liturgy," or the labor of the priests in the Temple in making offerings to God. In a moment, we shall understand why *abodah* can be a component of the life of the holy people: what work has to do with God.

But first, we have to face a striking fact. It is the Torah's answer to the question, why must we work? We must work, so far as Judaism is concerned, not merely so that we do not fall as a burden onto the backs of others. Work is

---

[1]Not to be confused with the contemporary State of Israel but to be understood as the principal theological category for the social order contemplated in the Torah. Christians will understand the category as the counterpart to "the Church, the mystical body of Christ."

natural to the human condition; it is what God does and what we, in his image, after his likeness, also are created to do. Everyone, by definition, has useful work to carry out, if not in a secular then in a sacred framework. "Unemployment," meaning having absolutely nothing of worth to do, no assigned task that possesses any value whatsoever, is a concept that the sages do not imagine (for a reason I shall give in a moment). Every human being has the capacity to engage in useful, worthwhile labor. And, along these same lines, while some tasks are easier and lighter than others, none in a secular framework (apart from labor in Torah-study, which we shall meet later on) is degraded.

Incumbent upon every human being are tasks of intrinsic merit, and no one can ever be unemployed in the sense of having no socially useful tasks to perform. Everyone from the smallest child to the oldest widow can and does contribute to sustaining the life of the community. All add to the treasury of scarce resources. But the scarce resource that must be rationally disposed of, so far as the Torah is concerned, has nothing to do with gold or silver; the scarce resource is piety, and that is to be "produced" and valued. And everyone is capable of acts of piety, for example, prayer or study of Torah, constituting *abodah* in the deepest sense: work in God's service. So unemployment in the contemporary sense is incomprehensible. That fixed idea comes to expression in a curious passage about the definition of a large town as against a village:[2]

> What is a large town?
> Any in which there are ten men available at all times [to form a quorum for prayer].
> [If there are] fewer than this number, lo, this is a village.
>
> Mishnah Megillah 1:3

What is the point? If you are a person of leisure, with resources to permit your being available at all times, for example, to participate in public prayer, it means you have no job; in a secular world you are "unemployed." But the idle rich, no less than the idle poor, have valued tasks to carry out. The Hebrew that I translate as "men available at all times" is *batlanim,* a word that in living Hebrew today means unemployed people, or in a broader sense, time wasters, worthless louts. But in the part of the Torah set forth in the Mishnah, ca. 200 C.E., men with no fixed obligations, people with no jobs to go to, form a public asset. That is because, without fixed schedules, they are always available to form a quorum for public prayer. Their presence defines a large town; a village cannot afford such a luxury as a permanent quorum for prayer; a town, with its amenities, can. What these people do, then, is say prayers and make it possible for others to do so in a quorum (there being certain prayers that can only be said in community, that is, among ten Israelites). By the definition of work of value that lies before us, every one of the faithful has valuable work to do, whether or not that work is conventional, and whether or not it is compensated in an everyday way.

---

[2]Translations are my own unless otherwise indicated.

And that brings us back to the connection between "work" and the life of holiness that the Torah demands of holy Israel. In the Torah, to be "holy" is to be like God, as at Leviticus 19:1: "You shall be holy, for I the Lord your God am holy," and to be Israel means to aspire to imitate God. To understand the connection between work and sanctification, therefore, we have to realize how sages frame the issue. Rather than explaining why we must work, sages ask, is work natural to the human condition? And, as we have already done, they turn to the Torah—in this case, to the account of creation in Genesis—to find the answer.

In the model of creation of the world in six days, with repose on the Sabbath, the whole sanctified at the very instant of perfection, sunset on the sixth day, work finds its context in the rhythm of the week. Six days are devoted to labor and one day to rest. That is how God made the world, and it is how we are to live our lives, six days of creation, a day of repose, called by the untranslatable Hebrew word *Shabbat* (English: Sabbath). Just as it is a religious duty to rest on the Sabbath, so it is a religious duty to work during the week. That is how we imitate God in everyday life. The Ten Commandments include that admonition: "Six days shall you labor and do all your work" (Exodus 20:9). When people work for the six days of creation, they act like God, and when they rest on the seventh day, they imitate God as well. But there is work, and then there is real labor. The Torah recognizes the difference and accounts for it. In Judaism we must work so that there can be the Sabbath. When you fully explore the depths of that proposition, you can understand any other statement that Judaism makes on any other critical subject: you enter the heart and soul of the Torah's system.

But, it goes without saying, the theology is one thing, the concrete activity, something else again. Most people do not feel that they are imitating God when they go to their jobs in the morning or in the middle of the night for that matter. But when the Sabbath defines the context of work, and creation the framework, the issue is not fatigue but something more:

> "and rested on the seventh day:"
> And does fatigue affect God? Is it not said, "The creator of the ends of the earth does not faint and is not weary" (Is. 40:28), "He gives power to the faint" (Is. 40:29); "By the word of the Lord the heavens were made" (Ps. 33:6)?
> How then can Scripture say, "and rested on the seventh day"?
> It is as if [God] had it written concerning himself that he created the world in six days and rested on the seventh.
> Now you may reason *a fortiori*:
> Now if the One who is not affected by fatigue had it written concerning himself that he created the world in six days and rested on the seventh, how much the more so should a human being, concerning whom it is written, "but man is born to trouble" (Job 5:7) [also rest on the Sabbath]?
>
> Mekhilta Attributed to R. Ishmael LIII:II.17

So work and repose form the framework within which life is lived: like God.

What about women and children? Predictably, all classes of the social order are assigned useful tasks. Women who manage the household and raise children are understood to work, and no one imagines that they are unemployed. Their work in the home carries out their obligation to their husband, which they undertook in agreeing to the marriage. Work is deemed a natural right that a woman has, and that cannot be denied her. For one principal reason that we must work is that idleness corrupts. When it comes to a wealthy woman, who does not have to work, and for whom, in the imagination of the sages of the Torah, a career outside of the home is unimaginable, she too has the right to work, not only the obligation. A husband who tries to keep his wife at leisure must divorce her and give her the opportunity to find a more humane world, in which she too may do things of value:

> These are the kinds of labor which a woman performs for her husband:
>   she (1) grinds flour, (2) bakes bread, (3) does laundry, (4) prepares meals, (5) gives suck to her child, (6) makes the bed, (7) works in wool.
>   [If] she brought with her a single slave girl, she does not (1) grind, (2) bake bread, or (3) do laundry.
>   [If she brought] two, she does not (4) prepare meals and does not (5) feed her child.
>   [If she brought] three, she does not (6) make the bed for him and does not (7) work in wool.
>   If she brought four, she sits on a throne.
>   R. Eliezer says, "Even if she brought him a hundred slave girls, he forces her to work in wool,
>   "for idleness leads to unchastity."
>   Rabban Simeon b. Gamaliel says, "Also: He who prohibits his wife by a vow from performing any labor puts her away and pays off her marriage contract. For idleness leads to boredom."
>
> Mishnah-tractate Ketubot 5:5

We see that the law assigns a fixed obligation of work to the wife; the burden may be diminished but not removed, for the reason Eliezer states. But Simeon b. Gamaliel gives a still more compelling explanation: idleness leads to boredom. So much for why we must work. But, in all candor, the real question is not, why must we work, but why must we work at jobs we do not necessarily like? Why is work a burden and not a joy? And the answer to these more cutting questions derives not from everyday experience but from the theology that animates Judaism in its classical statement.

Specifically, the Torah answers all questions by appeal to its own picture of the human condition, beginning with creation in Eden and the fall of humanity from grace by reason of sin. The classical statement of Judaism, in that reading of Scripture contained within the documents of the Oral Torah, points to the tragedy of Eden in explaining why we have to work. There the Judaic sages find that servile labor defines the human condition because of man's and woman's rebellion against God: "In the sweat of your face you shall eat bread until you return to the ground, for out of it you were taken; you are dust and to dust you shall return" (Genesis 3:19). The natural world ought to sustain man without his having to work. That is shown by the fact that nature sustains itself without menial labor. But with sin man has found it necessary to work, nature having lost its abundance:

> R. Simeon b. Eleazar says, "In your whole life, did you ever see a lion working as a porter, a deer working as a fruit-picker, a fox working as a storekeeper, a wolf selling pots, a domestic beast or a wild beast or a bird who had a trade?
>
> "Now these are created only to work for me, and I was made only to work for my Master.
>
> "Now is there not an argument a fortiori: Now if these, who were created only to work for me, lo, they make a living without anguish, I who have been created to work for my Master, is it not reasonable that I too should make a living without anguish!
>
> "But my deeds have ruined things, and I have spoiled my living."
>
> Tosefta Qiddushin 5:16

It is the natural order that has each species doing what it is created to do. Man is created to live without much trouble, but because of sin (Adam in Eden), he is condemned to hard labor.

Now if we examine work in the required context, namely, the workweek ending with the Sabbath of rest and repose, matters take on a different appearance. When we work, it is with the knowledge that we are destined to the Sabbath rest, so while we must work, we are not imprisoned by that obligation:

> "Six days you shall labor and do all your work:"
>   But can a mortal carry out all of one's work in only six days?
>   But the nature of Sabbath rest is such that it should be as though all of your labor has been carried out.
>
> Mekhilta Attributed to R. Ishmael LIII:II.9

> Another teaching [as to "Six days you shall labor and do all your work:"]
>   "Take a Sabbath rest from the very thought of work."
>   And so Scripture says, "If you turn away your foot because of the Sabbath" (Is. 58:13), and then, "Then you shall delight yourself in the Lord" (Is. 58:14).
>
> Mekhilta Attributed to R. Ishmael LIII:II.10

Man and woman have left Eden and entered the world of work. But the Sabbath, every seventh day, restores them for the moment to that world of Eden that they have lost. It gives them a foretaste of the age to come, when, the dead having been raised and life eternal having come, humanity will recover Eden.

But how to do so? Adam's sin finds its antidote in the Torah, which, sages maintain, is given to purify the heart of humanity. By keeping the Torah humanity learns to accept God's will, so to overcome the natural propensity to rebel. When humanity, in full freedom of will, accepts God's commandments, beginning with "You will love the Lord your God with all your heart, with all your soul, and with all your might" (Deuteronomy 6:5), then humanity regains Eden. The one thing God craves but cannot coerce is our love, freely given. That is what the Torah means to bring about. What appears to digress explains the very center of Judaism's doctrine of work: the most important work a person can do is study the Torah. For that is where God and humanity are to be reconciled: where humanity meets God in God's own self-revelation. In the Torah God sets forth what he wants us to know about himself, and it is in the labor of learning that we meet him, where he talks with us. In contemporary Judaism, centers of Torah-study, called yeshivot, flourish in every place in which the religion is practiced in its classical forms. The curriculum of such schools continues that process of transmitting the oral tradition of Sinai into the long future. To study in such places is to work very, very hard.

Israelites, in the Judaic conviction, were created to study the Torah. That fundamental conviction explains why, from sages' perspective, the kind of work that Israelites were made to carry out is labor in Torah-study. That position is expressed in so many words by a principal figure in the formation of the oral part of the Torah, Yohanan ben Zakkai, who flourished in the first century, at about the time of the destruction of the Jerusalem Temple in 70 C.E.:

> Rabban Yohanan b. Zakkai received [the tradition of the Oral Torah] from Hillel and Shammai.
>   He would say, "If you have learned much Torah, do not puff yourself up on that account, for it was for that purpose that you were created."
>
> Tractate Abot 2:8

Now the picture is complete, or so it would seem. We must work for three reasons, each quite distinct from the others. First, we must work to be like God, who created the world in six days of labor and rested on the seventh. Second, we must do servile labor because we are party to the human condition, cast from Eden by reason of our rebellion against God. Third, we ought to conduct the labor of divine service, particularly Torah-study, because that is how we may regain Eden. So work finds its place within a restorationist theology that aims at bringing Adam and Eve back to Eden.

HOW OUGHT WE TO WORK? KINDS OF WORK TO BE PREFERRED OR AVOIDED

The kind of work to be preferred unambiguously defines itself: Torah-study. Then the urgent question is, if we spend our time making a living, then how are we to find the time to study the Torah? And that question brings us to one of the great, and ongoing, debates in classical Judaism, which concerns what sort of work we must do. The issue is, may we divide our time between Torah-study and gainful labor, or must we devote our time only or mainly to Torah-study, and let the world bring what it may? What about knowledge of Torah as a way of making one's living?

The answers to these questions lead us into the Torah's theory of the kind of work to be preferred and avoided. The first position is the most practical:

> R. Meir says, "A man should always teach his son a clean and easy trade. And let him pray to him to whom belong riches and possessions.
> "For there is no trade which does not involve poverty or wealth.
> "For poverty does not come from one's trade, nor does wealth come from one's trade.
> "But all is in accord with a man's merit."
>
> Mishnah Qiddushin 4:14

Meir would hold that so far as one can provide for an easy living for one's children, one should do so, but in the end, everything is in God's hands, and God decides matters by reference to a person's merit (a conception that becomes urgent in the chapter on Judaism in the third volume of this series, since merit corresponds to virtue in the Torah). So the "clean and easy trade," such as tailoring, is to be preferred, but not for religious reasons, only for the simple, secular fact that it does not involve any heavy lifting.

> R. Simeon b. Eleazar says, "Have you ever seen a wild beast or a bird who has a trade? Yet they get along without difficulty. And were they not created only to serve me? And I was created to serve my Master. So is it not logical that I should get along without difficulty? But I have done evil and ruined my living."
>
> Mishnah Qiddushin 4:14

Here is the direct reference to the fall of Adam from Eden. How in practical, everyday terms that makes a difference then is explicit. One's merit makes the difference between poverty and wealth, or one's sinfulness. A more practical position is that which follows in the continuation of the passage:

> Abba Gurion of Sidon says in the name of Abba Gurya, "A man should not teach his son to be an ass-driver, a camel driver, a barber, a sailor, a herdsman, or a shopkeeper For their trade is the trade of thieves."
> R. Judah says in his name, "Most ass-drivers are evil, most camel drivers are decent, most sailors are saintly, the best among physicians is going to Gehenna, and the best of butchers is a partner of Amalek."
>
> Mishnah Qiddushin 4:14

Now comes the centerpiece, the view that "Torah"—meaning perpetual study of the Torah—suffices as a means for making a living. It is the most reliable medium of work, for it stays with the disciple of the sages through thick and thin:

> R. Nehorai says, "I should lay aside every trade in the world and teach my son only Torah.
> "For a man eats its fruits in this world, and the principal remains for the world to come.
> "But other trades are not that way.
> "When a man gets sick or old or has pains and cannot do his job, lo, he dies of starvation.
> "But with Torah it is not that way.

"But it keeps him from all evil when he is young, and it gives him a future and a hope when he is old.

"Concerning his youth, what does it say? 'They who wait upon the Lord shall renew their strength' (Is. 40:31). And concerning his old age what does it say? 'They shall still bring forth fruit in old age' (Ps. 92:14).

"And so it says with regard to the patriarch Abraham, may he rest in peace, 'And Abraham was old and well along in years, and the Lord blessed Abraham in all things' (Gen. 24:1).

"We find that the patriarch Abraham kept the entire Torah even before it was revealed, since it says, Since Abraham obeyed my voice and kept my charge, my commandments, my statutes, and my laws (Gen. 26:5)."

Mishnah Qiddushin 4:14

Why Torah works as it does is made explicit: "It keeps him from all evil when he is young." That is to say, the position of Meir and Simeon is repeated, only in a fresh way. If I know the Torah, I will not sin. The conception that, if I study Torah, I automatically get the food I need to eat and the roof I need for shelter is not at issue here, where our concern is with being kept from evil in youth and enjoying God's blessing in old age on account of keeping the Torah—a very different thing, as we shall see presently. But that position will emerge, as the successive documents record opinion unfolding over time.

Should one abandon all worldly occupations and only study the Torah? That is the position of hundreds of thousands of contemporary Israelites, men who spend all their time in yeshiva-learning, wives and children who live on the pittance that the yeshiva can give to support the men in their study. Within the society of Judaism are many, therefore, who may be compared to Catholic nuns and monks, living out their lives in sacred service. But the view that Torah-study suffices as the work one should do took shape only over time.

The first apologia for the Mishnah, ca. 200 C.E., which is tractate Abot, ca. 250 C.E., takes the view that one should not make one's living through study of the Torah. That is made explicit in Torah-sayings of tractate Abot, where we find explicit rejection of the theory of Torah-study as a means of avoiding one's obligation to earn a living. Torah-study without a craft is rejected, Torah-study along with labor at a craft is defined as the ideal way of life. The following sayings make that point quite clearly:

Rabban Gamaliel, a son of Rabbi Judah the Patriarch says: "Fitting is learning in the Torah along with a craft, for the labor put into the two of them makes one forget sin. And all learning of the Torah which is not joined with labor is destined to be null and causes sin."

M. Abot 2:2

R. Eleazar b. Azariah says, "… If there is no sustenance [lit.: flour], there is no Torah-learning. If there is no Torah-learning, there is no sustenance."

M. Abot 3:17

The way of virtue lies rather in economic activity in the conventional sense, joined to intellectual or philosophical activity in sages' sense. The labor in Torah is not an economic activity and produces no solutions to this-worldly problems of getting food, shelter, and clothing. To the contrary, labor in Torah defines the purpose of human life; it is the goal; but it is not the medium for maintaining life and avoiding starvation or exposure to the elements.

Why is Torah-study the preferred labor? Because that is where we meet God, in two ways. First, the Torah that is studied preserves the record of God's self-manifestation to humanity. If people want to know God, they learn in the Torah what God wants them to know. Second, for that very reason, when two or three people sit down to study Torah, God is present among them. That the context of Torah-study is religious and not economic in any sense is shown by Hananiah's saying, which is explicit: if people talk about the Torah, the Presence of God joins them to participate:

> R. Hananiah b. Teradion says, "[If] two sit together and between them do not pass teachings of the Torah, lo, this is a seat of the scornful, as it is said, 'Nor sits in the seat of the scornful' (Ps. 1:1). But two who are sitting, and words of the Torah do pass between them – the Presence is with them, as it is said, 'Then they that feared the Lord spoke with one another, and the Lord hearkened and heard, and a book of remembrance was written before him, for them that feared the Lord and gave thought to his name' (Mal. 3:16). I know that this applies to two. How do I know that even if a single person sits and works on the Torah, the Holy One, blessed be He, set aside a reward for him? As it is said, 'Let him sit alone and keep silent, because he has laid it upon him' (Lam. 3:28)."
>
> M. Abot 3:2

Do worldly benefits accrue to those who study the Torah? The rabbi cited in the following statement maintains that it is entirely inappropriate to use Torah-learning to gain either social standing or economic gain:

> R. Sadoq says, "Do not make [Torah-teachings] a crown in which to glorify yourself or a spade with which to dig. So did Hillel say, "He who uses the crown perishes. Thus have you learned: Whoever derives worldly benefit from teachings of the Torah takes his life out of this world."
>
> M. Abot 4:5

It is the simple fact that the bulk of opinion in the Mishnah and in tractate Abot identifies Torah-learning with status within a system of hierarchical classification, not with a medium for earning a living. Admittedly that is not the only position that is represented. The following contrasts "working for a living" with "studying Torah" and maintains that the latter will provide a living, without recourse to hard labor:

> R. Nehunia b. Haqqaneh says, "From whoever accepts upon himself the yoke of the Torah do they remove the yoke of the state and the yoke of hard labor. And upon whoever removes from himself the yoke of the Torah do they lay the yoke of the state and the yoke of hard labor."
>
> M. Abot 3:15

But the prevailing view, represented by the bulk of sayings, treats Torah-study as an activity that competes with economic venture and insists that Torah-study take precedence, even though it is not of economic value in any commonplace sense of the words. That is explicitly imputed to Meir and to Jonathan in the following:

> R. Meir says, "Keep your business to a minimum and make your business the Torah. And be humble before everybody. And if you treat the Torah as nothing, you will have many treating you as nothing. And if you have labored in the Torah, [the Torah] has a great reward to give you."
>
> M. Abot 4:10

Torah-study competes with, rather than replaces, economic activity. That is the simple position of tractate Abot, extending the conception of matters explicit in the Mishnah. If I had to make a simple statement of the situation prevailing at ca. 250, it would be that sages contrast their wealth, which is spiritual and intellectual, with material wealth; they do not deem the one to form the counterpart of the other, but only the opposite. But matters shift in the later documents of the Oral Torah in the formative age, for there are passages that are quite explicit that Torah-study is tantamount to wealth. Now, as a matter of fact, land is wealth, or Torah is wealth, but not both; owning land is power and studying Torah permits (re)gaining power.

A profound shift is represented by a story about first-century authorities that occurs in a fifth-century compilation, Leviticus Rabbah, a theological reading of passages in the book of Leviticus, which reached closure in ca. 450 C.E. Here is an explicit statement that study of the Torah forms a sufficient way to make a living—to make a life! To understand the passage, we must recall that in antiquity, "wealth" meant land, real estate, and people who had surplus to invest ordinarily bought land. So a this-worldly definition applies to "scarce resources." Here, however, we find a fundamental debate on the very definition of "wealth," or, in secular language, "scarce resources." It is a debate without precedent in any prior compilation, only adumbrated, as we saw, by minority opinion in tractate Abot. In this debate, the lesser figure, Tarfon, thought wealth took the form of land, while the greater figure, Aqiba, explained to him that wealth takes the form of Torah-learning. That the sense is material and concrete is explicit: land for Torah, Torah for land.

> R. Tarfon gave to R. Aqiba six silver centenarii, saying to him, "Go, buy us a piece of land, so we can get a living from it and labor in the study of Torah together."
>
> He took the money and handed it over to scribes, Mishnah-teachers, and those who study Torah.
>
> After some time R. Tarfon met him and said to him, "Did you buy the land that I mentioned to you?"
>
> He said to him, "Yes."
>
> He said to him, "Is it any good?"
>
> He said to him, "Yes."

He said to him, "And do you not want to show it to me?"

He took him and showed him the scribes, Mishnah-teachers, and people who were studying Torah, and the Torah that they had acquired.

He said to him, "Is there anyone who works for nothing? Where is the deed covering the field?"

He said to him, "It is with King David, concerning whom it is written, 'He has scattered, he has given to the poor, his righteousness endures forever' (Ps. 112:9)."

Leviticus Rabbah XXXIV:XVI

When "Torah" substitutes for real estate, what, exactly, do sages know as scarce resources, and how is the counterpart category constructed? We should err if we supposed that sages spoke in figurative or metaphorical language. When they identified "wealth" with "Torah-learning," they took a very concrete view. Just as "wealth" in real estate supports those who have it, so "wealth" in Torah-learning sustains those who have it. The spiritualization of the matter that we noted earlier—the Torah keeps us from sin—now moves to its logical next step, with the claim that, if we study the Torah, we gain that scarce resource that matters:

R. Yohanan was going up from Tiberias to Sepphoris. R. Hiyya bar Abba was supporting him. They came to a field. He said, "This field once belonged to me, but I sold it in order to acquire merit in the Torah."

They came to a vineyard, and he said, "This vineyard once belonged to me, but I sold it in order to acquire merit in the Torah."

They came to an olive grove, and he said, "This olive grove once belonged to me, but I sold it in order to acquire merit in the Torah."

R. Hiyya began to cry.

Said R. Yohanan, "Why are you crying?"

He said to him, "It is because you left nothing over to support you in your old age."

He said to him, "Hiyya, my disciple, is what I did such a light thing in your view? I sold something which was given in a spell of six days [of creation] and in exchange I acquired something which was given in a spell of forty days [of revelation].

"The entire world and everything in it was created in only six days, as it is written, 'For in six days the Lord made heaven and earth' [Ex. 20:11].

"But the Torah was given over a period of forty days, as it was said, 'And he was there with the Lord for forty days and forty nights' [Ex. 34:28].

"And it is written, 'And I remained on the mountain for forty days and forty nights' (Dt. 9:9)."

When R. Yohanan died, his generation recited concerning him [the following verse of Scripture]: "If a man should give all the wealth of his house for the love" (Song 8:7), with which R. Yohanan loved the Torah, "he would be utterly destitute" (Song 8:7). . . .

When R. Eleazar b. R. Simeon died, his generation recited concerning him [the following verse of Scripture]: "Who is this who comes up out of the wilderness like pillars of smoke, perfumed with myrrh and frankincense, with all the powders of the merchant?" (Song 3:6).

What is the meaning of the clause, "With all the powders of the merchant"?

[Like a merchant who carries all sorts of desired powders,] he was a master of Scripture, a repeater of Mishnah traditions, a writer of liturgical supplications, and a liturgical poet.

Leviticus Rabbah XXX:I.4–5

The importance of the statement lies in the second of the two, which deems land the counterpart—and clearly the opposite—of the Torah.

Now one can sell a field and acquire "Torah," meaning, in the context established by the exchange between Tarfon and Aqiba, the opportunity to gain leisure for (acquiring the merit gained by) the study of the Torah. That the sage has left himself nothing for his support in old age makes explicit the material meaning of the statement, and the comparison of the value of land, created in six days, and the Torah, created in forty days, is equally explicit. The comparison of knowledge of Torah to the merchandise of the merchant simply repeats the same point, but in a lower register. So too does the this-worldly power of study of the Torah make explicit in another framework the conviction that study of the Torah yields material and concrete benefit, not just spiritual renewal. Thus R. Huna states, "All of the exiles will be gathered together only on account of the study of Mishnah-teachings" (Pesiqta deRab Kahana VI:III.3.B). The point should not be missed: the in-gathering of the exiles marks the return of humanity to Eden, embodied in the return of holy Israel to the Land of Israel at the end of time. So Huna's statement fits into the larger system.

Not only so, but the sage devoted to study of the Torah has to be supported because he can no longer perform physical work. Study of the Torah deprives him of physical strength, and that contrast and counterpart represented by land and working of the land as against Torah and the study of the Torah comes to symbolic expression in yet another way:

R. Eleazar bar Simeon was appointed to impress men and beasts into forced labor [in the corvée]. One time Elijah, of blessed memory, appeared to him in the guise of an old man. Elijah said to him, "Get me a beast of burden."

Eleazar said to him, "What do you have as a cargo [to load on the beast]?"

He said to him, "This old skin-bottle of mine, my cloak, and me as rider."

He said, "Take a look at this old man! I [personally] can take him and carry him to the end of the world, and he says to me to get a beast ready!"

What did he do? He loaded him on his back and carried him up mountains and down valleys and over fields of thorns and fields of thistles.

In the end [Elijah] began to bear down on him. He said to him, "Old man, old man! Make yourself lighter, and if you don't, I'll toss you off."

[Elijah] said to him, "Now do you want to take a bit of a rest?"

He said to him, "Yes."

What did he do? [Elijah] took him to a field and set him down under a tree and gave him food and drink. When he had eaten and drunk, he [Elijah] said to him, "All this running about—what is in it for you? Would it not be better for you to take up the vocation of your fathers?"

He said to him, "And can you teach it to me?"

He said to him, "Yes."

And there are those who say that for thirteen years Elijah of blessed memory taught him until he could recite even Sifra [the exegesis of Leviticus, which is particularly difficult].

But once he could recite that document, [he had so lost his strength that] he could not lift up even a cloak.

The household of Rabban Gamaliel had a member who could carry forty *seahs* [of grain] to the baker [on his back].

He said to him, "All this vast power do you possess, and you do not devote yourself to the study of Sifra."

When he could recite that document, they say that even a single *seah* of grain he was unable to bear.

There are those who say that if someone else did not take it off him, he would not have been able to take it off himself.

Leviticus Rabbah XI:XXII.1–2

These stories about how a mark of the sage is physical weakness form part of a larger program of contrasting Torah-study with land ownership, intellectual prowess with physical power, the superiority of the one over the other. No wonder sages would in time claim that their power protected cities, which then needed neither police nor walls. These were concrete claims, affecting the rational use of scarce resources as much as the use and distribution of land constituted an expression of a rationality concerning scarce resources, their preservation and increase.

All of this is very well and good, but how are we going to put food on the table, if all we do is study? This brings us back to the matter of teaching one's son a trade. The contrast between the received position and that before us is found at the following, which occurs in the Talmud of the Land of Israel, a commentary to the Mishnah that came to closure at ca. 400 C.E., in the same time as the passages of Leviticus Rabbah we have examined:

It is forbidden to a person to teach his son a trade, in as much as it is written, "And you shall meditate therein day and night" (Joshua 1:8).

But has not R. Ishmael taught, "You shall choose life" (Dt. 30:19)—this refers to learning [Torah] and practicing a trade as well. [One both studies the Torah and also a trade.]

Yerushalmi Peah 1:1.VII

There is no harmonizing the two views by appeal to the rationalization before us. In fact, study of the Torah substituted for practicing a craft, and it was meant to do so. In all, therefore, the case in favor of the proposition that Torah has now become a material good, and, further, that Torah has now been transformed into the ultimate scarce resource—explicitly substituting for real estate, even in the Land of Israel—is firmly established.

No wonder then that sages protect cities. So it is claimed that sages are the guardians of cities, and later on that would yield the further allegation that sages do not have to pay taxes to build walls around cities, since their Torah-study protects the cities:

R. Abba bar Kahana commenced discourse by citing the following verse: "Who is the man so wise that he may understand this? To whom has the mouth of the Lord spoken, that he may declare it? Why is the land ruined and laid waste like a wilderness, [so that no one passes through? The Lord said, It is because they forsook my Torah which I set before them; they neither obeyed me nor conformed to it. They followed the promptings of their own stubborn hearts, they followed the Baalim as their forefathers had taught them. Therefore these are the words of the Lord of Hosts the God of Israel: I will feed this people with wormwood and give them bitter poison to drink. I will scatter them among nations whom neither they nor their forefathers have known; I will harry them with the sword until I have made an end of them]" (Jer. 9:16).

It was taught in the name of R. Simeon b. Yohai, "If you see towns uprooted from their place in the land of Israel, know that [it is because] the people did not pay the salaries of teachers of children and Mishnah-instructors.

"What is the verse of Scripture that indicates it? 'Why is the land ruined and laid waste like a wilderness, [so that no one passes through?]' What is written just following? 'It is because they forsook my Torah [which I set before them; they neither obeyed me nor conformed to it.]' "

Rabbi sent R. Yosé and R. Ammi to go and survey the towns of the Land of Israel. They would go into a town and say to the people, "Bring me the guardians of the town."

The people would bring out the head of the police and the local guard.

[The sages] would say, "These are not the guardians of the town, they are those who destroy the town. Who are the guardians of the town? They are the teachers of children and Mishnah-teachers, who keep watch by day and by night, in line with the verse, 'And you shall meditate in it day and night' (Josh. 1:8)."

"And so Scripture says, 'If the Lord does not build the house, in vain the builders labor' (Ps. 127:1)."

Said R. Abba bar Kahana, "No philosophers in the world ever arose of the quality of Balaam ben Beor and Abdymos of Gadara. The nations of the world came to Abnymos of Gadara. They said to him, 'Do you maintain that we can make war against this nation?'

"He said to them, 'Go and make the rounds of their synagogues and their study houses. So long as there are three children chirping out loud in their voices [and studying the Torah], then you cannot overcome them. If not, then you can conquer them, for so did their father promise them: "The voice is Jacob's voice" (Gen. 27:22), meaning that when Jacob's voice chirps in synagogues and study houses, The hands are not the hands of Esau [so Esau has no power].' "

"'So long as there are no children chirping out loud in their voices [and studying the Torah] in synagogues and study houses, The hands are the hands of Esau [so Esau has power].'"

Pesiqta deRab Kahana XV:V.1

To understand the message, we have to know that, when sages in the documents that reached closure in the fifth and later centuries referred to "Esau," they meant Rome. This was Christian Rome, Rome guided by the same Scriptures of ancient Israel that sages valued as "the Written Torah." So now Israel (Jacob) competed with Esau, as contemporary Israel of the fifth century competed with Rome. They were brothers and enemies. Then Rome was Christian, which accounts for the conviction that Rome was the brother, hence Esau, competing with Jacob, who is Israel, for the inheritance, the birthright of the Torah. The reference to Esau (Rome) thus links the whole to the contemporary context and alleges that if the Israelites will support those who study the Torah and teach it, then their cities will be safe, and the rule of Esau/Rome will come to an end; then the Messiah will come, so the stakes are not trivial.

So much for the work that really matters, the work that people should aspire to do. Sages also recognize that there are categories of work people should avoid, as we already have noticed. But what is the principle that explains which kind of work is to be avoided? It is work that demeans, and that means work that makes one dependent, or work that brings one into disrepute. A man should not depend on his wife's earnings:

Our rabbis have taught on Tannaite authority:
He who depends on the earnings of his wife or of a mill will never see a sign of blessing.
The earnings of his wife: this refers to her selling wool by weight.
A mill: this refers to renting it out.
But if she makes woolen things and sells them, Scripture certainly praises her: "She makes linen garments and sells them" (Prov. 31:24).

Bavli Pesahim 4:1–2 I.6–10/50B

Another kind of living that sages, for obvious reasons, condemn, brings the worker into disrepute. It is not necessarily illegal, but it is certainly destructive of the common interest. That may be because they trade in what is free for the taking, which is the produce of the seventh year of the seven-year cycle of agriculture, when the Holy Land is deemed ownerless, its produce available at no cost to everyone. Or it may be because they make a living by destroying the environment; sages condemn raising small cattle, particularly goats, which denude the land of trees and other sustaining growth, and cutting down trees. Or it may be that they want to rise beyond their assigned station and lot in life.

Our rabbis have taught on Tannaite authority:
Those who trade in produce of the Seventh Year, breed small cattle, cut down beautiful trees, or look for something better than their portion, will never see a sign of blessing.

How come?
People are scandalized by them.

Bavli Pesahim 4:1–2 I.6–10/50B

The striking point comes at the end: people who try to better themselves. Sages valued private property, regarding the right of ownership as a given. But they did not think that people should aspire to enrich themselves; they did not see as a worthy goal the increase of wealth defined as either gold or real estate. That is because, we recall, they defined wealth in other terms altogether. So they saw no point in trying to get more of what is worth less than something else, gold than Torah. Some money brings its own curse, as sages explain, and if people who work in the sacred professions, such as scribes, do the work just to make a living, they are profiting from God's interest.

Earlier we saw that within the system, all honorable ways of earning a living are treated with respect, though some are easier than others. But some ways of making a living do not bring honor and represent exploitation of one person by another. Here is how sages identify disreputable professions:

Our rabbis have taught on Tannaite authority:
Four pennies will never carry a sign of blessing.
The fee for a clerk, the fee for an interpreter, the fee paid by orphans to those who trade in their capital, and money that comes from overseas.
Now there is no problem understanding why that is the case of the fee for interpreters [who announce in a loud voice the teachings of the master], since it appears to be a fee paid for work on the Sabbath; there is no problem understanding the case of orphans' money, since they cannot renounce ownership [and the minor cannot renounce an excessive fee]; and there is no problem understanding the case of money from overseas, since miracles don't happen every day. [Overseas trading is so perilous that to make money in it requires a miracle from God. People should not depend on that.] But what's the problem with the fee for a clerk?
Said R. Joshua b. Levi, "Twenty-four fasts did the men of the great assembly conduct on account of those who write out scrolls, phylacteries, and doorpost Scriptures, so that they should never get rich, for if they get rich, they'll never write the necessary religious articles again."

Bavli Pesahim 4:1–2 I.6–10/50B

Our rabbis have taught on Tannaite authority:
Those who write out scrolls, phylacteries, and doorpost Scriptures, they, those who trade in what they make, and those who trade in what those who trade in what they make, and all who trade in the work of Heaven—including those who sell blue wool—will never see a sign of blessing. But if they do it for its own sake, they do.

Bavli Pesahim 4:1–2 I.6–10/50B

So much for work that the Torah does not advise or value; the reasons derive from the coherent system that identifies one kind of work as meritorious, another as neutral, and a third as disreputable. Essentially, the sages condemn making a living on God's account, that is, through trading in sacred objects.

Is there a form of labor that by definition is detestable? What sages condemn out of hand, for reasons that theology supplies, is sloth, and a simple statement of the matter suffices to show what is at stake:

R. Dosa b. Harkinas says, "Sleeping late in the morning, drinking wine at noon, chatting with children, and attending the synagogues of the ignorant drive a man out of the world."

Sleeping late in the morning: how so?

This teaches that a person should not intend to sleep until the time of reciting the *Shema* has passed.

For when someone sleeps until the time for reciting the Shema has passed, he turns out to waste time that should be spent studying the Torah.

As it is said, "The lazy one says, There is a lion in the way, yes, a lion is in the streets. The door is turning on its hinges and the lazy man is still in bed" (Prov. 26:13–14).

The Fathers According to Rabbi Nathan XXI:I.1

Drinking wine at noon: how so?

This teaches that someone should not plan to drink wine at night.

For when someone drinks wine at noon, he turns out to waste time that should be spent studying the Torah.

As it is said, "Woe to you, O land, when your king is a boy and your princes feast in the morning" (Qoh. 10:16).

And further: "Happy are you, O land, when your king is a free man, and your princes eat in due season, in strength and not in drunkenness" (Qoh. 10:17).

The Fathers According to Rabbi Nathan XXI:II.1

Chatting with children: how so?

This teaches that a person should not plan to sit by himself and repeat traditions [at home.]

For if someone sits by himself and repeats traditions at home, he chats with his children and dependents and turns out to waste time that should be spent in the study of the Torah.

For it is said, "This book of the Torah shall not depart out of your mouth, but you shall meditate in it day and night" (Josh. 1:8).

The Fathers According to Rabbi Nathan XXI:III.1

And attending the synagogues of the ignorant drive a man out of the world: how so?

This teaches that a person should not plan to join with the idle in the corners of the market place.

For if someone sits around with the idle in the corners of the market place, he turns out to waste time that he should spend in studying the Torah.

For so it is said, "Happy is the one who has not walked in the counsel of the wicked, stood in the way of the sinners, or sat in the seat of the scornful. . . . But his delight is in the Torah of the Lord" (Ps. 1:1–2).

The Fathers According to Rabbi Nathan XXI:IV.1

R. Meir says, "What is the meaning of the statement, 'sat in the seat of the scornful'?

"This refers to the theaters and circuses of the gentiles, in which people are sentenced to death,

"as it is said, 'I hate the gathering of evil doers and will not sit with the wicked' (Ps. 26:5).

"The word 'evil doers' refers only to the wicked, as it is said, 'For the evil doers shall be cut off, and yet a little while and the wicked is no more' (Ps. 37:9–10).

"And what will be the form of the punishment that is coming to them in time to come?

"'For behold the day comes, it burns as a furnace, and all the proud and all that do wickedness shall be stubble' (Ma. 3:19).

"And the proud are only the scorners, as it is said, 'A proud and haughty man—scorner is his name' (Prov. 21:24)."

The Fathers According to Rabbi Nathan XXI:IV.2

There was the case of R. Aqiba who was in session and repeating teachings for his disciples. He remembered something that he had done in his youth.

He said, "I give thanks for you, O Lord my God, that you have placed my portion among those who sit in the house of study and have not placed my portion with those who sit idly in the market place."

The Fathers According to Rabbi Nathan XXI:V.1

It would be difficult to state the matter more clearly than Aqiba does: work to be desired is Torah-study, work to be avoided demeans. But any form of useful labor gains its blessing, and all modes of sloth, their curse.

WHY MUST WE HELP OTHERS? PRIVATE GAIN AND PUBLIC BENEFIT

We cannot understand the answer to this question that the Judaism under study here puts forth without keeping in mind a single fact. The Torah contemplates Israel within the Land of Israel, the Promised Land, and the Torah further regards God as the owner of the Land: "The earth is the Lord's, and the fulness thereof" (Ps. 24:1). Hence when we help others, it is because we are using what God owns and has given to us in such a way as to carry out the will of the one who owns it all.

Viewing holy Israel as a society made up of households engaged in farming, the Torah provides for sharing crops with the needy as well as those engaged in public service. Scripture forms the basis for that provision, with its program of offerings and tithes to support the poor, the priesthood, and pilgrimage to Jerusalem on the festivals. Farmers are to leave the corner of the field, not taking every last bit of grain; the poor then are free to glean the remnant of the crops. Within this system, why must we help others? It is because what we have belongs to God. God has designated his share for those who need his help, especially the poor. In the context of holy Israel living in the Holy Land, Roger L. Brooks explains, the matter is worked out in concrete terms as follows:

> The Land worked by Israelite farmers did not belong to them, but to God. Israelites worked the soil as tenant farmers, and benefited from the Land through God's munificence. Each crop they reaped constituted a reaffirmation of God's gift of the Land to them alone. In return for this gift, the Rabbinic authors of Tractate Peah (following Scripture's commands) deemed the product of the Land of Israel subject to a variety of taxes and transfer payments. These dues were paid, so to speak, to God himself, or at least to his representatives. Thus Israelite farmers, within the Rabbinic system of agriculture, were required to hand over a portion of their crops to priests, in exchange for their service in the holy Temple. A separate portion of the Land's produce was to be set aside for poor people. The poor, in the early Rabbinic world, were deemed to be under God's special protection, because otherwise they would not share equally in the benefit of God's Holy Land. All of these taxes flowed directly out of the Rabbis' conviction that God alone owned and controlled the entire Land of Israel. In an age of competing claims for ownership and right to settlement, perhaps we may refocus our attention on the true owner of the Land of Israel. . . .
>
> These passages in the Torah specified constraints upon normal agricultural procedures, all designed to allow poor and indigent Israelites to eke out a living by gathering scraps of food from fields and orchards. Leviticus 19:9 commanded Israelites to leave a corner of their fields unharvested, so that poor people might reap a bit of grain; Leviticus 19:10 extended this provision by ruling that stalks of grain or clusters of grapes that accidentally fell to the earth were not to be gathered by the harvesters, but left behind for the poor. Deuteronomy 26:19 ruled that produce that workers left behind in a field, orchard, or vineyard, should be abandoned so that the poor, once again, might gain some benefit of the Land's yield. And finally, Deuteronomy 26:12–13 described poorman's tithe, a portion of the yield set aside during the third and sixth years of the Sabbatical cycle.[3]

Brooks's exposition requires no comment; it is a reliable and clear account of how Israelites provide for the less fortunate classes of society. It is by sharing the wealth. In an agricultural economy, that meant the crops. In this context, the poor are not beggars, the rich are not patrons. The rich do their duty, and the poor collect what is owing to them, what God has assigned to them. In addition to the tithes and offerings to the poor, the farmer contributed to the support of the Temple priests and Levites. In the seven-year cycle, a further tithe, set aside in years 1, 2, 4, and 5, was for the poor, and in years 3 and 6 for the pilgrimage to Jerusalem. So a simple and clear answer responds to the question at hand.

---

[3]Roger Brooks, *The Talmud of the Land of Israel. A Preliminary Translation and Explanation.* Edited by Jacob Neusner. Volume Two. *Tractate Peah: Support for the Poor* (Chicago: University of Chicago Press, 1987), 1.

How does the Torah situate charity in the hierarchy of virtues and meritorious deeds? As in Islam, charity (called by the same Hebrew word that is used
for "righteousness," *sedaqah*) forms a principal religious obligation. But when it
comes to hierarchizing the virtues of charity, loving-kindness, and justice, when
they are to be compared with one another, they are shown in the end to be
equivalent in God's eyes:

> Said R. Eleazar, "Greater is the one who carries out an act of charity than
> one who offers all the sacrifices.
> 　　"For it is said, 'To do charity and justice is more desired by the Lord than
> sacrifice' (Prov. 21:3)."

So far we have set the world on its head, by declaring charity for the poor a
greater act of service to God than the offering of sacrifices to God in heaven.
But an act of loving-kindness takes priority over an act of charity:

> And R. Eleazar said, "An act of loving kindness is greater than an act of charity.
> 　　"For it is said, 'Sow to yourselves according to your charity, but reap ac-
> cording to your loving kindness' (Hos. 10:12).
> 　　"If a man sows seed, it is a matter of doubt whether he will eat a crop or
> not. But if a man harvests the crop, he most certainly will eat it."
> 　　And R. Eleazar said, "An act of charity is rewarded only in accord with
> the loving kindness that is connected with it.
> 　　"For it is said, 'Sow to yourselves according to your charity, but reap ac-
> cording to your loving kindness' (Hos. 10:12)."

The point is, if an act of charity is done out of a sense of obligation and devotion to the other, then it has value, but if it is done in a spirit of arrogance and
condescension, then it does not. Not only so, but an act of personal service takes
priority over an act of charity in the form of mere money:

> Our rabbis have taught on Tannaite authority:
> 　　In three aspects are acts of loving kindness greater than an act of charity.
> 　　An act of charity is done only with money, but an act of loving kindness
> someone carries out either with his own person or with his money.
> 　　An act of charity is done only for the poor, while an act of loving kindness
> may be done either for the poor or for the rich.
> 　　An act of charity is done only for the living. An act of loving kindness may
> be done either for the living or for the dead.

Charity and justice are the same thing. We give to the poor because it is an act
of righteousness, it is owing from us, not a matter of volition but of obligation:

> And R. Eleazar has said, "Whoever does an act of charity and justice is as if
> he has filled the entire world with mercy.
> 　　"For it is said, 'He loves charity and justice, the earth is full of the loving
> kindness of the Lord' (Ps. 33:5).
> 　　"Now you might wish to say that whoever comes to jump may take a leap
> [whoever wishes to do good succeeds without difficulty]."

"Scripture accordingly states, 'How precious is your loving kindness, O God' (Ps. 36:8). [The opportunity of doing real, well-deserved charity and dispensing it in a judicious manner is rare].

"Now you might wish to say that the same is the case for fear of Heaven [so that one who fears Heaven nonetheless has trouble in carrying out charity and justice].

"Scripture accordingly states, 'But the loving kindness of the Lord is from everlasting to everlasting upon them that fear him' (Ps. 103:17)."

Said R. Hama bar Papa, "Every man who enjoys grace is assuredly a God-fearer.

"For it is said, 'But the loving kindness of the Lord is from everlasting to everlasting upon them that fear him' (Ps. 103:17)."

Bavli Sukkah 4:10 V.8/49b

The hierarchizing of loving kindness and charity produces the result that the former takes priority, for specified reasons, deriving from Scripture.

WHEN WORK DOES NOT WORK: UNEMPLOYMENT, EXPLOITATION, AND ALTERNATIVES TO PROPER WORK

If, as we noted at the very outset, the situation of unemployment simply lies beyond the imagination of the sages of the Torah, they fully appreciated the mutual obligations of worker and employer. Employers exploit workers when they pay them less than the going wage. Workers swindle employers when they do not show up for work they have contracted to do. How then to sort out the conflicting claims? In some cases the deceived party may complain but not gain reparations:

He who hires craftsmen,

and one party deceived the other—

one has no claim on the other party except a complaint [which is not subject to legal recourse].

But what if one can demonstrate that the worker has caused the employer a genuine loss? Then the employer has recourse even to deception:

[If] one hired an ass driver or wagon driver to bring porters and pipes for a bride or a corpse,

or workers to take his flax out of the steep,

or anything which goes to waste [if there is a delay],

and [the workers] went back on their word—

in a situation in which there is no one else [available for hire],

he hires others at their expense,

or he deceives them [by promising to pay more and then not paying up more than his originally stipulated commitment].

Mishnah-tractate Baba Mesia 6:1

The same principle of equity governs not only workers, but also craftsmen. And workers and craftsmen are protected by the rule: if the employer changes the terms of the original agreement, he must pay up:

> He who hires craftsmen and they retracted—
>   their hand is on the bottom.
>   If the householder retracts,
>   his hand is on the bottom.
>   Whoever changes [the original terms of the agreement]—
>   his hand is on the bottom.
>   And whoever retracts—
>   his hand is on the bottom.
>
> Mishnah-tractate Baba Mesia 6:2

The extent to which workers bear responsibility for deceit is spelled out by the first systematic commentary to the Mishnah, the Tosefta, in detailed terms. We see that the Mishnah's treatment of the basic transaction—one party deceives another, neither then has much of a concrete claim—applies only if the workers did not show up. But if these day workers did show up, then they have lost a day of work, and living from pay check to pay check and day to day, they cannot afford to lose the salary. The householder must pay it.

> He who hires workers and they deceived the householder, or the householder deceived them, they have no claim on one another except a complaint.
> Under what circumstances? When the workers did not show up.
>   But if ass-drivers came but did not find grain, but found the field too wet to work and not suitable for ploughing, he pays them their wages in full.
>   But one who actually travels with a load is not the same as one who travels empty-handed, and one who does the work is not treated as equivalent to one who comes and sits and does nothing.

What happens if the work has gotten under way? Then we proportion the settlement, paying for the work actually done:

> Under what circumstances? It is in a case in which they did not actually begin the work. But if they had actually begun the work, lo, they make an estimate for him of how much work had actually been done.
>   How so? If one undertook for the householder to cut down his standing grain for two selas, and he had cut down half of it but left half of it, or if he undertook to weave a cloak for two selas, and had woven half of it but left half of it, the portion that is done is assessed.
>   How so? If what he had made was worth six denars, they hand over to him a sela [four denars] or he completes the work. And if it was worth a sela, they hand over to him a sela.
>   R. Dosa says, "They make an estimate of the value of what is going to be made. If that which was going to be made was worth five denars, they give him a sheqel or he finishes the work. And if it was worth a sheqel, they give him a sheqel."

Now we revert to the main point of the Mishnah: when the employer may take high-handed action, replacing the workers or promising to pay them more and then adhering to the original agreement. That is when time is of the essence. But if time is of the essence, then the generous provision of the Mishnah's law pertains.

> Under what circumstances? If it is a case of something that does not go to waste. But in the case of something that goes to waste if there is a delay, he hires others at their expense or deceives them by promising to pay more and then not paying up more than his originally stated commitment.
>
> How so? He says to the worker, "I agreed to pay you a sela. Lo, I'm going to give you two." He then goes and hires workers from another location and comes and takes the money from this party and hands it over to that party. To what extent? Even up to forty or fifty zuz.
>
> Under what circumstances? In a situation in which he comes to an agreement with him while he cannot find others to hire. But if he saw ass-drivers coming along, the worker may say to him, "Go and hire one of these for your needs," and the employer has no claim on him except a complaint.
>
> Tosefta Baba Mesia 7:1A–LL]

In this way we see how the law provides fair arrangements for both parties to the transaction of work, the employer and the employee. And we note, further, that the law limits the workers' liability: if other workers are at hand, those that have chosen not to work cannot be penalized.

The established rules of the community govern; one may not make up his own work regulations for his employees. Exploitation involves not only the employer's deceiving the workers, it also covers the employer's adhering to the accepted practices of the locale. The employer may not impose upon the workers regulations that are not generally required:

> He who hires day workers and told them to start work early or to stay late— in a place in which they are accustomed not to start work early or not to stay late, he has no right to force them to do so. In a place in which they are accustomed to provide a meal, he must provide a meal. In a place in which they are accustomed to make do with a sweet, he provides it.
>
> Mishnah-tractate Baba Mesia 7:1

The Torah provides that one may not muzzle an ox when it is ploughing: "You shall not muzzle an ox when it treads out the grain" (Deuteronomy 25:4). The ox has the right to nibble on the crop that it is helping to produce. The same rule applies to workers. If they are working in vineyards, they have the right to nibble on the grapes while they work; that is not deemed thievery.

> And these have the right to eat the produce on which they work by right accorded to them in the Torah: he who works on what is as yet unplucked may eat from the produce at the end of the time of processing; and he who works on plucked produce may eat from the produce before processing is done; in both instances solely in regard to what grows from the ground.
>
> But these do not have the right to eat the produce on which they labor by right accorded to them in the Torah: he who works on what is as yet

unplucked, before the end of the time of processing; and he who works on plucked produce after the processing is done, in both instances solely in regard to what does not grow from the ground.

Mishnah-tractate Baba Mesia 7:2

But here too, the employer has rights; the workers may not gorge themselves or take advantage, and they also may eat only the crop on which they are working:

> If the laborer was working on figs, he has not got the right to eat grapes. If he was working on grapes, he has not got the right to eat figs.
>
> But he does have the right to refrain from eating until he gets to the best produce and then to exercise his right to eat.
>
> And in all instances they have said that he may eat from the produce on which he is laboring only in the time of work. But on grounds of restoring lost property to the owner, they have said in addition:
>
> Workers have the right to eat as they go from furrow to furrow even though they do not then work, and when they are coming back from the press so saving time for the employer.

Mishnah-tractate Baba Mesia 7:4

> A worker has the right to eat cucumbers, even to a denar's worth, or dates, even to a denar's worth.
>
> R. Eleazar Hisma says, "A worker should not eat more than the value of his wages."
>
> But sages permit.
>
> But they instruct the man not to be a glutton and thereby slam the door in his own face to future employment.

Mishnah-tractate Baba Mesia 7:5

So here again, the workers may not exploit their rights, and the employers may not limit those same rights. A further form of exploitation of workers involves not paying them promptly. The Written Torah forbids such a practice, "In his day you shall give him his fee" (Deuteronomy 24:15), so too, "The wages of a hired worker will not abide with you at night until the morning" (Lev. 19:13). The Oral Torah interprets the law to mean, one who has worked all day must be paid by nightfall, and one who has worked all night must be paid by dawn:

> (1) A day worker collects his wage any time of the night. (2) And a night worker collects his wage any time of the day. (3) A worker by the hour collects his wage any time of the night or day.
>
> A worker hired by the week, a worker hired by the month, a worker hired by the year, a worker hired by the septennate—if he completed his period of labor by day, collects any time that day. If he completed his period of labor by night, he collects his wage any time during the rest of that night and the following day.

Mishnah-tractate Baba Mesia 9:11

Not paying promptly is deemed an oppression of the workers:

> He who holds back the wages of a hired hand transgresses on account of five negative commandments, because of not oppressing (Lev. 19:13),
>> because of not stealing (Lev. 19:13),
>> because of the verse that says, "The wages of a hired worker will not abide with you all night until morning" (Lev. 19:13);
>> "you shall give him hire on the day he earns it before the sun goes down, because he is poor" (Dt. 24:15).
>
> Tosefta Baba Mesia 10:3A–C

But that is the case only if the worker lays claim for his wages. If he does not do so, the employer does not violate the law of paying promptly. The worker's responsibility to take care of himself triggers the working of the law.

The Torah takes account of all manner of exploitation of workers in its quest for justice for poor and rich alike. But, as we have seen, the sages find little to say about matters that fall outside of their categorical structure. Just as unemployment lies beyond the imagination of the sages of the Torah, so they would find it difficult to differentiate "proper" from "improper" work. True, the Torah as sages interpret it values some kinds of work over others. It further recognizes the difference between hard physical labor and the less physically enervating demands of certain crafts. But in the end, work is work, and the system treats workers with dignity and respect, without regard to the kind of work that they do.

UNCONVENTIONAL WORK: WORKING FOR GOD

Who are the people who work for God? There are three types: those who study Torah, those who carry on the sacred service in the Temple (when it is standing), and those who without coercion treat others with generosity of spirit. Giving what God values but cannot command or coerce represents the highest form of unconventional work. The priests and Levites of the Temple would certainly present themselves as candidates. Their work is hard, involving much heavy lifting. To do the work properly, they must be punctilious—for example, avoiding those sources of cultic contamination or uncleanness that Scripture specifies at Leviticus chapters 11–15. And the children of Aaron, the priests, bring peace to the community and work for peace between Israel and their father in heaven:

> Hillel says, "Be disciples of Aaron, loving peace and pursuing peace, loving people and drawing them near to the Torah."
>
> Tractate Abot 1:12

The leaders of the community, judges and administrators, would offer themselves as a choice. They provide for the general welfare; they hold things together; they make provision for the needs of the community. They work not only for themselves but for everyone, realizing Hillel's famous saying:

Hillel would say, "If I am not for myself, who is for me? And when I am for myself, what am I? And if not now, when?"

Tractate Abot 1:14

The householders, responsible for the working of the social order, organizing and maintaining the natural processes that feed the community and sustain the entire life of Israel—they too would say they do God's work. And all would present a strong case for themselves, one that no one would reject.

But it will not surprise readers of this chapter to learn that, for its part, the Torah identifies as those who work for God, above all, the disciples of the sages, who study the Torah, provide the model of true piety; they study the Torah in poverty and among nonbelievers. To make that point, the fourth-century sage, Raba, reads the verse of the Song of Songs 7:12, "Come . . . let us go forth into the fields." Since all of Judaism knows that the Song of Solomon speaks of the intense, passionate love of God for Israel and Israel for God, the meaning of the verse will prove self-evident. Here Israel speaks to God and asks God to join Israel in the fields, not in the cities but in the villages—where the disciples of the Torah, in penury, labor at study of the Torah:

> Expounded Raba, "What is the meaning of the verse of Scripture, 'Come my beloved, let us go forth into the field, let us lodge in the villages, let us get up early to the vineyards, let us see whether the vine has budded, whether the vine blossom be opened, and the pomegranates be in flower; there will I give you my love' (Song 7:12)?
>
> "'Come my beloved, let us go forth into the field': Said the congregation of Israel before the Holy One, blessed be He, 'Lord of the world, don't judge me like those who live in the cities, who are full of thievery and fornication and vain oaths and false swearing.'
>
> "'Let us go forth into the field': 'Come and I shall show you disciples of sages, who are engaged in the Torah in the midst of want.'
>
> "'Let us lodge in the villages': Read the letters for villages as though they bore vowels to yield, 'among the infidels,' 'come and I shall show you those upon whom you have bestowed much good, and who have denied you.'
>
> "'Let us get up early to the vineyards': This refers to the synagogues and study houses.
>
> "'Let us see whether the vine has budded': This refers to masters of Scripture.
>
> "'Whether the vine blossom be opened': This refers to masters of the Mishnah.
>
> "'And the pomegranates be in flower': This refers to the masters of analysis.
>
> "'There will I give you my love': 'I shall show you my glory, my greatness, the praise of my sons and my daughters.'"

Bavli-tractate Erubin 2:1–2 V.16/21B–22A

So the Oral Torah is explicit in the matter: those who do God's work are those who spend their lives at Torah-study. But when in the third volume of this series we come to the matter of virtue, we shall find a quite surprising judgment on that view: there are forms of virtue that transcend in importance even Torah-study, and those who do God's work turn out to be those who surrender their will to the need and outcry of another.

This brings us to the third category of unconventional labor: deeds that the law of the Torah cannot require but must favor: what one does on one's own volition, beyond the measure of the law. Such deeds elicit from him a response comparable to grace: divine favor that cannot be coerced but that can be merited. The Hebrew word is *zekhut,* sometimes translated "merit," but really untranslatable. It is best understood as the opposite of sin. A sin is what one has done by one's own volition beyond all limits of the law. So an act that generates *zekhut* for the individual is the counterpart and opposite: what one does by one's own volition that also is beyond all requirements of the law. Here are those acts of labor of such a remarkable generosity as to bring about a response in heaven:

> A certain ass-driver appeared before the rabbis [the context requires: in a dream] and prayed, and rain came. The rabbis sent and brought him and said to him, "What is your trade?"
>
> He said to them, "I am an ass-driver."
>
> They said to him, "And how do you conduct your business?"
>
> He said to them, "One time I rented my ass to a certain woman, and she was weeping on the way, and I said to her, 'What's with you?' and she said to me, 'The husband of that woman [me] is in prison [for debt], and I wanted to see what I can do to free him.' So I sold my ass and I gave her the proceeds, and I said to her, 'Here is your money, free your husband, but do not sin [by becoming a prostitute to raise the necessary funds].'"
>
> They said to him, "You are worthy of praying and having your prayers answered."

The ass-driver clearly has a powerful lien on heaven, so that his prayers are answered, even while those of others are not. What did he do to get that entitlement? He did what no law could demand: impoverished himself to save the woman from a "fate worse than death."

> In a dream of R. Abbahu, Mr. Pentakaka ["Five sins"] appeared, who prayed that rain would come, and it rained. R. Abbahu sent and summoned him. He said to him, "What is your trade?"
>
> He said to him, "Five sins does that man [I] do every day, [for I am a pimp:] hiring whores, cleaning up the theater, bringing home their garments for washing, dancing, and performing before them."
>
> He said to him, "And what sort of decent thing have you ever done?"
>
> He said to him, "One day that man [I] was cleaning the theater, and a woman came and stood behind a pillar and cried. I said to her, 'What's with you?' And she said to me, 'That woman's [my] husband is in prison, and I wanted to see what I can do to free him,' so I sold my bed and cover, and I gave the proceeds to her. I said to her, 'Here is your money, free your husband, but do not sin.'"
>
> He said to him, "You are worthy of praying and having your prayers answered."

This moves us still further, since the named man has done everything sinful that one can do, and, more to the point, he does it every day. So the singularity of the act of *zekhut,* which suffices if done only one time, encompasses its power to outweigh a life of sin—again, an act of *zekhut* as the mirror image and opposite of sin. Here again, the single act of saving a woman from a "fate worse than death" has sufficed.

A pious man from Kefar Imi appeared [in a dream] to the rabbis. He prayed for rain and it rained. The rabbis went up to him. His householders told them that he was sitting on a hill. They went out to him, saying to him, "Greetings," but he did not answer them.

He was sitting and eating, and he did not say to them, "You break bread too."

When he went back home, he made a bundle of faggots and put his cloak on top of the bundle [instead of on his shoulder].

When he came home, he said to his household [wife], "These rabbis are here [because] they want me to pray for rain. If I pray and it rains, it is a disgrace for them, and if not, it is a profanation of the Name of Heaven. But come, you and I will go up [to the roof] and pray. If it rains, we shall tell them, 'We are not worthy to pray and have our prayers answered.'"

They went up and prayed and it rained.

They came down to them [and asked], "Why have the rabbis troubled themselves to come here today?"

They said to him, "We wanted you to pray so that it would rain."

He said to them, "Now do you really need my prayers? Heaven already has done its miracle."

They said to him, "Why, when you were on the hill, did we say hello to you, and you did not reply?"

He said to them, "I was then doing my job. Should I then interrupt my concentration [on my work]?"

They said to him, "And why, when you sat down to eat, did you not say to us 'You break bread too'?"

He said to them, "Because I had only my small ration of bread. Why would I have invited you to eat by way of mere flattery [when I knew I could not give you anything at all]?"

They said to him, "And why when you came to go down, did you put your cloak on top of the bundle?"

He said to them, "Because the cloak was not mine. It was borrowed for use at prayer. I did not want to tear it."

They said to him, "And why, when you were on the hill, did your wife wear dirty clothes, but when you came down from the mountain, did she put on clean clothes?"

He said to them, "When I was on the hill, she put on dirty clothes, so that no one would gaze at her. But when I came home from the hill, she put on clean clothes, so that I would not gaze on any other woman."

They said to him, "It is well that you pray and have your prayers answered."

The pious man, finally, enjoys the recognition of the sages by reason of his lien upon Heaven, able as he is to pray and bring rain. What has so endowed him with *zekhut*? Acts of punctiliousness of a moral order: concentrating on his work, avoiding an act of dissimulation, integrity in the disposition of a borrowed object, his wife's concern not to attract other men and her equal concern to make herself attractive to her husband. None of these stories refers explicitly to *zekhut*; all of them tell us about what it means to enjoy not an entitlement by inheritance but a lien accomplished by one's own supererogatory acts of restraint.

When, at the outset, we placed the matter of work—what we owe the community—into the larger context of the theology of the Torah (a.k.a. Judaism), we turned out to predetermine our results at every point. We cannot explain why we must work, what kinds of work are to be preferred or avoided, why we must help others through our work, what constitutes exploitation of workers, or what it means to work for God—we cannot explain anything to do with Israel in community without invoking the governing principle throughout. It is that Israel through the Torah will make of itself that community faithful to God such that God will respond with the work of restoration: Adam and Eve lost Eden, as Israel has lost the Land (so matters appeared to the sages after 70 C.E., when the Temple was destroyed, and in the centuries thereafter). Through the regeneration brought about by the Torah, Israel will so purify its heart as to accept God's will over its own will—and the restoration of holy Israel to the Land, signifying the return of Adam and Eve to Eden, is sure to follow. To the drama of humanity's restoration to grace, work forms a worthy overture.

COMMENTARIES

Christianity on Judaism

by BRUCE CHILTON

The First Letter of Peter takes up the language of "a royal priesthood, a holy nation," but applies it, rather than to Israel in the Land, to all those who are built into the spiritual house of sacrifice established by Jesus (1 Peter 2:5, 9). The act of following in the steps of Jesus, especially in a willingness to suffer for others on behalf of what is right (2:21), realizes the offering of which the Temple in Jerusalem was the model, but not the essence. Naturally, this move implies that all those who believe in Christ, led by the spirit of God, are in fact sons of Abraham and as such, joined to Israel. That principle—explicitly spelled out by Paul (Galatians 3:6–9)—is embraced by the author of 1 Peter (ca. 90 C.E.), who uses the language of the sanctification by God's Spirit (1:2) of those who "once were no people but now are God's people" (2:10).

The logic of this sacrificial inclusion of non-Jews with Israel is rooted in the final chapter of the book of Zechariah, which envisions a sacrifice on Mount Zion that includes the nations. Just that chapter, of course, inspired Jesus when he expelled traders from the Great Court of the Temple (Zechariah 14:21; Matthew 21:12–13; Mark 11:15–19; Luke 19:45–49; John 2:13–16), and the elimination of commercial dealings from the community of Christians in Jerusalem under Peter's leadership (Acts 4:32–5:11). By the time 1 Peter was written, however, Peter had died (in 64 C.E.), the Jerusalem community had been dispersed, and the Temple itself destroyed (in 70 C.E.). This epistle is written to "exiles" (1 Peter 1:1), because that was the experience of living in the Graeco-Roman world without the visible sacrifice and public recognition that were once possible in Jerusalem. This was a world to be skeptical of, and the author exhorts his readers "as aliens and exiles to abstain from the passions of the flesh that wage war against the soul" (2:11). So it is no surprise that, to Christianity, work looks more like a necessary evil than a blessing.

Genesis 3:19 indeed supports that sort of wariness about work, and leads to a certain reserve about finding reasons for doing it. If work is part of the curse of disobedience, is it really an imitation of God and the means of restoring us to Eden? For Christianity, work is more what you do to make a living, while the spiritual sacrifice of imitating Jesus is what enables people to apprehend the sovereignty of God. That is why the community described in Acts pools its property to address common needs, rather than selling it to acquire leisure. The imperative of a world being transformed by God's influence involves giving up the structures of authority and profit that govern the status quo.

So the household is addressed in 1 Peter (2:18–3:7), but as a reality rather than as a privileged ideal, simply as the place where salvation may peacefully be worked out for all if all attend to the example of Christ. It is evident from the pages of the New Testament itself that this lesson was learned only too well by some people. In the name of Paul, the authors of 2 Thessalonians set out the apostlic commandment, "If anyone does not wish to work, let one not eat" (2 Thessalonians 3:10). Simple idleness, which in later centuries was an occasion for the contemplative tradition in Christianity, was in the earliest stages a vexing problem, because it could claim justification in the widespread agreement among Christians about the vanity of the present world (2 Thessalonians 3:6–13). But it is notable that the putative authors of 2 Thessalonians, Paul with Silvanus and Timothy (1:1), do not in any way desist from the fundamental hope that the form of this world is passing away. Indeed, they emphasize that the final transformation is already under way (2:1–12). The almost petulant tone of the linkage between working and eating conceals a more subtle insight: in the world we presently live in, cursed as it is, work is simply a necessity, as is eating. Until that world has been comprehensively transformed, the one is the condition of the other. But that is simply an analysis of where we are, not part of the hope of where we are to be.

Islam on Judaism

by TAMARA SONN

As in Judaism, in Islam everyone has a role in society and the efforts necessary to fulfill those roles are considered each person's proper work. Women's roles in the home are included in that category; this is their work and it is respected as such. In fact, the word used for "dowry" in the Qur'an is not one that means "bride price" or any such thing; it is *ujur,* which actually means "wages." The same term is used for the maintenance paid for a nursing mother in the case of divorce. However, in contrast to Judaism, people's social roles/work are not considered a punishment for sin in Islam. Islam does not view daily life as un-natural, a state deviant from the perfect world of Eden. Rather, human beings are seen as God's deputies or stewards (Qur'an 2:31). We were created with a purpose and that purpose is to carry on the work of God by working to create a just world, one in which the equality all humans share in the eyes of their cre-ator is reflected in the social order. The story of Eden explains the reality of human ignorance and weakness. We must overcome these in order to fulfill God's will. But the perfect existence of which Judaism speaks is not the "nor-mal" existence for humans; it will be the reward for efforts to fulfill the divine will in a less-than-perfect world. Thus, no sabbath as such is necessary to remind people of something they have lost. Instead, daily prayer reminds people of the purpose of their existence. The Friday communal prayer allows Muslims to draw strength and encouragement from one another. It reminds them that they are not alone in their struggle, nor can they hope to fulfill the divine will alone. It in-spires them to work toward a future of social justice and ultimate reward in the afterlife, rather than reminding them of a more perfect past. Because all people in Islam are charged with the "trust," the task to contribute to social justice to the extent they are capable, no individual or particular kind of work is favored in Islam above any others in this regard. Each will be judged according to her or his intentions and capacity. Any act of charity—whether financial or otherwise, such as an act of kindness—is a part of that effort. Good deeds, including sup-port of those in need and the social services that sustain any community, are therefore integral to the Islamic mission.

Hinduism on Judaism

by BRIAN K. SMITH

Judaism and Hinduism agree on a fundamental point: work should be a sacred activity. Beginning with the etymological similarities (both traditions derive their term for "work" from words originally meaning "ritual activity"), both re-ligions conceive of human labor as an integral part of the divine plan. The no-tion in Judaism that one's workweek imitates God's labor of creation (and rest) in the beginning also finds a parallel in the teachings of the Bhagavad Gita, where Krishna tells Arjuna that humans should work *because* God does; but here also one should work *in the way* God does (i.e., with detachment): "Whatever a leader does, the ordinary people also do. He sets the standard for the world to follow. In the three worlds, there is nothing I must do, nothing unattained to be attained, yet I engage in action. . . . Men retrace my path at every turn, Ar-juna. . . . As the ignorant act with attachment to actions, Arjuna, so wise men should act with detachment to preserve the world." Here the traditions part ways: if, in Judaism, human work imitates God's work "so that there can be the Sabbath," the "foretaste of the age to come, when . . . humanity will recover Eden," in Hinduism no such eschatological expectations drive the principle:

humans should work simply because it is their duty to do so, and through fulfilling their duty (*in the right way*), individual salvation is possible. Nor is there
any sense in most forms of Hinduism that work is a punishment for some kind
of "fall" from an original paradise, although within the ideology of caste the
lower classes are supposedly assigned their relatively demeaning occupations as a
kind of karmic retribution for past bad actions.

The two traditions also agree on another major point. The best work is the
work of studying, memorizing, and reciting the sacred texts. The tension in the
Jewish tradition between this highest occupation and making an actual living is
mitigated in Hinduism, however. Those who engage in this activity in Hinduism—the student of the Veda regardless of caste, and members of the Brahmin class who, ideally at least, pursue this work throughout their lifetimes—are
supported by others. Among other ways of keeping themselves afloat economically, students of the Veda are allowed to beg for their sustenance, a practice apparently unknown in Judaism. Nor is there in Hinduism any real, developed
notion that what we own belongs to God and therefore must be charitably re-
distributed to others. Charity in Hinduism is said to be a means of collecting
merit for the donor and the primary means by which the religious are supported
in their holy endeavors.

The idea in Judaism that "work is work, and the system treats workers with
dignity and respect, without regard to the kind of work that they do" is both affirmed in theory and denied in practice in Hinduism. While in theory all occupations are regarded as at least necessary to the cosmic-moral scheme of things
(for even thieves and other criminals are engaged in their *svadharma* or "own
duty" according to some Hindu texts), in practice there are what are regarded as
pure and impure occupations within caste Hinduism. The fact that some people
are assigned, by virtue of their birth, to work that others regarded as polluting is
at the heart of the injustices perpetrated by caste, and has stimulated modern
Hindu leaders like Gandhi to reform if not the system as a whole then at least
the attitudes many Hindus have toward those engaged in certain kinds of work.

Buddhism on Judaism

by Charles Hallisey

Striking differences between Buddhism and the three great monotheistic religions—Judaism, Christianity, and Islam—are immediately apparent. The ab-
sence of a Creator God and the assumption that beings have more than one life
can be named as two of the most obvious, but we should not allow such strong
contrasts to blind us to important similarities or to equally important, but more
subtle differences.

A careful comparison between Jewish and Buddhist materials helps us to see,
for example, an important similarity that illuminates each. This similarity is a structural one. That is, both Judaism and Buddhism seem to take the measure of work,
and what we owe to others, by recourse to a religious vision of a whole human
life. The sages of the Torah were concerned to see work as a sacred activity that
could be connected to and contrasted with Torah-study. As Jacob Neusner says,
"labor in Torah defines the purpose of human life; it is the goal; but it is not the

medium for maintaining life and avoiding starvation or exposure to the elements."
This basic position is one in which work and an ideal religious life are each put in
their place by the way they fit together into a broad pattern of human flourishing.
Buddhists did something similar when they made such religious practices as charity and meditation the goals of human life, rather than work itself.

Another similarity between Judaism and Buddhism on work also belies the
obvious differences: it is one's merit that makes the difference between poverty
and wealth, and certain occupations inevitably bring the consequences of sin for
those who engage in such occupations. Such ideas are very similar to Hindu and
Buddhist ideas of karma, the law of moral cause and effect, in which one's status in the present, including one's occupation, is determined by one's actions in
the past, just as one's actions now will determine one's future conditions for life.

SUMMARY

God made the world in six days and rested on the Seventh, and humanity, in
God's image, does the same. Work is natural to the human condition. Everyone
has worthwhile tasks: women, children, and men alike. But the most valuable
work lies in study of the Torah: for that purpose we are created. Among two or
three or more who engage in Torah-study, God is present. Torah-learning is
more valued than possession of land. The reason that people have to perform less
desirable tasks is that humanity embodies the condition of Adam and Eve after
Eden, required to perform hard labor to earn a living. It is a matter of one's merit
that a particular vocation is assigned. Everyone in society has a claim to a digni-
fied living. God is the ultimate owner of all things, human beings possess and use
them by God's grace. So sharing one's wealth is giving back to God what belongs to God anyhow. In this context, there is no such thing as "unemployment," since everyone has a task.

GLOSSARY

Abodah   labor; also, Temple service, performing the sacrificial cult in the Temple
of Jerusalem; also prayer

Abot   "the Fathers," the sayings of the principal authorities of the Oral Torah of
Judaism; a tractate attached to the Mishnah, ca. 200 C.E., at about 250 C.E.

Aggadah   lore, narrative, exegesis of Scripture, theology

B.C.E.   before the Common Era = B.C.

Baba Mesia   The Middle Gate, a tractate of the Mishnah that deals with aspects
of civil law, subject to commentary in the Bavli and the Yerushalmi

Bavli   the Talmud of Babylonia, ca. 600 C.E., a systematic commentary to thirty-
seven of the sixty-three tractates of the Mishnah

C.E.   Common Era = A.D.

Erubin a tractate of the Mishnah that deals with transporting objects on the Sabbath from public to private domain and vice versa; and the provision of a Sabbath boundary, mingling ownership of property within the boundary into a single domain for purpose of Sabbath observance

Fathers According to Rabbi Nathan, a talmud to Abot

Fathers see Abot

Halakhah law, norms of behavior

Hillel and Shammai Two principal authorities of the Mishnah, flourished around the beginning of the first century C.E.

Ketubot a tractate of the Mishnah that deals with marriage-agreements, guaranteeing support for a wife in the event of death or divorce

Leviticus Rabbah Commentary to the book of Leviticus, ca. 450 C.E.

Megillah a tractate of the Mishnah that deals with the festival of Purim, described in the biblical book of Esther; and with the life of synagogues, with special attention to the public declamation of the Torah

Mekhilta attributed to R. Ishmael Commentary to the book of Exodus, probably of ca. 250 C.E.

Mishnah a six part exposition of the law, divided into sixty-three tractates, or subject-areas, of the Oral Torah revealed by God to Moses at Mount Sinai and formulated and transmitted wholly in memory until formalized in ca. 200 C.E. under the auspices of Judah the Patriarch, the ruler of the Jewish population of Roman Palestine of that period

Pesahim a tractate of the Mishnah that deals with the festival of Passover, with special attention to the prohibition of leaven on that holy day and the sacrifice of the Pascal lamb; and the Passover meal in the home

Pesiqta deRab Kahana Rabbinic commentary on passages of Scripture highlighted on various Sabbaths and festivals

Qiddushin a tractate of the Mishnah that deals with betrothals

Shabbat Hebrew word for the Sabbath; the seventh day, a day of rest, commemorating the creation of the world in six days and God's repose on the Seventh

Taanit a tractate of the Mishnah that deals with fasting in times of crisis, and also the delegation of priests of a given village and its activities when it goes up to Jerusalem to conduct the Temple rites

Talmud a systematic commentary to a tractate of the Mishnah, clarifying the source in Scripture of a law in the Mishnah, the meanings of words and phrases, and the broader implications of a rule; also augmenting the presentation of the law by the Mishnah through a systematic exposition of correlative topics, whether of law or of theology; the whole characterized by contentious analytical argument

Torah the Five books of Moses, Genesis, Exodus, Leviticus Numbers, Deuteronomy; more generally, God's teaching to Moses at Mount Sinai, written and oral

Tosefta A compilation of legal rulings that complement those in the Mishnah and are attributed to the same authorities as are cited in the Mishnah

Tractate   a topical exposition of a category of law (halakhah) in Judaism, with special reference to the Mishnah's, Tosefta's, Yerushalmi's, and Bavli's topical divisions

Yerushalmi   The Talmud of the Land of Israel ("Jerusalem"), produced in ca. 400 C.E. in Galilee by the sages of the Torah

Yohanan ben Zakkai   The Rabbinic leader who escaped from Jerusalem before it fell to the Romans in the summer of 68 C.E. and who founded the study-circle that preserved knowledge of the Torah after the calamity and that produced the Mishnah and related traditions

Zekhut   unearned, uncoerced grace, bestowed by God in response to unearned acts of self-sacrifice or of other unusual merit that God craves but cannot coerce

DISCUSSION QUESTIONS

1. How does Judaism define "labor" or "work"? What is the model upon which Judaism calls for its definition?

2. How does the basic mythic narrative of Judaism come to concrete expression in the theory of work?

3. Why does Judaism teach that the highest form of labor is study of the Torah?

4. How does Judaism define ownership and possession, and how does it distinguish between ownership and the right to make use of something? In the context of the theology of Judaism, how does this distinction come to the surface in the Halakhah (law) of support for the poor in particular?

5. Why does Judaism deny the concept of "unemployment" altogether?

6. How does Judaism balance the rights of workers and management?

 **INFOTRAC**

If you would like additional information related to the material discussed here, you can visit our Web site: http://www.wadsworth.com

2

Christianity

BY BRUCE CHILTON

WHY MUST WE WORK?

One of the most revolutionary moments in the experience of the Church occurred when the Roman Empire tolerated Christianity, and then came to embrace it. That event, unanticipated and largely unpredictable, changed the terms in which Christians engaged the society in which they lived. Honest work became a religious duty, because the nature of the world itself had changed in the Christian estimation. There were certainly examples of economic teaching within the Church prior to Constantine, as we shall see in the sections that follow. But our first section is devoted to the way in which the events leading up to and culminating during the fourth century C.E. changed the constitution of the Roman world in a way that suddenly made Christians more responsible for that world. A reason was given for work that had not existed before.

The emergence of a group of followers around a Galilean rabbi named Jesus seems to have occasioned no official concern from the Romans prior to Jesus' action in the Temple, with one exception. Herod Antipas ruled Galilee and Peraea (east of the Jordan) as a client king of Rome, in succession to his father, Herod the Great (who died in 4 B.C.E.). His reign was notably stable, largely because he assiduously repressed critics. John the Baptist denounced Antipas' marriage to his brother's former wife, and Antipas had him beheaded (Matthew 14:3–12; Mark 6:17–29; Luke 3:19–20 and Josephus' *Antiquities* 18 § 109–119). His execution was not occasioned by placing an unusual requirement upon Antipas, but for insisting Antipas keep the Torah of purity as any person might understand it (Leviticus 20:21). When Jesus, who had been a disciple of John's for a time, enjoyed popular success, Antipas' suspicion turned to him (Matthew 14:1–2; Mark 6:14–16; Luke 9:7–9). One saying of Jesus probably reflects a period in which he fled from Antipas, and that may have been a reason for his final visit to Jerusalem (Luke 13:31–33).

But the execution of John the Baptist by Herod Antipas, and the execution of Jesus by Pontius Pilate, were not examples of religious oppression. In each case, the representative of Roman power was insisting (from his own point of view) upon recognition of the legitimacy of the Roman settlement. Herod's marriage was a public arrangement; the good order of the Temple was part and parcel of the Roman recognition of Judaism as a sanctioned religion. Provided routine worship in the Temple continued, and imperial sacrifices were accepted there, the old alliance from the time of Judas Maccabaeus was remembered (1 Maccabees 8), and Judaism would enjoy the status of *religio licita,* a legal religion.[1]

The value of being considered licit was the avoidance of the potential or actual danger of being violently repressed as a conspiratorial threat. Within the active memory of writers during the first century, the bloody removal of those who practiced the Bacchanalia in 186 B.C.E. was vivid. During the reign of Claudius (41–54 C.E.) a Roman officer who attended the imperial court was immediately sentenced to death, because he wore a Druid talisman (Pliny, *Natural History* 29 § 53–4). Since the Druids of Britain remained an untamed and rebellious people, their very symbols were considered a threat.

Followers of Jesus, especially those who had long practiced Judaism (and continued to do so after baptism), naturally assumed that their meetings were as licit as Judaism itself. After the Sabbath closed at sunset (which was seen as the end of one day and the beginning of another), followers of Jesus would continue their observance, concluding at dawn on Sunday, the day and the time of the resurrection. The rising of the heaven's sun corresponded to the rising of God's son within this practice.

With the inclusion of non-Jews within their community by baptism, and with their refusal to require circumcision and (in some cases) other laws of purity, followers of Jesus ran the risk of being denounced as followers of a *superstitio,* rather than as practitioners of what a *religio licita* (such as Judaism) did. The book of Acts consistently presents Paul as hounded by leaders of synagogues who, having given him a hearing, resisted his message (Acts 13–14). The very name given to Jesus' followers, *Christiani,* was a sign of coming trouble. Adherents of the movement came to be known as "Christians" (meaning partisans of Christ) in Antioch by around the year 45 C.E., and they embraced that term of intended ridicule.[2] The use of the term by outsiders highlights the marginal status of non-Jews who accepted baptism. Without conversion to Judaism, they were not Jews in the usual understanding; having rejected the gods of Hellenism by being baptized, they were also no longer representative of the Graeco-Roman syncretism, which was then fashionable. By calling disciples *Christiani,* a term analogous to *Caesariani* and *Pompeiani,* outsiders compared the movement more to a political faction than to a religion. It would be as if, in English, we called a disciple a "Christite," on the model of Thatcherite, Reaganite, Clintonite, and so on.

In the year 64 C.E., the emperor Nero used the marginal status of Christians to get out of a difficult political situation of his own. In that year, the great fire of Rome broke out, and it was rumored that it had been set at Nero's order.

---

[1]See Amnon Linder, *The Jews in Roman Imperial Legislation* (Detroit: Wayne State University Press, 1987).

[2]See C. K. Barrett, *The Acts of the Apostles:* The International Critical Commentary (Edinburgh: Clark, 1994), 556.

There is no doubt but that the opportunity for him to rebuild Rome along the lines he preferred was one he exploited to the greatest possible extent. Nero attempted to deflect suspicion from himself by fastening blame for the fire on Christians. They were rounded up, interrogated, and slaughtered, often with elaborate means of torture. Nero's excesses in regard to the Christians were obvious even to those who held that their religion was superstitious. The result seems to have been a reduction of attacks upon Christians for several decades (Tacitus, *Annals* 15.37–44).

In Jerusalem, meanwhile, trouble of a different kind was brewing for both Judaism and Christianity. A new spirit of nationalism influenced the priestly aristocracy. Josephus reports that James, the brother of Jesus, was killed in the Temple in 62 C.E. at the instigation of the high priest Ananus during the interregnum of the Roman governors Festus and Albinus (*Antiquities* 20 § 197–203). To have the most prominent leader within Christian Judaism removed was obviously a momentous event within Christianity, but arguably the execution was even more ominous for the prospects of Judaism within the empire. Ananus was deposed from the high priesthood for his action, but Josephus' account of the period makes it clear that, from the time of Albinus onward, Rome had to contend with a rising tide of nationalistic violence in and around Jerusalem.

The tide rose fatefully in the year 66 C.E., when Eleazar (the *sagan,* or manager, of the Temple) convinced priests not to accept offerings from non-Jews (Jewish War 2 § 409). That included the sacrifices paid for by Rome: the authorities of the Temple were breaching terms basic to the recognition of Judaism as *religio licita.* Insurgents took the Antonia, the fortress adjacent to the Temple, and killed the soldiers within. War had been irrevocably declared, and the victor could only have been Rome. The Temple itself was destroyed by fire in 70 C.E. after a protracted siege, and the suicide of the Zealots at Masada in 73 C.E. was the last public act of the revolt.

The strategy of the empire in the wake of the revolt was simple, direct, and punitive. The *fiscus Iudaicus,* a tax that adult males had paid for the maintenance of the Temple, was now demanded by Rome to be paid to the Temple of Jupiter Capitolinus in Rome. Moreover, the Roman version of *fiscus Iudaicus* was to be paid by all Jews, minors and women included, not only by adult males.[3] It is not surprising that, in the wake of those events, Judaic hopes centered on the restoration of the Temple. Works such as 2 Esdras (in the Apocrypha, also known as 4 Ezra), written around 100 C.E., openly represent the messianic vindication that was the object of much prayer and action. Such hopes were in cruel contrast to the political reality that the *fiscus Iudaicus* was now the price of being considered *religio licita.*

That period also saw much unrest among Jews outside of geographical Israel, especially during the reign of Trajan (98–117 C.E.). Trajan also had to deal with the question of what to do with Christians. Although Nero had discredited vigorous persecution, the association of Christianity with Judaism raised the question of Christian loyalty to Rome anew. Even within the New Testament, there are

---

[3]See E. Mary Smallwood, *The Jews under Roman Rule: Studies in Judaism in Late Antiquity* 20 (Leiden: Brill, 1976), 371–376.

hints of an unwillingness of the new community to pay the *fiscus Iudaicus* (Matthew 17:24–27, from a Gospel composed ca. 80 C.E.). Moreover, the Davidic descent of Jesus and his relatives could easily be understood as a challenge to Roman hegemony. During the time of the emperor Domitian (81–96), the surviving relatives of Jesus, grandsons of Jesus' brother Judas, were interrogated concerning their understanding of the kingdom preached by Jesus (Eusebius, *History of the Church* 3.19–20). So Trajan inevitably had to deal with the issue of Christians.

In a letter written in 111 C.E. to Pliny, governor of Bithynia and Pontus in Asia Minor, Trajan sets out a moderating policy.[4] Recognition of the gods of Rome (including the emperor as *Divi filius,* son of God) is said by Trajan to be all that should be required of those denounced as Christians. The question was not their identity or their practice as such, only whether they were loyal to the empire. By this time, however, there is no question of Christianity as such being included under the umbrella of Judaism.

Indeed, the empire may be said to have recognized a separation between Judaism and Christianity before Jews and Christians did.[5] Nero never considered extending the rights of a *religio licita* to Christians in 64, when followers of Jesus still worshipped in the Temple in Jerusalem. Not until around 85 C.E. would the framers of a principal prayer of Judaism, the "Eighteen Benedictions," compose a curse to be included, against the "Nazoraeans," followers of Jesus. On the Christian side the claim to replace Judaism only came with the Epistle to the Hebrews, around 95 C.E. Trajan simply takes the separation for granted, but in effect treats Christianity as a harmless superstition.

The relative tolerance of Trajan's policy, as articulated to Pliny, ironically resulted in the extraordinary phenomenon of Christian martyrdom. In effect, Trajan stood down from the open persecution of a Nero, and simply insisted upon the equivalent of an oath of loyalty. But the loyalty involved was to the gods of Rome, and to the emperor as divine son. In good conscience, Christians could not comply with the relatively lenient policy, since swearing allegiance to the emperor as *Divi filius* was an act conventionally performed before his image, with an oblation of wine and the burning of incense. It was, however perfunctory, an imperial sacrifice, and an obvious example of idolatry, as well as a betrayal of one's worship of Jesus as the son of God. Ignatius of Antioch was put to death during the reign of Trajan, and encouraged others to follow his example of holy obstinacy. On the other hand, devotion to the divine ideal of the empire could also lead to the use of the loyalty test to seek out Christians. That occurred in 177 C.E. in the Rhone valley, at the instigation of the emperor (and noted Stoic philosopher) Marcus Aurelius.

The emperor Severus issued an edict against Christians making converts (and against Jewish proselytism, as well) in 202 C.E. Apparently the former policy, ultimately derived from Trajan, was not an effective instrument of repression. It

---

[4]For the text of the letter, see Bruce Chilton and Jacob Neusner, editors, *Trading Places Sourcebook: Readings in the Intersecting Histories of Judaism and Christianity* (Cleveland: Pilgrim Press, 1996), 179–181.

[5]See E. A. Judge, "Judaism and the Rise of Christianity: A Roman Perpsective," *Tyndale Bulletin* 45.2 (1994), 355–368.

is of note that Severus' edict also included Judaism: for the first time, Judaism was classed with Christianity (instead of the reverse, as in the first century). The Severine persecution that followed was severe, but short-lived. One unfortunate effect (from the Roman point of view) was that it provoked Tertullian in North Africa to write his encouragement of martyrdom, and to utter the words that were to prove prophetic, "the blood of the martyrs is the seed of the Church."[6] Others in North Africa, such as Cyprian, were later to wrestle with the truth of those words.

In 250 C.E., the emperor Decius decreed that all citizens were to take part in sacrifice to the gods, and the inevitable result was a widespread persecution of Christians. During that persecution, the greatest theologian of the time, Origen, was imprisoned and tortured. Origen died during the reign of Valerian (253–260), who attempted to suppress Christian worship itself for the first time. But Valerian was captured and killed by Shapur, the Sassanid monarch. In important rescripts, the emperor Gallien actually restored Christian churches and cemeteries. Valerian's death is therefore an important transitional point from the point of view of official policy toward Christianity: it marks the moment from which Christians will begin to acquire rights. At the same time, Valerian's death marks the importance of the Sassanid Empire as a counterweight to the Roman Empire.[7]

The emperor Diocletian (284–305) was the last great persecutor of Christianity during the period of the empire. His motives appear to have been patriotic. After all, he branded the Manichaeans as criminal (in an edict of 297) before he acted against the Christians. But when his persecution came, it was systematic and savage. Beginning in 303, property was seized and clergy were arrested. Trajan's old test, of offering sacrifice to the gods, was resumed and made universal. Diocletian himself abdicated in 305, but the persecution went on until 313. It was the last gasp of the ideal of a universal civic religion of the Roman Empire based upon the ancestral gods.

Among the rivals for the title of emperor was Constantine, who defeated Maxentius at the Milvian Bridge in 312. Legend has it that as a result of a vision, Constantine permitted the display of crosses on shields within his army. His victory assured the restoration of Christian worship and Christian property. Christian symbols even appear on coins from 315, and the older references to the gods disappear in 323. Constantine would accept baptism himself only at the time of his death, but there was no question that Christianity was now, de facto, the religion of the empire.

A brief coda marks the extraordinary reversal of fortunes experienced by Judaism and Christianity between the first and the fourth centuries. Under the emperor Julian (361–363), a return to the old gods was attempted, and authorization for the rebuilding of the Temple in Jerusalem was given. Here Judaism is treated as belonging to ancestral religion, rather than one of the new movements such as

---

[6]See Henry Chadwick, *The Early Church* (London: Penguin Books, 1993), 29.

[7]The transition of Rabbinic authority from Galilee to Babylonia is to some extent explicable on that basis.

Christianity and Manichaeanism. An earthquake greeted the attempt to bring the project off, which only encouraged the Christian mobs that resisted the policies of Julian. The emperor himself was killed in battle with the Sassanids. His death left Rome to the Christians, and Jewish hopes for the restoration of the Temple in ruins. Babylonia, which had long offered a more congenial environment than Rome for a Judaism that would order its own affairs, now appeared to be no less a land of promise than a Jerusalem that could no longer host the Temple.

The discovery of the significance of historical sequence within Christianity was perhaps the most radical inheritance of the Constantinian settlement. In most of the areas of its life, the Church had at least some slight preparation for the transformations that were involved. In politics, Christians had no experience of leadership, but they had already thought through the relationship between secular power and eternal salvation. In their values, they had faced up to the question of the goods of this world, so that they could react to the blandishments of the empire with the thriving movements of asceticism that multiplied from the fourth century onward. Whatever grandeur the empire might offer could only pale into insignificance in comparison with the glory that was to come. But history—specifically, history as a sequence of events—could scarcely be ignored or slighted, when it seemed actually to validate the claims of the gospel. There was a before Constantine and an after Constantine in a way there has not been a before and after Marcus Aurelius, or even Augustus. Something happened that demanded a sequential explanation.

That explanation, and the beginning of Christian history, came with Eusebius (260–340), bishop of Caesarea. Through Pamphilus, his teacher and model, Eusebius had been deeply influenced by the thought of Origen. So before there was a consciously Christian history, there was an irony of history: from the least historical perspective there was provided the first comprehensively historical account of the meaning of Christ. His prominence in the ecumenical Church at various councils from Nicea onward, as well as his friendship with Constantine, go a long way toward explaining why Eusebius should have made the contribution that makes him the Herodotus of ecclesiastical history.

As he attempted to express the startling breakthrough under Constantine, Eusebius portrayed the new emperor as chosen by God himself. The most famous result of his meditation on the significance of the new order is his *History of the Church*, a vitally important document that takes up the Christian story from the time of Christ. The settlement under Constantine is his goal, however, and his portrayal of the emperor is perhaps most vividly conveyed in his *Praise of Constantine*. After speaking of Christ the word of God which holds dominion over the whole world, Eusebius goes on to make a comparison with Constantine (*Praise of Constantine* 1.6):

> Our Emperor, beloved of God, bearing a kind of image of the supreme rule as it were in imitation of the greater, directs the course of all things upon earth.

Here the old Stoic idea of the rule of the emperor as commensurate with the divine rule is provided with a new substance: the emperor who obeys Christ himself imitates Christ's glory.

Eusebius was inclined to describe himself as moderately capable (*History of the Church* 1.1; 10.4), and that may be an accurate assessment of him as a theologian and historian. But as a political theorist, he is one of the most influential thinkers in the West. He provided the basis upon which the Roman Empire could be presented as the Holy Roman Empire, and the grounds for claiming the divine rights of rulers. At the same time, his reference to the conditional nature of those rights, as dependent upon the imitation of Christ, has provided a basis upon which political revolution may be encouraged on religious grounds. Throughout the whole of his contribution, Eusebius conveys the vision of social order permeated as well as influenced by Christ, in which work is implicitly sanctioned in a way it was not before. When the empire became God's, Christians became responsible for the empire.

Part of Eusebius' argument was that Constantine restored the united form of the empire, which had been the ideal of Augustus. After a preface that sets out Christ's divine and human natures, Eusebius carefully places Christ's birth during Augustus' reign, after the Roman subjugation of Egypt (*History of the Church* 1.5). The pairing of Augustus and Christ, Christ and Constantine is therefore symmetrical, and defines the scope of the work. The result is to present a theologically structured political history.

The extent of that history is determined by its political horizon, much as in the case of Eusebius' predecessors in classical history. Whether we think of Herodotus in his explanation of the Persian War, or of Thucydides in the case of the Peloponnesian War, the impetus of writing history seems to be the experience of political change and dislocation. The scope of such work would be extended by such writers as Polybius (the apologist for Rome) and Josephus (the apologist for Judaism), but the desire to learn from the past in the effort to construct a politically viable present is evident throughout.

Many readers of Eusebius feel uncomfortable about his apology for Constantine. Although the form is political history, the substance seems embarrassingly like flattery. How could Eusebius so thoroughly fail to be critical, whether as historian or as theologian? As a historian, he knew that kings and their flatterers were transient; as a theologian in the line of Origen, he knew that perfection eluded human flesh. The key to this riddle lies in Eusebius' conviction that Christ was at work in Constantine's conversion (*History of the Church* 10.1):

> From that time on a day bright and radiant, with no cloud overshadowing it, shone down with shafts of heavenly light on the churches of Christ throughout the world, nor was there any reluctance to grant even those outside our community the enjoyment, if not of equal blessings, at least of an effluence from and a share in the things that God had bestowed on us.

The sharp change from persecution and all it involved was as disorienting for Eusebius as the Peloponnesian War had been to Thucydides, and an explanation was demanded. In that explanation, ecclesiastical history was born: that is, not simply the anecdotes of experience, but a rational account of God's activity within human events. The sequence of those events seemed to express revelation itself, and Eusebius' history seeks to map that congruence.

The intervention of Constantine and his colleague Licinius (who at first reigned with Constantine) was nothing less than the appointed plan of God within a definite sequence of events. Eusebius reminds the reader of the terrible tortures Christians had experienced, and then proceeds (*History of the Church* 10.4):

> But once again the Angel of the great counsel, God's great Commander-in-Chief, after the thoroughgoing training of which the greatest soldiers in his kingdom gave proof by their patience and endurance in all trials, appeared suddenly and thereby swept all that was hostile and inimical into oblivion and nothingness, so that its very existence was forgotten. But all that was near and dear to Him He advanced beyond glory in the sight of all, not men only but the heavenly powers as well—sun, moon, and stars, and the entire heaven and earth.

Only the language of apocalypse, of the sequenced revelation of God himself in Christ, can explain to Eusebius' satisfaction how the former agony can so quickly have been transformed into festivity. In Constantine, the promised future had begun, and there was no room for a return to the past.

The picture that Eusebius draws of the contemporary scene might have been drawn from an apocalyptic work in Hellenistic dress (10.9, after the narrative of the removal of Licinius):

> Men had now lost all fear of their former oppressors; day after day they kept dazzling festival; light was everywhere, and men who once dared not look up greeted each other with smiling faces and shining eyes. They danced and sang in city and country alike, giving honor first to God our Sovereign Lord, as they had been instructed, and then to the pious emperor with his sons, so dear to God.

History for Eusebius was not just an account of the past; it was an apocalypse moving through the course of human events, rather than from heaven to earth. His account was designed to set out the sequence of events that brought about the dawn of a new age.

Long before Eusebius, Origen had written that Rome would prosper better by worshipping the true God than even the children of Israel had (*Against Celsus* 8.69). For Origen, the argument was hypothetical; for Eusebius, it had become a reality. The new unity of the empire, under God, in Christ, and through the piety of the emperor himself, constituted for Eusebius a divine polity (*politeia* or *politeuma*), literally a breath away from paradise. And together with his contemporaries, he confronted the responsibility of articulating the order of that new dispensation and contributing to its prosperity. Christianity went to work.

HOW OUGHT WE TO WORK? KINDS OF WORK TO BE PREFERRED OR AVOIDED

Even while Christianity was enduring persecution within the Roman Empire, many of its prominent teachers provided a theology of engagement with the world, which could be activated into overt support for and hierarchical loyalty to the empire from the time of Eusebius. That theology of engagement was the foundation of the categorical insistence after Constantine that the order of the empire was also God's order.

During the last decade of the second century, Clement of Alexandria offered instruction to Christians in that great city and intellectual center. He was active there until the persecution that broke out in 202 under Septimus Severus. Clement developed a brilliant philosophy of Christian faith, which he produced in conscious opposition to Gnostic teachings. His greatest works constitute a trilogy. The first is an introduction to Christianity as a superior philosophical teaching (the *Protrepticos*); the second, the *Paidagogos* or "Tutor," is an account of how Christ serves as our moral guide in the quest for true knowledge and perfection. Finally, his "Miscellanies," the *Stromateis* (literally, "Carpetbags"), is a wide-ranging and complex work. Initially, it was intended as a defense of Clement's thesis that Christian revelation surpasses the achievements of human reason, but its structure and expression are obscure. The entire corpus of his work may be understood as a dialog with Gnosticism.

When Christianity emerged, other popular movements were also taking shape; taken together the members of those other groups at times greatly outnumbered Christians. Among those movements, the ones called "Gnostic" exerted the strongest influence on the Church, and provided so serious a challenge that Christian theology spelled itself out as an alternative to Gnosticism. The debate between Christians and Gnostics enables us clearly to see the articulation of Christian values.

"Gnostic" and "Gnosticism" derive from the Greek term *gnosis,* which means "knowledge." The knowledge that was in mind in the religious usage of the term was not simply a matter of data or information. Gnostics claimed that they enjoyed insight into the divine realm itself. The origins of Gnosticism have been hotly debated in the history of scholarship. It has been seen, to give some examples, as just an elite, intellectual phase within Christianity, or as a typically Hellenistic tendency, or as the transformation of Jewish apocalyptic speculation into a new key. All of those suggestions have merit, but it is not possible to fix upon a single origin of Gnosticism. It is a very widespread phenomenon of the Hellenistic world, and thrived in an environment of syncretism, in which the contributions of many different religions were brought together into new configurations. Gnosticism is one of those syncretistic configurations.

The emergence of Gnosticism reflects the appeal of dualism within the period. Dualism refers to any bifurcation of experience into two distinct realms. Gnostics typically made a radical distinction between the present, material world and ineffable nature of God. This world is subject to decay and the rule of evil forces; only release from it can bring the spiritual awakening and freedom of gnosis.

A good example of a Gnostic text from the second century is *The Gospel of Truth,* which begins:

> The gospel of truth is a joy for those who have received from the Father of truth the gift of knowing him, through the power of the Word that came forth from the fullness—the one who is in the thought and the mind of the Father, that is, the one who is addressed as the Savior, that being the name of

the work he is to perform for the redemption of those who were ignorant of the Father, while the name of the gospel is the proclamation of hope, being discovery for those who search for him.

What is useful about that initial statement is that it is a very simplified summary of major precepts and assumptions of Gnosticism.

"Knowledge" here comes only as a gift of the Father, and is mediated by the "Word," a designation for Jesus taken from the first chapter of John's Gospel. But that Word comes forth from "the fullness," emanations outward from the Father. The complexity of the divine world around the Father is often emphasized in Gnostic texts, and developed to a bewildering degree of detail. The fascination with schemes representing the generation of the world is probably an inheritance from Greek and Roman mythology and perhaps from the religions of India. The mastery of that detail is held to mean that one has successfully become one who knows, a Gnostic.

A firm distinction is made in *The Gospel of Truth* between those who are spiritual, capable of receiving illumination, and those who are material, ignorant of what is being offered (*The Gospel of Truth* 28–31). Failure to attain gnosis, then, is a mark of one's incapacity to be rescued from the conditions of this world. The assumption throughout is that the material world is a pit of ignorance and decay, from which the Gnostic must be extricated. That explains what is otherwise a puzzling feature of Gnosticism: the wide variance between ascetical self-denial and the encouragement of libertine behavior. In both cases, freedom from what is material was being claimed and put into practice.

Charges against Gnostics of libertinism should not be pressed literally. The same sorts of accusations—of such crimes as incest, cannibalism, and debauchery—were brought against Christians during the same period.[8] Both Gnostics and Christians fell under suspicion of being practitioners of nontraditional religions (superstitions), which would not support the interests of the empire. Also in both cases, the emphasis upon esoteric doctrine opened the way for the charge that secrecy was intended to conceal something shameful.

Christianity and Gnosticism also challenged the sensibilities of Graeco-Roman religious philosophies. During the second century, both of them had discovered the idiom of philosophy itself in order to develop and convey their claims. Particularly, each crafted a distinctive view of the divine "Word" (Logos), which conveys the truth of God to humanity. For most Christians, that Logos was Jesus Christ, understood as the human teacher who at last fully incarnated what philosophers and prophets had been searching for and had partially seen.

Justin Martyr initially articulated that doctrine most clearly from the perspective of Christianity, on the basis of the Gospel according to John. In 151 C.E. he addressed his *Apology* to the emperor, Antoninus Pius himself. Such was his confidence that the "true philosophy" represented by Christ, attested in the Hebrew Scriptures, would triumph among the other options available at the time. Justin himself had been trained within some of those traditions, and by his

---

[8]See Stephen Benko, *Pagan Rome and the Early Christians* (Bloomington: Indiana University Press, 1986), 54–78.

Samaritan birth he could claim to represent something of the wisdom of the east. Somewhere between 162 and 168, however, Justin was martyred in Rome, a victim of the increasing hostility to Christianity under the reign of Marcus Aurelius.[9] Justin argued that the light of reason in people is put there by God, and is to be equated with the Word of God incarnate in Jesus. His belief in the salvation of people as they actually are is attested by his attachment to millenarianism, the conviction that Christ would return to reign with his saints for a thousand years. That conviction, derived from Revelation 20, was fervently maintained by many Catholic Christians during the second century, in opposition to the abstract view of salvation that Gnostics preferred.

As we saw in the passage from *The Gospel of Truth,* the Gnostic perspective on the Logos was very different. It had to do first of all with an emanation from the Father in the fullness of the divine realm, and had less to do with Jesus personally and historically. Indeed, some Gnostics did not find it necessary to use Christian traditions at all in order to articulate their position, and even those who did adopt Christian materials transformed them in the interests of abstraction.

The emerging difference between Christians and Gnostics over the question of Christology was inevitable, in that the issue of dualism separated them. Some Gnostics, such as Marcion, believed that the God of the Hebrew Bible was a false pretender, and that the Christian canon should be reduced to the nub of those portions of Luke and Paul that portray Christianity as superseding Judaism. It must be stressed that not all Gnostics were Christians, and not all rejected the God of Israel as firmly as Marcion did, but the tendency of the Gnostic movements in all their variety was in a dualistic direction.

In his response to the claims of Gnosticism, Clement of Alexandria, who was active in the catechetical school in that great city during the latter part of the second century, stands out as a leader among Christians. Alexandria was a center for Gnosticism as well as Christianity, and the two groups contended over a similar constituency. Clement's strategy was to insist that the gospel offered its own gnosis in the form of Jesus Christ himself, whom Clement portrayed as "the Paedagogue." That term in Greek had a particular meaning. It did not refer to a schoolmaster, but to someone who leads children to school. So Clement's choice of words conceives of Jesus as a companion on the way to learning. He frames our habits according to divine wisdom, brings us to the point where we can decide to act according to his Word (for he is the Logos), and even offers us the prospect of control over our passions.

The role of Christ as the Paedagogue is a daring conception. Clement deliberately avoids the more exalted terminology of divine emanation that had been developed by that time within Gnostic circles. Instead, Clement stresses the offer of mediation to all that is involved in Christ. By choosing an example from a rather low social status, Clement also hit upon a resonance with the social experience of his own constituency. But that choice had another—and more profound—implication. The Paedagogue who leads the children to school is less exalted than the teacher in the academy, but he also knows those children in

[9]See Chadwick, *The Early Church,* 29, 74–79.

ways the teacher does not. Clement understands Jesus to be involved in the formation of passions, as well as of reason.

Reason is certainly at the center of Clement's view of education. It is the point from which one might decide to learn from the Logos. But that decision takes place in a particular social and individual context. Socially, there are habits of behavior and speech that the Paedagogue instills; they are the habits that make the personal decision to learn possible and even likely. Individually, the power of the Logos is such that even human passions may fall within its influence. Clement is quite clear that passions are more recalcitrant than reason, and that inadvertent disobedience is inevitable, but he is also insistent in the claim that emotions as well as intellect are reformed in the light of the Logos. Dedication to that continuous reformation, including the social relations of Christians and the feelings those relations involve, gave Christianity a foundation for its theology of work before there was a Christian empire to articulate it in.

Clement's developmental model expresses the anthropology of early Christianity in a way that distinguishes it from Gnosticism. He aggressively reclaims the realm of human passion as part of the potential and actual rule of Christ. Where Gnosticism focuses on the issue of intellectual illumination alone, to the exclusion of the realm of moral and emotional engagement, Christianity during the second century came to insist upon a more integrative understanding of salvation. That integration explicitly includes the personal and the social realms in Clement's exposition (Clement of Alexandria, *Paidagogos* 1.1–1.5.13):

> There are these three attributes in man: habits, deeds, and passions. Of these, habits come under the influence of the word of persuasion, the guide to godliness. This is the word that underlies and supports, like the keel of a ship, the whole structure of the faith. Under its spell, we joyfully surrender our old ideas, become young again to gain salvation, and sing in the inspired words of the psalm: "How good is God to Israel, to those who are upright of heart." As for deeds, they are affected by the word of counsel, and passions are healed by that of consolation. This word is one in operation: the self-same Word who forcibly draws men from their natural, worldly way of life and educates them to the only true salvation: faith in God. That is to say, the heavenly guide, the Word, once he begins to call men to salvation, takes to himself the name of persuasion. This kind of appeal, although only one part of the appeal, is properly given the name of persuasion, that is, word, since the whole worship of God has a persuasive appeal, instilling in a receptive mind the desire for life now and for the life to come. But the Word also heals and counsels, all at the same time. In fact, he follows up his own activity by encouraging the one he has already persuaded, and particularly by offering a cure for his passions.
>
> Let us call him, then, by the one title: Paedagogue of little ones, a Paedagogue who does not simply follow behind, but who leads the way, for his aim is to improve the soul, not just to instruct it; to guide to a life of virtue, not merely to one of knowledge. Yet, that same Word does teach. It is simply that we are not now considering him in that light. As Teacher, he explains and

reveals through instruction, but as Paedagogue he is practical. First he persuades men to form habits of life, then he encourages them to fulfill their duties by laying down clear-cut counsels and by exhibiting, for those who follow, examples of those who have erred in the past. Both are most useful: the advice, that it may be obeyed; the other, given in the form of example, has a twofold object—that we may choose the good and imitate it or condemn and avoid the bad.

Healing of the passions follows as a consequence. The Paedagogue strengthens souls with the persuasion implied in these examples, and he gives the mild medicine of his loving counsels to the sick man that he may come to a full knowledge of the truth. Health and knowledge are not the same; one is a result of study, the other of healing. In fact, if a person is sick, he cannot master any of the things taught him until he is first completely cured. We give instructions to someone who is sick for an entirely different reason than we do to someone who is learning; the latter, we instruct that he may acquire knowledge, the first, that he may regain health. Just as those diseased in body require a physician, so too, those weak in soul require the Paedagogue to cure its ills. Only then does it need the Teacher to guide it and develop its capacity to know, once it is made pure and capable of retaining the revelation of the Word.

Therefore, the all-loving Word, anxious to perfect us in a way that leads progressively to salvation, observes an order well adapted to our development; at first, he persuades, then he educates, and after all this he teaches. Our Educator, you children, resembles his Father, God, whose Son he is. He is without sin, without blame, without passion of soul, God undefiled in form of man, accomplishing his Father's will. He is God the Word, who is in the Father, and also at the right hand of the Father, with even the form of God.

He is to us the spotless image. We must try, then, to resemble him in soul as far as we are able. It is true that he himself is entirely free from human passion; that is why he alone is sinless and he alone is judge. Yet we must strive, to the best of our ability, to be as sinless as we can. There is nothing more important for us than first to be rid of sin and weakness, and then to uproot any habitual sinful inclination. The highest perfection, of course, is never to sin in any least way; but this can be said of God alone. The next highest is never deliberately to commit wrong; this is the state proper to the man who possesses wisdom. In the third place comes not sinning greatly by involuntary wrongs; this marks a man who is well educated. Finally, in the lowest degree, we must place not continuing long in sin; even this, for those who are called to recover their loss and repent, is a step on the path to salvation.

It seems to me that the Paedagogue expresses it aptly through Moses when he says: "If anyone dies suddenly before the priest, the head of his consecration shall be defiled; and he shall immediately shave it." By sudden death he means an involuntary sin, and says that it defiles because it pollutes the soul. For the cure he prescribes that the head be shaved as soon as possible, meaning that the locks of ignorance that darken the reason should be shorn so that the reason (which has its seat in the head), stripped of hair, that is, wickedness, may the better continue its course to repentance.

Then a little afterwards he adds: "The former days were without reason," by which he surely means that deliberate sin is an act done contrary to reason. Involuntary sin he calls "sudden," but deliberate sin "without reason." It is precisely for this purpose that the Word, Reason itself, has taken upon himself, as the Paedagogue, the task of preventing sins against reason. Consider in this light that expression in the Scriptures: "For this reason, thus says the Lord. . . ." The words that follow ("For this reason . . .") describe and condemn some sin that has been committed. The judgment contained in these words is just, for it is as if he were giving notice in the words of the prophets that, if you had not sinned, he would not have made these threats. The same is true of those other words: "For this reason, the Lord says these things . . . ,"and "Because you have not heard these words, the Lord says these things . . . ," and "Behold, for this reason, the Lord says. . . ." In fact, the inspired Word exists because of both obedience and disobedience: that we may be saved by obeying it, and corrected because we have disobeyed.

Therefore, the Word is our Paedagogue who heals the unnatural passions of our soul with his counsel. The art of healing, strictly speaking, is the relief of the ills of the body, an art learned by man's wisdom. Yet the only true divine healer of human sickness, the holy relief of the soul when it is ill, is the Word of the Father. Scripture says: "Save thy servant, O my God, who puts his trust in thee. Have mercy on me, O Lord, because I have cried to thee the whole day through." In the words of Democritus, "The healer, by his art, cures the body of its diseases, but it is wisdom that rids the soul of its passions." The good Paedagogue, however, Wisdom, the Word of the Father, who created man, concerns himself with the whole creature, and as the Physician of the whole man heals both body and soul.

"Arise," he said to the paralytic, "take up the bed on which you are lying and go home." And immediately the sick man regained his health. To the man who was dead he said: "Lazarus, come forth." And the man came forth from his tomb, the same as he had been before he suffered, having experienced resurrection.

But the soul he heals in a way suitable to the nature of the soul: by his commandments and by his gifts. He is ready to heal with his counsels, but, generous with his gifts, he also says to us sinners: "Your sins are forgiven you." With this thought we have become an infant of his providence, for we share in his magnificent and unvarying order. That providence begins by ordering the world and the heavens, the course of the sun's orbit and the movements of the other heavenly bodies, all for the sake of man. Then, it concerns itself with man himself, for whom it had undertaken all these other labors. And because it considers this as its most important work, it guides man's soul on the right path by the virtues of prudence and temperance, and equips his body with beauty and harmony. Finally, into the actions of mankind it infuses uprightness and some of its own good order.

Both as God and as man, the Lord renders us every kind of service and assistance. As God, he forgives sin; as man, he educates us to avoid sin completely. Man is the work of God; he is naturally dear to him. Other things God made by a simple word of command, but man he fashioned by his own direct action and breathed into him something proper to himself. Now, a being which God himself has fashioned, and in such a way that it resembles himself closely, must have been created either because it is desirable to God in itself, or because it is useful for some other creature. If man has been created as desirable in himself, then God loves him as good since he himself is good; there is a certain affectiveness in man, which is the very quality breathed into him by God.

But, if God made man only because he considered him useful for some other creature, then he could have had no other reason for actually creating him than that with him he could become a good Creator, and man could not attain the knowledge of God. In this case, unless man had been created, God would not have made the other creature for whose sake man was being created. So, the strength of will which God already possessed, hidden deep within himself, he actualized by this display of the external power of creating, taking this supposed other man from the man he had made. But according to this idea, he saw what he possessed all along, and the creature whom God had willed to be, actually came into existence in the first place. For there is nothing that God cannot do.

Therefore, man, whom God made, is desirable in himself. But being desirable in oneself means being related to the person to whom one is desirable, and being acceptable and pleasing. But what does being pleasing to someone mean, if not being loved by him? Man is, then, an object of love; indeed, man is loved by God. It must be so, for it was on man's account that the only-begotten was sent from the bosom of the Father, as the Word of faith, faith which has a wealth of resources. The Lord clearly attests this when he says: "The Father himself loves you, because you have loved me." And again: "And you have loved them, just as you have loved me." What the Educator desires and what he proclaims, what he has in mind in his words and in his deeds, in his commands of what we are to do and what we are to avoid, is already clear. It is clear, too, that the other kind of discourse, that of the Teacher, is at once strong and spiritual, in accurate terms, but meant only for those who are initiated. But, for the present, let that be.

As for him who lovingly guides us along the way to the better life, we ought to return him love and live according to the dictate of his principles. This we should do not only by fulfilling his commandments and obeying his prohibitions, but also by turning away from the evil examples we just mentioned and imitating the good. In this way, we shall make our own actions, as far as we are able, like those of our Paedagogue, that the ancient saying, "according to his own image and likeness," may be accomplished.

For we wander in thick darkness; we need a sure and unerring guide in life. The best guide is not that blind one who, in the words of Scripture, "leads the blind into a ditch," but the Word, keen of sight, penetrating into the secret places of the heart. Just as there cannot be a light that does not give light, nor a movement that does not move nor a lover unless he loves, just so he can not be good unless he rendered us service and led us to salvation.

Let us, then, perform the commandments through works of the Lord. Indeed, the Word himself, when he became flesh in visible form, unceasingly showed not only the theory but also the practice of virtue. Further, considering the Word as our law, let us see in his commandments and counsels direct and sure paths to eternity. For his precepts are filled, not with fear, but with persuasion.

Let us welcome more and more gladly this holy obedience, and let us surrender ourselves more and more completely to the Lord, holding to the steadfast cable of his faith. Let us recognize, too, that both men and women practice the same sort of virtue. Surely, if there is but one God for both, then there is but one Paedagogue for both.

One Church, one temperance, one modesty, a common food, equality in marriage; breath, sight, hearing, knowledge, hope, obedience, love, all are alike. They who possess life in common, grace in common, and salvation in common have also love in common and education too. The Scripture says: "For in this world, they marry and are given in marriage," for this world is the only place in which the female is distinguished from the male, "but in that other world, no longer." There, the rewards of this common and holy life, based on equality, await not male or female as such, but man, removed from the lust that in this life divided man from himself.

The very name "mankind" is a name common to both males and women. Similarly, the Attic Greeks called not only the boy but also the girl by the one name of "child," if Meander, the comic poet, is to be believed in a passage of his play *Rapizomene*: "My little daughter, . . . indeed, she is by nature an exceedingly loving child." Notice, too, that "sheep" is the general name used for the male and female. Yet the Lord shepherds us for ever, Amen. Now, neither sheep nor any other animal should live without a shepherd, nor should children, without a paedagogue, nor servants without a master.

That paedagogy is the training given children (*paidon*) is evident from the name itself. It remains for us to consider who the children are as explained by the Scriptures and, from the same Scriptural passages, to understand the Paedagogue.

We are the children. Scripture celebrates us very often and in many different ways, and refers to us under different titles, thereby introducing variety in the simple language of the faith. For example, in the Gospel, it says: "And the Lord, standing on the shore, said to his disciples"—they were fishing— "Children, do you have no fish?" Those who already had the position of disciples he now calls "children."

Again, we read: "And they brought the children to him, that he might lay hands on them and bless them, and when the disciples tried to prevent it, Jesus said: Let the little children be and do not hinder them from coming to me, for of such is the kingdom of heaven." What such a remark means the Lord himself explains plainly later on: "Unless you turn and become like little children, you shall not enter into the kingdom of heaven." Those words are not a figure of speech for some kind of rebirth, but recommend the simplicity of childhood for our imitation.

The prophetic Spirit also describes us as children: "Plucking branches of olives," Scripture says, "or of palm, the children came out to meet the Lord, and they cried out, saying: Hosanna to the Son of David, blessed is he who

comes in the name of the Lord." The word "Hosanna," translated into
Greek, means "light, glory, praise, supplication to the Lord."

Incidentally, it seems to me that the Scripture, in this inspired passage, intends to accuse and condemn the careless: "Have you never read that out of
the mouths of babes and sucklings, you have brought forth praise?"

In the same way again in the Gospel, the Lord shocked his companions,
attempting to arouse their attention when he was about to go to his father.
To urge them to listen more intently, he tells them in advance that in a little
while he will go away; so he would make them understand that while the
Word has not yet ascended into heaven, they must gather in the fruits of truth
with greater care. So it is that once more he calls them children: "Children,"
he says, "yet a little while and I am with you."

In Clement's analysis, the Word of God works through human reason, into one's
passions and actions, and on to relationships in marriage and community. In a
philosophical key, Clement spells out the dynamic already discovered in the
Shepherd of Hermas (discussed in the first volume in the chapter on Christianity).

But because Clement does develop the idea further, an implicit social policy
begins to emerge. Here, within the Church, members are encouraged to imitate
Christ as educator, in the intellectual and social ordering of the individual and
the community. During this same period, Christians were barred from holding
positions of responsibility within the Roman Empire, such as teacher, magistrate,
and officer, because they required taking an oath of allegiance to the emperor.[10]
But Clement's advice would have them take up cognate functions within the
Church. That was one reason for which, when the Constantinian revolution
came, Christians were in a position to take on responsibilities of public trust. In
Christianity, work is more a personal vocation than it is a public duty. That it is
because, before it is a matter of profit or community service or even loyalty to
one's group, work is a stable social relationship within which an individual and
a community are called to feel and realize the influence of the divine Paedagogue, shaping reason, passions, and actions. The selection of particular kinds of
employment (assuming that is an option) is geared to the specific habits that are
most in need of reformation.

WHY MUST WE HELP OTHERS?
PRIVATE GAIN AND PUBLIC BENEFIT

The prosecution and persecution of Christians elicited from them carefully argued explanations of how a tolerant treatment of their faith would bring good
to the Roman Empire. Those articulations of the nexus between Christianity's
gain and the empire's benefit served as the model of social policy in the Church

---

[10]See Robert M. Grant, *Early Christianity and Society* (San Francisco: Harper & Row,
1977), 66–95. Naturally, the imperative to imitate Christ also resulted in the proscription
of immoral occupations within the Church.

for centuries to come. Tertullian addressed his *Apology* to those who might be called upon to judge Christians, but in fact it is intended to counter the common prejudice that Christianity encountered. It is as effective an example of rhetoric as one will find, and at the same time it illustrates both the legal situation and the popular reaction to the new religion. The *Apology* was written in 197 C.E., shortly after Tertullian's conversion. It is a good example of Christianity in North Africa, coming from Carthage (which was Tertullian's birthplace). The uncompromising stance is characteristic of the climate of the movement there, and may explain why, around 207 C.E., Tertullian himself became a Montanist, attracted by the asceticism that comported with the conviction that each believer was a vessel of the holy Spirit.

Throughout, Tertullian insists that the comportment of Christians is proof of the justice of their cause. The rhetoric is directed against Roman persecution, but its impact equally serves to put the case to Christian readers that a thorough integrity is demanded of them by the environment of prejudice in which they live (*Apology* I):

> If you, the masters of the Roman Empire—you who, openly and loftily at the very head of the state, preside to do justice—if you are not allowed openly to investigate, to examine face to face, the Christian issue, to learn what it is in truth; if, in this particular matter, and this alone, your authority either dreads or blushes to inquire in public, with all the care that justice demands; if finally (as recently befell) the persecution of this school is so avid in the domestic tribunal as to block the way of defense;—then let truth be allowed to reach your ears at least by the hidden path of silent literature.
>
> Truth asks no favors in her cause, since she has no surprise at her present position. Truth knows that she is a stranger on earth and easily finds enemies among men of another descent, but she knows that her descent, home, hope, recompense, honor, are in heaven. For one thing meanwhile she is eager—not to be condemned without being known. The laws are supreme in their own sphere; what loss can they suffer, if truth be heard? Why, would it not enhance the glory of their supremacy to condemn truth after hearing her? But, if they condemn her unheard—aside from the odium of such injustice—they will merit the suspicion that they knowingly refuse to hear what, once heard, they cannot condemn.
>
> This, then, is the first plea we lodge with you—the injustice of your hatred of the names of the Christians. The very excuse that seems to acquit it, at once aggravates and convicts that injustice—namely, ignorance. For what could be more unjust than for men to hate a thing they do not know, even if it really deserves hatred? It can only deserve hatred when it is known whether it does deserve it.
>
> But so long as nothing at all is known of what it deserves, how can you defend the justice of the hatred? That must be established, not on the bare fact of its existence, but on knowledge. When men hate a thing simply because they do not know the character of what they hate, what prevents it being of a nature that does not deserve hate at all? Whichever alternative obtains, we

maintain both points: they are ignorant so long as they hate, and their hate is unjust as long as they are ignorant. It is evidence of an ignorance which, while it is made an excuse for their injustice, really condemns it, that all who once hated Christianity because they were ignorant of the nature of what they hated, as soon as they cease to be ignorant of it, leave off hating it.

From their number come the Christians; it is on the basis of knowledge, nothing else; and they begin to hate what once they were and to profess what once they hated; and we are as many as we are alleged to be. Men proclaim aloud that the state is beset with us; in countryside, in villages, in islands— Christians; every sex, age, condition, and even rank going over to this name. They lament it as an injury; and yet even so they do not bestir their minds to reflect whether there may not be in it something good that escapes them. It is forbidden to suspect more shrewdly; it does not please them to test it at closer quarters. Here, of all places, human curiosity grows torpid. They love to be ignorant, though others rejoice to know. How much better the saying of Anacharsis about the ignorant judging the expert would have fitted them, than the unmusical who judge the musicians! They prefer not to know because they already hate. Their prejudice implies that what they do not know really is what, if they were to know, they could not hate. Because, if no just ground for hatred be found, surely it is best to leave off hating unjustly. But if the hatred prove to be deserved, so far from any of it being abated, more hatred should be added to keep it up; and justice itself would authorize it.

But, one could reply, a thing is not necessarily good because it wins many adherents; how many are predisposed to evil, how many desert to error! Who denies that? Yet a thing that is really bad, not even those who are caught by it dare to defend or to call good. Nature steeps every evil thing with either fear or shame. Evil-doers are eager to escape notice; they avoid appearing; they are anxious when caught; they deny when accused; even under torture they do not easily or always confess; when condemned they always lament. They count up how often they have felt the impulses of a mind distraught; they set their deeds down to fate or to the stars; they will not admit to being what they are because they recognize it is evil. In what way is a Christian comparable? Not a man of them is ashamed of it, not a man regrets—except only that he was not a Christian earlier. If he is denounced, he glories in it; if he is accused, he does not defend himself; when he is questioned, he confesses without any pressure; when he is condemned, he renders thanks. What sort of evil is that which has none of the native marks of evil—fear, shame, evasion, regret, lament? What? Is that evil where the criminal is glad, where accusation is the thing he prays for, and punishment is his felicity? It is not for you to call it madness—*you,* a man convicted of sheer ignorance of it!

But now, if it is really certain that we are of all men the most noxious, why do you yourselves treat us otherwise than those like us, the rest of the noxious classes, when the same treatment belongs to the same fault? Whatever you charge against us, when you so charge others, they use their own eloquence, they hire the advocacy of others, to plead their innocence. There is freedom to answer, to cross-examine, since in fact it is against the law for men to be condemned, undefended and unheard. But to Christians alone it is forbidden to say anything to clear their case, to defend truth, to stop the judge from being unjust. One thing is looked for, one alone, the one thing needful for popular hatred—the confession of the name. Not investigation of the crime! Yet, if you are trying any other criminal, it does not follow at once from his confessing to the name of a murderer, or temple-robber, or sex-criminal, or enemy of the state (to touch on *our* indictments), that you are satisfied to pronounce sentence, unless you pursue all the consequent investigation, such as the character of the act, how often, where, how, when, he did it, the accessories, the confederates. In our case—nothing of the kind! Yet it ought just as much to be wrung out of us (whenever that false charge is made) how many murdered babies each of us had tasted, how many acts of incest he had done in the dark, what cooks were there, and what dogs. Think of the glory of that judge who had brought to light some Christian who had eaten a hundred babies!

And yet we find it is forbidden even to hunt us down. For when Plinius Secundus was governing his province and had condemned some Christians and driven others from their position, and still the sheer numbers concerned worried him as to what he ought to do thereafter, he consulted the Emperor Trajan. He asserted that, apart from an obstinacy that refused to sacrifice, he had learnt nothing about the Christian mysteries—nothing beyond meetings before dawn to sing to Christ and to God, and to band themselves together in discipline, forbidding murder, adultery, fraud, treachery, and such wickedness. Trajan replied in a rescript that men of this kind were not to be sought out, but if they were brought before Pliny they must be punished.

What a decision, how inevitably confused! He says they must not be sought out, implying they are innocent; and he orders them to be punished, implying they are guilty. He spares them and rages against them, he pretends not to see and punishes. Why cheat yourself with your judgment? If you condemn them, why not hunt them down? If you do not hunt them down, why not also acquit them? To track down bandits through all the provinces is a duty assigned by lot to the garrisons. Against those answerable for treason, against public enemies, every man is a soldier; inquiry is extended to confederates, to accessories. The Christian alone may not be hunted down; but he may be summoned before the magistrate; as if hunting down led to anything but summoning to the court. So you condemn a man when summoned to court—a man whom nobody wished to be sought out, who (I suppose) really has not deserved punishment because he is guilty, but because, forbidden to be looked for, he was found!

Then, again, in that vein, you do not deal with us in accordance with your procedure in judging criminals. If the other criminals plead "Not guilty," you torture them to make them confess; the Christians alone you torture to make them deny. Yet if it were really something evil, we should deny our guilt, and you would use torture to force us to confess it. And you would not dispense with judicial investigation of our crimes on the sole ground that you were certain of their commission from the confession of the name; for to this day, though the murderer confesses, and though you know what murder is, none the less you wring out of him the story of his crime. How perverse, when you presume our crimes from our confession of the name and then try by torture to force us to cancel our confession, in order that, by denying the name, we may really deny the crimes too, which you had presumed from our confession of the name! I do not suppose you do not want us to be done to death—because you believe us the worst of men. For that is your way—to say to the murderer, "Deny!" and to order the temple-thief to be mangled, if he will insist on confession! If that is not your procedure with regard to us in our guilt, then it is clear you count us the most innocent of men. You will not have us (as being the most innocent of men) persist with a confession which you know you will have to condemn, not because justice requires it, but because of legal requirement.

A man shouts, "I am a Christian." He says what he is. You wish to hear what he is *not*. Presiding to extort the truth, you take infinite pains in our case, and ours alone, to hear a lie. "I am," says he, "what you ask if I am; why torture me to twist the facts? I confess, and you torture me. What would you do if I denied?" Clearly, when others deny, you do not readily believe them; if we have denied, you at once believe us. Let this perversity of yours arouse the suspicion that there may be some hidden power which makes you serve against the form, yes, against the very nature of judicial procedure, against the laws themselves. For, unless I am mistaken, these laws bid evil men to be brought to light, not hidden; they enact that those confessing be condemned, not acquitted. This is laid down by decrees of the Senate, by rescripts of the Emperors.

This Empire of which you are ministers is the rule of citizens, not of tyrants. With tyrants torture was also used as penalty; with you, it is moderated and used for examination only. Maintain your law by this method until the necessary confession is made. If a confession intervenes, it serves no purpose. It is the sentence that is called for then; the guilty man must cancel the penalty due by enduring it, not by being relieved of it. In the end, nobody desires to acquit him; it is not permissible to wish it; that is why no man is forced to deny his guilt. But you conceive the Christian to be a man guilty of every crime, the enemy of gods, emperors, laws, morals, of all nature together. And then you force him to deny the charge, in order to acquit him— a man you will not be able to acquit unless he has denied. You are colluding to obstruct the laws. You want him, then, to deny that he is guilty, in order to *make* him innocent—and quite against his will; and even his past is not to count against him.

What is the meaning of this perversity? this failure to reflect that more credence is to be given to a voluntary confession than to a forced denial? to reflect that, when compelled to deny, he may not honestly deny; and, once acquitted, he may again after your tribunal laugh at your exercise, once more a Christian?

So, when in every detail you treat us differently from all other criminals— as you do in concentrating on the one object of dissociating us from that name (for we are dissociated from it, if we do what non-Christians do)—you can gather then the gravamen of the case is not any crime but a name. Conscious rivalry is set up against this name, with the primary effect that men are unwilling to know for certain, what they certainly know they do not know. So they believe things about us which are not proved, and they are unwilling for inquiry to be made, in case things they prefer to have believed should be proved untrue. The object is that the name, which is the enemy of that conscious rivalry, may, because of crimes presumed but not proven, be condemned simply on its own confession. So we are tortured when we confess; we are punished when we persist; we are acquitted when we deny; all because the battle is for a name. Finally, in reading the charge, why do you call the man a Christian, why not a murderer too, if a Christian is a murderer? Why not incestuous, or anything else you believe us to be? Or is it that in our case and ours alone, it shames you, or vexes you, to use the actual names of our crimes? If a Christian, with no charge laid against him, is defendant because of a name, how shocking the name must be, if the charge consist of a name and nothing more.

What does it mean, when most people shut their eyes and run so blindfold into hatred of that name, that, even if they bear favorable testimony to a man, they throw in some detestation of the name? "A good man," they say, "this Caius Seius, only that he is a Christian." Then another says: "I am surprised that that wise man, Lucius Titius, has suddenly become a Christian." Nobody reflects whether Caius is good, and Lucius sensible, just because he is a Christian, or is a Christian because he is sensible and good. They praise what they know and blame what they do not know. They spoil their knowledge with their ignorance because it is fairer to prejudge what is hidden by what is evident, than to condemn in advance what is evident because of what is hidden. Other people, persons known before they had the name to have been vagabond, worthless, and wicked, they condemn and praise in one breath. In the blindness of hate they stumble into commendation. "What a woman! how wanton, how frivolous! What a young man! how wanton, how gallant! They have become Christians." So the name follows the reformation as a fresh charge. Some men even play their own advantage with this hatred, content with injustice, provided they do not have at home what they hate. The wife is chaste now; but the husband has ceased to be jealous, and has turned her out. The son is now submissive; but the father, who used to bear with his ways, has disinherited him. The slave is faithful now; but the master, once so gentle, has banished him from his sight. As sure as a man is reformed by the name, he gives offense. The advantage does not balance the hatred felt for Christians.

Now, then, if it is hatred of a name, how can a name be indicted? What charge can lie against words, unless the pronunciation of some name has a barbarous sound about it—something unlucky or scurrilous or lewd? "Christian," so far as translation goes, is derived from "anointing." Yes, and when it is mispronounced by you "Chrestian" (for you have not even certain knowledge of the mere name) it is framed from "sweetness" or "kindness." So in innocent men you hate even the innocent name.

But the school is in fact hated for the name of its founder! What novelty is it, if some way of life gives its followers a name drawn from their teacher?

Are not the philosophers called after their founders—Platonists, Epicureans, Pythagoreans? and also from the places where they gathered, where they took their stand—Stoics, Academics? and physicians in the same way from Erasistratus, and grammarians from Aristarchus—cooks too from Apicius? Yet nobody is ever offended by the avowal of a name, handed down with his teaching from the teacher. Clearly, if a man has proved the school a bad one and its founder as bad, he will prove the bad name also to be worthy of hate because of the guilt of the school and the founder. So before you hated the name, it would have been proper first to judge the school in the light of the founder, or the founder in the light of the school. But, as things are, inquiry as to both and knowledge of both are allowed to slide; the name is picked out; the name is the object of attack. The school is unknown; the founder is unknown; a word of itself condemns both in advance—because they bear a name, not because they are convicted of anything.

In Tertullian's overt formulation, Roman magistrates are exhorted not to punish Christians for the good they do, on the sole grounds that they are called Christians. But the underside of that rhetoric is the imperative already discussed in the first volume in the chapter on Christianity, articulated in 1 Peter 2:18–3:7, that Christians themselves should so conduct their private lives that the public benefit of the faith becomes evident as widely as possible. Exemplary living in private is made into a communal virtue, and the continuity of the public and private spheres is a characteristic feature of Christianity. Loving one's neighbor as oneself, a principle Jesus took from his own heritage (Matthew 22:39; Mark 12:31; Leviticus 19:18) becomes more than a matter of being helpful when and as necessary. Jesus' innovation in citing this commandment lay in insisting that loving one's neighbor was "like" loving God, and that is the source of the exacting integrity in social contact that Tertullian demanded. Private gain and public benefit are indistinguishable from one another, when both are measured by a truth whose descent, home, hope, recompense, and honor are in heaven.

WHEN WORK DOES NOT WORK: UNEMPLOYMENT, EXPLOITATION, AND ALTERNATIVES TO PROPER WORK

The imperative to live in a publicly exemplary way, coupled with the conception of Christian communities as households, resulted in a passionate and eloquent program for the response to and alleviation of poverty among believers. In his correspondence with the Corinthians (around 56 C.E.), Paul sets out a simple and direct policy for how to deal with the problems of the inequality inherent in wealth (2 Corinthians 8:1–15):

But I want you to know, brothers, the grace of God which has been given to the churches of Macedonia. Because in a great test of pressure, the overflow of their joy and their deep poverty abounded in the wealth of their generosity. Because according to their power and—I attest—beyond their power, of their own accord they petitioned us with much summoning for the grace and fellowship of providing for the saints. And not only as we had hoped: they gave themselves first to the Lord and to us through God's will. So we summoned Titus so that just as he commenced, so also he might complete this grace among you. But just as you abound in everything, in faith and reason and knowledge and in all eagerness and love from us among you, so abound in this grace. I speak not by command, but through others' eagerness, and testing the genuineness of your love. For you know the grace of Christ Jesus our lord, that being rich he became poor for you, so that you might become rich through that poverty. And I give an opinion in this: this is beneficial for you, such as last year began not only to act, but to will, now also to complete the action, so that just as there was readiness of will, there might be completion from what you have. For if readiness subsisted, what one has is pleasing, not what one does not have. Because this is not pressure among you for the ease of others, but a matter of equality. In the present time your abundance is for their lack, so that their abundance might be for your lack: so that it becomes equal. Just as it is written, The one who has much did not exceed, and the one who has little did not want.

Paul's concern for the poor church in Jerusalem was an earmark of his apostolate (Galatians 2:10), and he engaged in this collection for the saints consistently. What he here makes plain, however, is that the underlying principle is that our inheritance in Christ is communal, just as wealth in the church in Jerusalem was also communal (Acts 4:32–5:11).

UNCONVENTIONAL WORK: WORKING FOR GOD

For all that Christian teaching came to emphasize the importance of social responsibility, as we have seen, a deep skepticism regarding the capacity of any economic order to correspond to the sovereign will of God has persisted. In large measure, that persistence may be attributed to the unconventional setting that was Jesus' original context. As Richard Horsley has explained, until the most recent study, there has been a tendency over the past decade to exaggerate the integration of Galilee within the Graeco-Roman world. Because the sites of Sepphoris and Tiberias, both substantial cities, had been excavated, the supposition was that they represented Galilean culture as such. The problem is first that both cities were not of the importance or influence of Ptolemais, Scythopolis, Caesarea Maritima, and Jerusalem, all of which were outside Galilee.[11] Second, neither city could be said to have deserved the loyalty of those who live around them. Sepphoris was essentially a fortress town for Herod and Herod Antipas. When Herod himself died, Judas (the son of an outlaw whom Herod had killed) led a group on a raid of the royal fortress (Josephus, *Antiquities* 17

---

[11]See Richard A. Horsley, *Archaeology, History, and Society in Galilee: The Social Context of Jesus and the Rabbis* (Valley Forge, Pennsylvania: Trinity Press International, 1996), 43–47.

§ 271–272). It was then up to the Roman legate Varus to retake Sepphoris, and punish the populace (*Antiquities* 17 § 289), and up to Herod Antipas later to repair and even enhance the city (*Antiquities* 18 § 27), renaming it "Imperial City." Not even Herod Antipas showed much faith in the future of Sepphoris as the seat of his power. In 18 C.E., he founded Tiberias (named after the emperor) on the Sea of Galilee,[12] on a site that included a disused cemetery. Josephus goes out of his way to emphasize the poor background of the Galileans who were encouraged and even compelled to settle there, among whom some were involved in the collection of taxes (*Antiquities* 18 § 36–38).

The consequences of recognizing these difficulties are quite dramatic for an understanding of the context of earliest Christianity, as Horsley goes on to say:

> To say that the culture was already urban as well as rural and therefore prepared for Roman dominance is untrue both of Galilee and of Judea proper. In fact, such a generalization flies in the face of the history of Palestine during what archaeologists call the "Early Roman" period (Pompey through Bar Kokhba). In late second-temple Judea proper the only city was Jerusalem itself. Prior to Antipas, with only the administrative town of Sepphoris (the size of which at that time is still unclear), Galilee was hardly urbanized. The popular rebellions against the Roman conquerors and/or their client-rulers in 40–37 B.C.E., 4 B.C.E., and 66–70 C.E., as well as several ad hoc protests and resistance movements among both Judeans and Galileans in the Early Roman period hardly indicates a people prepared for Roman domination and favorable to urbanization.[13]

Resistance to the Roman city is much more characteristic among the Galileans than an acceptance of Greco-Roman urbanization, and urbanization of Galilee in any case only became a Roman policy during the second century, after the revolt of Simeon bar Kosiba (132–135 C.E.).[14]

Horsley develops a model of what he calls the regionalism of Galilee that represents a major advance in understanding. He refutes the attempt to characterize Lower Galilee as urban and Upper Galilee as rural during the time of Jesus, and argues that the more basic cultural differences throughout Galilee "were probably between the cities and the villages, not between Upper Galilean villages and Lower Galilean villages."[15] But aside from some resistance to urban, Roman culture, what was the ethos of these villages? Horsley suggests that some "separate development" of "Israelite traditions such as the Mosaic covenant," which he calls a "'little tradition' or popular customs," in contrast to the "'great tradition'" of "the Jerusalem temple-state."[16]

---

[12]See Horsley, 49–51.

[13]Horsley, 54–55. He also rightly observes that the hypothesis of Jesus as a Cynic philosopher, an attempt to "de-Judaize Jesus and place him into a more cosmopolitan cultural context" (p. 1), is simply ruled out by a consideration of the archaeological and historical sources, pp. 179–185.

[14]See Lee I. Levine, *The Rabbinic Class of Palestine in Late Antiquity* (New York: Jewish Theological Seminary of America, 1989).

[15]Horsley, 93, and see the discussion on pp. 88–95 as a whole.

[16]Horsley, 95; see also p. 122.

That characterization is basic to Horsley's take on Galilean regionalism, and it must be refined in order to understand Jesus' activity, even as the real strengths of this scheme should be acknowledged. Here we find a thematic emphasis that Aramaic was the language of the Galileans,[17] that the "oral 'little' tradition of the traditional village life" would likely have recalled the stories of Saul, David, Jeroboam, Jehu, as well as Mount Tabor, and—above all—Elijah,[18] that the synagogue in first-century Galilee was not a building but a congregation for the purpose of guiding the community.[19] All that has been argued on the basis of literary sources alone, especially viewed from the angle of cultural anthropology,[20] but Horsley provides a much-needed collation with archaeological evidence.

That work needs to go on, but particular attention should be paid to a perspective James F. Strange has recently referred to:

> A unique item in the material culture of the Early Roman Jewish world was a class of soft, white stone vessels which appear in no less than sixty-five sites all over ancient Palestine. At least fourteen of these sites are in Upper and Lower Galilee (Gush Halav, Nabratein, Meiron, Kefar Hananiah, Capernaum, Yodfat, Jotapata, Ibelin, Kefar Kenna, Sepphoris, Reina, Nazareth, Bethlehem of Galilee, Migdal Ha-Emeq, and Tiberias). . . . These vessels were evidently designed to meet the requirements of laws of purity. They seem to be distinctively Jewish, as they only superficially resemble the marble vessels well known in the Roman world.[21]

Evidently, purity is a perspective of analysis that the mounting archaeological evidence demands, and that Horsley all but ignores.

That perspective is vital to understanding an observation Horsley himself makes. He sees the importance of the fact that, in many Galilean villages, hordes of coins were found. In these hordes, all types of coins—those actually in currency and those not—are mixed together, sometimes with weights. Stashed together in this way, nothing is in place for regular usage. As Horsley rightly says,[22] that implies that the economy of Jewish Galilee was primarily a matter, not of transactions of currency, but of exchanging goods and services. Indeed, this

---

[17]Horsley, 106, 154–171, 177. On the last page cited, he acknowledges that his mind has changed in this regard.

[18]Horsley, 112, 171–175.

[19]Horsley, 145–153. This section is especially interesting for its reference to the Mishnah in order to characterize synagogues in Galilee. But Horsley's assumption that communal regulation of this sort was "democratic" needs to be tested against both historical and ethnographic evidence. See also Kenneth Atkinson, "On Further Defining the First-Century CE Synagogue: Fact or Fiction?" *New Testament Studies* 43.4 (1997), 491–502.

[20]Indeed, I am struck with the overlap with Chilton, *A Galilean Rabbi and His Bible: Jesus' Use of the Interpreted Scripture of His Time* (Wilmington: Glazier, 1984), also published with the subtitle *Jesus' Own Interpretation of Isaiah* (London: SPCK, 1984), and *The Temple of Jesus: His Sacrificial Program Within a Cultural History of Sacrifice* (University Park: Pennsylvania State University Press, 1992).

[21]James F. Strange, "First Century Galilee from Archaeology and from the Texts," in *Archaeology and the Galilee* (Atlanta: Scholars Press, 1997), 39–48, 44.

[22]He takes this point up in greater detail in *Galilee. History, Politics, People* (Valley Forge: Trinity Press International, 1995), 189–221.

exchange was probably not even usually a matter of bartering one thing for another. Once the provision of some product was agreed, it became a regular feature of life in that community. Jesus' own perspective on money as impure, his
sense that it was "unjust mammon" (Luke 16:9) and Caesar's rather than God's
(Matthew 22:21; Mark 12:17; Luke 20:25), stems from his own experience in
the Galilean exchange economy, where currency appeared to be the instrument
of a foreign sovereignty, alien to the sovereignty of God.

Jesus' rejection of currency makes his teaching appear opaque from the point
of view of modern economics and the conventionally positive evaluation of work.
Our assumption of the value and necessity of currency seems to put him on the
other side of the watershed of economic development. But one might ask: just
who is on which side of what watershed? In the end, currency is only an abstract
form of the products an economy permits it to buy. The standard policies of interest and confiscation by taxes and other means are, of course, much easier to
implement with money than with products, but only the give-and-take of products measures how each of us lives within our communities. "Gross domestic
product" and "average income per household" are sensible measures of how states
might fashion their policies of interest and confiscation, and they will presumably
remain so. They are Caesar's measures, designed to serve Caesar's ends. But
alongside them, the Galilean measure also has its place. That measure does not
concern what I have or what I earn, but what I really make: how am I productive? And in the nexus of relations in which I am productive, with whom do I
live, what do I eat, where do I sleep, how am I healed of injury or disease, when
am I entertained and nurtured and encouraged and disciplined? And from the
perspective of Christianity, of course, there is always the reminder that the measure I measure with is the one by which I will be measured (Mark 4:24; Matthew
7:2; and see the Targum of Isaiah 27:8).[23] The Galilean minimum that is owed
to me is owed to all. Taken on its own terms, Christianity itself is an alternative
to work, because its motivating concern is the transformation of this world according to the principles of the world that is to come.

COMMENTARIES

Judaism on Christianity

by JACOB NEUSNER

With Gnostic Christianity, Judaism has a considerable dispute. For the distinction between spirit and material, which is fundamental to Gnosticism, is lost on
Judaism. When it comes to work, the spiritual—Torah-study—and the material—making a living in a conventional sense—are intertwined. The sages of Judaism do not condemn the ignorant as "materialist," they encourage them to

---

[23]The relationship among the texts is dealt with in *A Galilean Rabbi and His Bible*, 123–
124; see also *The Isaiah Targum. Introduction, Translation, Apparatus, and Notes:* The Aramaic
Bible 11 (Wilmington: Glazier and Edinburgh: Clark, 1987), 53.

study the Torah. But when we come to Orthodox, Catholic Christianity, we find ourselves with a doctrine of learning as an act of virtuous labor that the sages of Judaism will have found entirely suitable. People are expected to join moral, emotional, and intellectual components of their personality, to integrate habits, deeds, and passions. Deeds are shaped by deliberation, just as Torah-study comes to realization in deeds. Christ as Paedagogue corresponds to the sage as the embodiment of the Torah, and the deeds of learning of Christian theology to the activities of Torah-study of Judaism. The mode of expression is different, but the fundamental attitude, which encompasses under virtuous labor the entire life of intellect and character, heart and soul, surely corresponds.

The doctrine of helping others in classical Christianity, as Professor Chilton portrays matters, forms part of the larger program for maintaining a persecuted community, and considerations of assisting those who suffer by reason of their faith predominate. In the context of Judaism, helping others takes its place within the larger program of guiding a community formed at God's initiative. In Judaism one helps others as part of a larger obligation to serve God and share with God the gifts that God has bestowed on the person. While the result may be the same—assisting the persecuted or the poor—the motivation and context differ. In each case, we see how the larger system imparts context and meaning to each detail of the system. And that is so even though, in the corresponding religion, the action that is required will be precisely the same.

Where the two systems come closest is in the Judaic and Christian concurrence that there are things of value that transcend material interest. Money is not the only thing that counts, and it is not the main thing either. The sages of Judaism do not condemn money as impure; there are religious obligations that can be carried out only in specie, the payment of the half-shekel that every Israelite male owes for the upkeep of the public offerings of the Temple being a good example. But then money serves as a symbol, not as a thing of intrinsic value. Indeed, the Rabbinic sages maintain that goods have a true value. Money fluctuates. Comparing investment in a field and investment in Torah-study says it all. And a reading of Jesus' view of unconventional ways of making a living will show that in his terms and context, he will have concurred.

Islam on Christianity

by TAMARA SONN

Christianity and Islam are both such varied phenomena that generalizations about either one of them are difficult. Each tradition accounts for more than one-fifth of the world's population, spread worldwide, and living in conditions ranging from the most sophisticated urban centers to remote village outposts. Each has had a triumphal, worldly, and imperial past that, in fact, brought them into direct confrontation with one another. But in the case of Christianity, that triumphal legacy has been largely bequeathed to Western secular society, and in the case of Islam it has been overshadowed by centuries of colonial domination. Each developed as well distinct ascetic traditions, some of that have survived to the present era. But Christianity and Islam do share a dominant value that influences attitudes toward work in both traditions. That value is compassion. Islam agrees with Christianity that "whatever you do for the least of me, you do for me." Muslims are taught that any wealth they attain is not for its own sake but for the sake of those for whom they are responsible. Wealth that is acquired dishonestly or dishonorably, or that is not shared, is of no benefit to believers. Indeed, their wealth must be "purified" through charity; that is the literal meaning of the Arabic term (*zakat*) used for the required annual giving. The similarity between Islamic and Christian values in this regard can best be seen in the development of liberation theology in the modern Roman Catholic world. Liberation theologians agree with modern Muslim activists that believers have a responsibility to work for the well-being of society rather than simply accept negative conditions as a reflection of the divine will. More than simply praying for relief from suffering, believers must actively engage in efforts to change the conditions responsible for the suffering. Interestingly, the shared nature of this commitment has allowed many Muslims and Christians to overcome traditional sectarian differences and work together on shared goals. (Farid Esack, *Qur'an, Liberation and Pluralism* [Oxford: One World, 1997], describes such shared efforts in South Africa.)

Hinduism on Christianity
by Brian K. Smith

The enduring legacy of eschatological hope, together with the memory (and potential religious significance) of persecution persisting long after Constantine, has seemingly engendered suspicions in Christianity regarding the value of this world as a whole and of work within it that are entirely foreign to Hinduism. The latter has never experienced the kind of persecution Christianity suffered in its formative early years; nor has it ever generated the same kind of millenarianism and apocalyptic expectations that run as undercurrents in Christian thinking. From this point of view, the early Christian opposition of this world and the "kingdom of heaven," between things "belonging to Caesar" and things "belonging to God," finds no parallels in Hinduism.

The opposition between worldly activity and the renunciatory, other-world-directed religious quest is, however, represented in certain strains of the Hindu tradition. The world of work, of karma, has for some Hindu sages and philosophers been constituted as extremely problematic; indeed, for most strands of Hinduism it is the escape from such a world of karma and the perpetual rebirth it causes, that is held up as the ultimate religious goal. In most Hindu traditions, however, this does not obviate the value of work in this world. Rather, renunciatory goals and attitudes have been infused into the worldly life (as in some forms of Christianity), thus allowing for a religiously validated form of worldly activity, or have been separated out into a separate "stage of life" that follows upon the successful pursuit of work in the world. In general, however, Hinduism does not really recognize "two worlds," this one and the next, but regards the ultimate as the true foundation and essence of this world, which is ordinarily perceived in an illusory fashion.

Buddhism on Christianity

by CHARLES HALLISEY

There is a sharp contrast between Buddhism and Christianity in a matter of deep sociology and we are able to see this important contrast clearly because of Bruce Chilton's historical approach to the topic of this volume. Chilton emphasizes how a process of development that culminated in the fourth century C.E. changed the way that Christians assumed responsibility for the world, but he also shows how this process of development took place within a context of extreme persecution of the fledgling Christian community. As a result, an emphasis on exemplary living in every area of private life, including work, was tied to the well-being not only of the individual, but of the Christian community as a whole. Exemplary living of individuals in private was tied to maintaining the good reputation of the Christian community, and it is obvious that self-consciousness about one's persona as a representative of a community before the hostile eyes of others was a key component in moral self-reflection for Christians.

A comparison with Buddhism makes it clear that the notion of membership in an imagined community can take many forms and that membership in such a community does not have to be intimately connected to issues of self-identity. It would appear that Christians thought of themselves, first and foremost, as Christians. They saw themselves as individuals who had lives that others would judge "the faith" by. In contrast, Buddhists rarely used the category of "Buddhist" as a key component of individual self-identity, nor did they identify a community that all Buddhists should see themselves as representing in public work-lives to non-Buddhists or that established unique bonds and obligations among its members. The closest one might come to something analogous to the notion of "Christian community" is the community of Buddhist monks, but remember that monks do not work in any conventional sense and are supported by charity. In other words, the difference between Buddhist and Christian notions of work is reflected in quite different conceptions of the "community" alluded to in the title of this volume. For Buddhists, the community to which we owe something is weakly defined. It is the community of all sentient beings, and work is part of a grand religious program to end their suffering. For Christians, it is a community that is given quite a strong definition: the Christian community.

SUMMARY

"Who ever does not wish to work should not eat!" That outburst in 2 Thessalonians 3:10 is often taken as the point of departure for discussing the Christian ethics of work. But what is startling about this statement is not its content, but the fact that it had to be made at all. Why should Christian teachers have to emphasize that productive labor is a virtue, and that laziness should be avoided?

The simple answer to that question is that Christianity does not "work," in the usual sense of that word. The insistence that the world is to be transformed makes Christians strangers to conventional moralities embedded in the status quo, however much a matter of common sense they may seem to be. The basic issue of Christians' attitude toward the world, in its historical development, is taken up in the section "Why must we work?" Christianity was only put to work when the empire that had persecuted it suddenly seemed to have become an instrument of the world's transformation.

Even so, the "how" of working, as we see in "How ought we to work?" is distinctly odd. The emphasis is not on producing, but on becoming different by virtue of what one does. As Catholic Christianity pursued its debate with Gnosticism, the physical dimension of that transformation came to acquire increasing importance. Within it, the distinction between public and private was dissolved, just as self-interest and altruism also coalesced. Yet even as these perspectives have developed and become dominate, Christianity persisted in its deep skepticism concerning what the world—and therefore ordinary work—could really offer.

GLOSSARY

Christian   the Latin name given followers of Jesus, *Christiani,* signaled contempt for them. First used in Antioch by around the year 50 C.E., this term of intended ridicule designated them as partisans of Christ, rather than practitioners of a respected religion.

Divi filius   "God's son," was a title sometimes borne by the Emperors of Rome. Swearing obeisance to the emperor was a religious act, including a sacrifice of wine and incense, and this particular designation made such acts of allegiance all the more abhorrent to Christians. Many suffered torture and death, rather than conform to the custom.

fiscus Iudaicus   a tax which adult males had paid for the maintenance of the Temple, was commandeered after 70 C.E. by the Romans for the Temple of Jupiter Capitolinus in Rome. Moreover, the Roman version of *fiscus Iudaicus* was to be paid by all Jews, minors and women included, not only by adult males.

Gnosticism   a radical distinction between the present, material world and ineffable nature of God. This world is subject to decay and the rule of evil forces; only release from it can bring the spiritual awakening and freedom of knowledge (*gnosis*).

Religio licita   the status of a permitted religion enabled Jews to congregate in the Roman world, and to be exempt from the requirement of offering obeisance to the Emperor. In exchange, the priests in Jerusalem accepted the sacrificial animals that the Emperor donated for daily worship.

Sassanid dynasty   ruled Persia between the third and the seventh century C.E., instituted Zoroastrianism, and often posed a direct threat to the stability and hegemony of the Roman Empire.

DISCUSSION QUESTIONS

1. Prior to the toleration of Christianity under Constantine, what was the official attitude toward the new religion?

2. During this formative period, what adjustments do you see in Christian literature which address the problem of Roman persecution?

3. Assess the importance of Eusebius as an early Christian teacher.

4. What were the preeminent issues involved in the confrontation between Catholic Christianity and Gnosticism?

5. Why does Tertullian's argument turn so insistently on how personal virtue should be taken into account by public magistrates?

6. How might Jesus' attitude to work and profit be said to have influenced Christian theology at a later period?

INFOTRAC

If you would like additional information related to the material discussed here, you can visit our Web site: http://www.wadsworth.com

3

Islam

BY TAMARA SONN

WHY MUST WE WORK?

The Qur'an assumes that human beings work. Unlike Jewish scripture, the Qur'an does not describe work as a punishment. The story of the fall of humanity from divine grace in the garden, according to the Qur'an, does not include labor as punishment. The story, told several times, begins with God informing the angels that he intends to create a human being as his deputy on earth and they are to kneel before the human in respect. All did so except Iblis, whose pride did not allow paying such respect to human beings. God therefore dismissed Iblis from the heavens, cursing him. When Iblis begged for a reprieve, "until the day when they will be raised [from the dead]," God relented and put off Iblis' final judgment until "the appointed time." Iblis then vowed to try to distract as many people as possible from doing the will of God, and God promised him that he would "fill hell with you and those who follow you" (38:72–86). Iblis then tempts Adam and his wife (who remains nameless in the Qur'an) to eat from the forbidden tree:

> [God said,] "Adam, you and your wife live in the garden and eat whatever you want from it, but do not go near this tree or you will be sinners." But Satan whispered to them, making them aware of their hidden shame, and said, "Your Lord has only forbidden this tree so you will not become angels or immortals." And he swore to them, "Surely, I am a sincere advisor to you." So he caused them to fall through lies, and when they tasted the tree, their shame became obvious to them and they started sticking leaves from the garden over themselves. And their Lord called them, "Didn't I forbid that tree to you and tell you that indeed Satan is your clear enemy?" They said, "Our lord, we have wronged ourselves, and if you do not forgive us and have mercy on us, we will surely be lost." He said, "Go, some of you enemies of the others. And there is a place for you on earth and provision for a time." He said, "You shall live there and you shall die there, and from there you will be brought forth. O children of Adam, we have sent down to you a garment to cover your shame and a covering, but the garment of righteousness is the best. That is one of the signs of God that they may remember. O children of Adam, do not let Satan tempt you, as he turned your parents from the garden,

stripping them of their garments to show them their shame. Indeed, he and his group see you from a place where you do not see them." (7:20–28)

The story of the expulsion of Adam and his wife from the garden, therefore, is used in the Qur'an to explain the human condition: living in imperfection and enmity among peoples, with a tendency to be misled through deceit, but in ultimate dependence upon God and only until such time as God either "calls us forth" or banishes us to hell with Satan and other wrongdoers. It is only in oral tradition (hadith) that the story is augmented with explanations that men must toil for their livelihood and women must suffer in childbirth as punishment for violating God's command in the garden.

For whatever reason, the fact that human beings must work to sustain themselves is assumed in Islamic teaching. The need to struggle is part of the overall picture of creation in Islam, and the Qur'an presents itself as a guide for people in all their efforts. Acknowledging the stressful nature of human existence, the Qur'an describes life as an integrated process, beginning with repeated assurance that we were created for a purpose. God says, "Did you think we created you as a joke and that you wouldn't be brought back to us?" (23:116). Elsewhere, "We have not created heaven and earth and everything between them without purpose" (38:28). That purpose is summed up in the term *khalifah*. The Qur'an says in another telling of the creation story, that God said, "I am about to place a *khalifah* on earth" (2:31). The term *khalifah* technically means "successor," and is often translated—rather opaquely—as "vicegerent." But it stands for one of the central teachings of Islam: that human beings were designated by their creator as assistants or even vicars, meaning that human beings are charged with doing the work God has assigned to us. We are called upon to recreate in society the equality all human beings share in the eyes of God. In short, the purpose of humans' existence is to "establish justice": "You who believe, witness for God, even if it goes against yourselves or your parents or relatives. Whether rich or poor, God is closer than either" (4:136). As the Qur'an puts it, our job is to "expend every effort in the way of God" (9:41), to "enjoin good and prevent evil" (3:105, 111). The community established by those who accept the Qur'an is called the "median" community: "Thus we have made you as a median community that you show witness to the people and that the messenger be a witness over you" (2:144). Elsewhere, "You are the best community produced for humanity who command good and forbid evil and believe in God" (3:111).

This responsibility is the *amanah*, the task God entrusted us with at creation: "Indeed, we offered the *amanah* to the heavens and the earth and the mountains but they refused to carry it and were afraid of it. But human beings accepted it" (33:73). It is the covenant in which humans have been involved with God since creation. The Qur'an precedes the telling of the story of the garden by reminding listeners that Adam himself was a party to the covenant, but he was not perfect in carrying it out: "Indeed we had made a covenant with Adam before, but he forgot, and we found in him no determination" (20:116). Therefore, the Qur'an reminds people of the need for steadfastness, for constant effort (jihad), to do the will of God. We are weak and prone to fear: "Indeed, human beings are born impatient and greedy. When evil comes to them, they are full of fear and when good things come, they are greedy" (70:20–22). But we are given the guidance needed through revelation, and are assured that we will be rewarded for our efforts. Indeed, that ability to choose good over evil is the source of human moral superiority over those creatures who instinctively do the will of God, signified in God's insistence that the angels kneel before human beings. We are far from perfect, and many of us have different ways of going about our responsibilities. That is why the Qur'an tells us that we should compete in goodness: "For each of you we have established a law and a way. And if God had willed it, he would have made you one people. But to test you by what he has given you, so compete with one another in goodness. To God you all return, and then he will inform you about your differences" (5:49). In other words, if it had been part of the divine plan that we all be the same, that is how we would have been created; instead, we were created with differences. Prophet Muhammad is commanded in the Qur'an to tell all believers—whether Jewish, Christian, or Muslim—that they should learn to cooperate in a common goal: "Say, 'People of the Book [i.e., those who believe their scripture is from the one God], come together in agreement on a word, that we worship only God, and that we not associate anything with him'" (3:65). The goal, therefore, is not a uniform humanity or belief system, but a just society; and morality consists in sincere and constant efforts to achieve that goal.

Doing—or submitting to—the will of God is the very meaning of the term *islam*. Efforts in that regard are the basis of our ultimate reward. Another term for that concept is *'ibadah*, service or servitude to God. And every effort sincerely devoted to fulfilling the will of God is a part of that service. This includes even daily labor. Arabic, the language of the Qur'an, has other words for "work" as such, but all of them amount to *'ibadah* when properly oriented to fulfilling the will of God because the Qur'an provides guidance for every aspect of human life.

HOW OUGHT WE TO WORK? KINDS OF WORK TO BE PREFERRED OR AVOIDED

Not everyone is called upon to make the kinds of heroic contributions to the human effort we hear about in the epics. The Qur'an says, "God does not require from anyone what is beyond her/his capacity" (2:287). But each is called upon to fulfill her/his responsibilities within a properly ordered and just society. Children are called upon to respect their elders, parents are called upon to nurture their children and each other; and all are called upon to "read the signs," to seek knowledge, to understand their environment so as to be able to make meaningful contributions to it. All are called upon to behave humanely and decently in all their dealings. Whatever work we do, we must be honest, steadfast, and generous. In the Qur'an's words:

> Indeed whoever surrenders to God, male and female,
> those who believe, male and female,

those who obey, male and female,
those who are truthful, male and female,
those who are patient, male and female,
those who are humble, male and female,
those who give charity, male and female,
those who fast, male and female,
those who are chaste, male and female,
those who remember God often, male and female—
God has prepared for them forgiveness and great reward. (33:35)

More specifically, the Qur'an warns that all merchants must practice fair trade: "Woe to those who, when they take by measure from people, take full measure, but when they give to them or weigh for them, they give less" (83:2–4). And, "Do not cheat people of their things" (11:86; 26:184); "Do not . . . consume the wealth of [other] people unjustly" (2:189; 4:29). Historian N. J. Coulson characterizes the general Islamic orientation as codified in Islamic law as follows:

> Compassion for the weaker members of society, fairness and good faith in commercial dealings, incorruptibility in the administration of justice are all enjoined as desirable norms of behavior without being translated into any legal structure of rights and duties.[1]

In the context of these overall principles, Islamic teaching has a basic positive attitude toward the accumulation of wealth in general, and trade in particular. The Qur'an says, "Those people who aim at the life of this world and its beauty, we fully reward their labor in this [regard] and they will not be denied" (11:16). Much of the language of the Qur'an is based on commercial analogies, such as "store up credit with God," or "compete with one another in goodness." Furthermore, just as in English, the terms used for moral *good*ness in the Qur'an (*khair, fadl*) are also used for material *goods*. (Compare, e.g., 2:181 and 100:9 with 4:128.) This interchangeable terminology would not be likely in a society that does not consider honestly earned wealth to be a blessing from God. In fact, in oral tradition (hadith), we find the opinion that engaging in honest trade is a moral duty. Fazlur Rahman cites a hadith commentary according to which one of the early legal scholars said, "The honest merchant is more dear to me because he is like the holy warrior: the devil comes to him [to seduce him] in the matter of his weights and measures . . . and thus he unleashes a *jihad* against him."[2] In other words, the effort undertaken to avoid temptations to be greedy and corrupt in business is a moral good, worthy of reward.

But there are certain kinds of activities Muslims are not allowed to participate in. The Qur'an assumes commercial activity as a basic element of human economic life. It therefore seeks to protect the legitimacy of trade by insisting on

---

[1] N. J. Coulson, *A History of Islamic Law* (Edinburgh: University Press, 1964), 11.

[2] See Tamara Sonn, "Islam and Economic Issues," in *Religious Belief and Economic Behavior* (Atlanta: Scholars Press for the University of South Florida, 1999). See also Fazlur Rahman, "Islam and [the] Problem of Economic Justice," *Pakistan Economist* (24 August 1974), 19.

honesty and fairness. But even fair trade practices would not be sufficient to allow Muslims to participate in commerce involving prohibited substances such as alcohol, drugs, and pork, or activities such as prostitution or gambling.

Beyond these obvious limits, Islamic teaching condemns only fraudulent practices and those that put one party at a disadvantage. It begins by setting out the way to conduct transactions so as to ensure fairness:

> Believers, when you borrow from one another for a fixed period, write it down. And let a writer write in your presence fairly, and no writer should refuse to write as God has taught him, so let him write and let the debtor dictate and let him fear God, his lord, and not take anything away from it. But if the debtor is of low intelligence or weak or unable to dictate himself, then let someone who can watch over his interest dictate fairly. And call in two male witnesses and if not two men then one man and two women, of whom you approve as witnesses, so that if either of them should make a mistake, the other may remind her. And the witnesses should not refuse when they are called. And do not begrudgingly write it down, whether it is small or large, along with its term. This is more fair in the sight of God and makes testimony more definite and is more likely to keep you away from doubt, except if what you exchange is merchandise, then it is no offense not to write it down. (2:283)[3]

Precision in financial dealings is therefore required by the Qur'an, in order to avoid confusion and disputes arising from claims that cannot be substantiated.

Further, the Qur'an insists on equitable trade conditions, prohibiting practices that allow one individual or group to dominate another. The charging of interest on loans—*riba*—is the most obvious exploitation of the disadvantaged.[4] It allows those with wealth to augment their capital at the expense of those without it, potentially resulting in chronic indebtedness. The Qur'an, therefore, prohibits this practice outright: "Those who consume usury (*riba*) do not rise except as one whom Satan has afflicted with insanity. . . . God has made trade lawful and made usury unlawful" (2:276; cf. 3:125). Therefore, Muslim law disallows transactions in which one party is required to return more than she or he borrowed if that amount continually increases. Associated with the prohibition of interest is the Qur'an's prohibition of games of chance: "They ask you about wine and games of chance. Say, 'In both there is serious

---

[3]The requirement that two female witnesses substitute for a male witness has been taken in traditional interpretations to mean that women's testimony is only half as reliable as that of men in general. Many reformers today believe this interpretation is unsubstantiated in view of the Qur'an's insistence on the equality of females and males. They believe this requirement applies only in circumstances in which women are not familiar with the kind of transaction taking place. See, for example, Fazlur Rahman, *Major Themes of the Qur'an* (Minneapolis and Chicago: Bibliotheca Islamica, 1980), 48ff.

[4]Some commentators argue that *riba'* refers only to excessive interest rates (usury), allowing reasonable interest rates to be charged. The majority, however, believe the Qur'an's prohibition pertains to the charging of any interest on loans or other transactions whatsoever.

sin and advantage for people but their sin is greater than their advantage'"
(2:220; cf. 5:91). Gambling of any sort is therefore not allowed in Islam. The
prohibition of profiting from gambling, like the prohibition of profiting from
interest, was interpreted by the classical legists as a general prohibition of two
kinds of economic activities. First, those that produce unearned income are dis-
allowed. This includes not only gaining interest from loans but also from speculation on the prices of commodities. For example, one is not allowed to
purchase an amount of grain at a certain price and then sell it again at a higher
price without ever even receiving the goods, since this would only be done in
order to capitalize on fluctuations in the market price. Second, transactions
based on exchange of uncertain amounts are not allowed. Both parties to a con-
tract must be fully aware of their obligations and what they will receive. Thus,
for example, one may not sell a plot of land with an orchard on it, factoring in
the projected value of the fruit the trees will produce before the fruit has actually matured. If a drought or a blight struck and the trees did not produce or
the fruit was bad or failed to ripen, the buyer would have paid for something
that did not materialize.

A third aspect of Islamic law affecting economic issues, in addition to the
prohibition of unearned profit and uncertainty in transactions, is the requirement
that all participants in a commercial transaction share liability. This is different
from Western law that allows the legal fiction of corporations. Corporations are
entities in which shareholders are entitled to profit but whose risk is limited to
the amount of capital invested. Officers in corporations are also protected from
personal liability for things the corporation may do. This legal device allows for
the accumulation of significant profit, with limited risk. In the Islamic view, such
limited-risk enterprises potentially mitigate the sense of responsibility ideally
shared by all involved in economic associations.

Islamic law concerning trade and contractual obligations is very detailed,
and there are slight differences in opinion concerning application of certain
principles among the various schools of law.[5] Because the purpose of law concerning economic transactions is to safeguard fair trade in which all may participate, however, the law does allow for exceptions in cases where strict
application of the general law would result in hardship or negative results for
the community. In addition, institutions were developed to allow for complex
economic transactions that might otherwise be precluded by the dual prohibition of interest and uncertainty, such as banking as we know it, using credit
cards, or investing in the stock market. Such institutions operate as partnerships
in which all participants share risk and potential benefits. There are several kinds
of these partnerships. Some, for example, are associations in which partners
share investments, work, and profits or losses. Others are partnerships in which
some participants put up the money and others do the work; those who do the
work also share in the profit, but not the loss, while the financial partner(s) share

---

[5]For a good summary, see Joseph Schacht, *An Introduction to Islamic Law* (Oxford:
Clarendon Press, 1982), 134–160.

also in the loss. Such institutions operate as counterparts of Western corporations and banks but avoid Islamic prohibitions on interest, uncertainty, and contracts with legal fictions. Islamic banks, for example, operate on the basis of profit sharing and fixed fees rather than the charging or paying interest.[6]

WHY MUST WE HELP OTHERS?
PRIVATE GAIN AND PUBLIC BENEFIT

If the subheadings in this chapter were arranged according to Islamic priorities, this section would undoubtedly be the first. Among the Qur'an's most extensive discussions are those concerning charity. The Qur'an was delivered in a specific historical context, seventh-century Arabia, that was characterized by enormous suffering on the part of the majority as a result of the maldistribution of resources. Mercantile trade by means of camel caravans was the dominant economic factor in the region, yet only a few were wealthy enough to participate directly in this trade. The vast majority simply worked for the caravan owners and the suppliers of provisions. Many families were chronically in debt because debts left unpaid at death were inherited by the debtor's survivors. As in all cases of economic disparity, the burden was heaviest on the most vulnerable: widows and orphans. Women were often so desperate that they had no economic recourse but prostitution; some families were forced by poverty to kill their female children, since women had no direct access to economic independence. The Qur'an therefore addresses this situation repeatedly.

> Say, "Come, I will recite what your lord has forbidden you: that you associate anything with Him, and [you must] be good to parents and not kill your children because of poverty. We will provide for you and them. . . ." (6:152)

Greed and exploitation are condemned outright:

> Give the orphans their property, and do not consume their property with your property; surely that is a great crime. (4:3)

> They will ask you for a pronouncement concerning women. Say: "God pronounces to you concerning them and what is recited to you in the book concerning the orphan girls to whom you do not give what is prescribed for them and yet desire to marry them, and the oppressed children, and that you secure justice for orphans. Whatever good you do, God knows of it." (4:128)

> Woe to every fault-finder, slanderer, who collects wealth and counts it repeatedly. He thinks his wealth will bring him eternal life. No, he will certainly be thrown into *hutama* and you know what *hutama* is? It is God's fire that he lights and that descends upon the heart. (104:2–6)

---

[6]For a detailed discussion of Islamic banks, see Muhammad Nejatullah Siddiqi, *Banking without Interest* (Leicester, UK: The Islamic Foundation, 1983).

Have you seen the one who makes a mockery of religion? It is the one who mistreats orphans and works little for the feeding of the poor. Woe, then, to those who pray, yet are neglectful of their prayers—those who pray for show and withhold charity. (107:2–8)

We have seen that social justice, through equitable distribution of resources and prohibition of exploitative practices, is a major theme of the Qur'an. The giving of charity is another aspect of this theme.

> Whatever God has given to His Messenger . . . is for God and the Messenger and for relatives and orphans and the needy and the travelers, so it may not circulate [only] among the wealthy." (59:8)

> If you give charity openly, it is good, but if you conceal it and give it to the poor, it is better for you, and [God] will remove from you your sins. And God is aware of what you do. (2:272)

> Those who spend their wealth by night and day [in charity], secretly and openly, have their reward with their lord; on them [there will be] no fear, and they will not sorrow. (2:275)

In fact, giving charity in order to correct the social injustices resulting from maldistribution of wealth is more important, in the Qur'an's view, than converting people:

> It is not your responsibility to make them follow the right path, but God guides whomever he pleases. And whatever wealth you spend, it is for yourselves, if you spend only to seek the favor of God. And whatever wealth you spend [for charity], it shall be repaid to you in full and you shall not be wronged. (2:273)

So important is the giving of charity that it is one of the five basic requirements of all Muslims—the five "pillars" of Islam. In this form it is called *zakat*. Charity in general, *sadaqah,* is strongly encouraged, but all adult Muslims are required to give a portion of their wealth over and above that necessary to provide for themselves and their dependents, for the support of the needy and the well-being of society. This is to be done every year and is considered an essential component of serving God. In addition, it is the only way to legitimate or "purify" wealth. As discussed above, Islam's general attitude toward the acquisition of wealth is positive, but only provided the wealth does not result from exploitative practices and that it is used for the well-being of society, particularly the needy. Thus, those who seek moral guidance are advised to focus on helping the poor:

> Good is the one who believes in God and the last day and the angels and the book and the prophets and who spends money for love of Him on relatives and orphans and the needy and travelers and beggars, and for captives and who observes prayer and gives charity [pays *zakat*]. (2:178)

The causes for which charity are to be spent are also specified:

> [This charity] is for the poor who are detained in the way of God and are unable to move about in the land. The ignorant think of them as free from want

because of [their] abstaining [from begging]. You will know them by their appearance; they do not beg openly. And whatever wealth you spend, surely God has perfect knowledge of it. (2:274)

Indeed, the Qur'an stipulates the precise areas on which charity is to be spent:

Charity is for the poor and the needy and for those who work with them, those whose hearts are to be won over, for captives, for debtors, for the cause of God, and for travellers, a ruling from God. (9:60)

Charity may be left to individuals' consciences to pay, or it may be collected officially by the government, as the eleventh-century Andalusian jurist Ibn Hazm summarized:

It is the obligation of the rich in every society to fulfill the needs of the poor. The government has to compel them to undertake this if [voluntary] zakat is insufficient for their needs. The poor must be insured for their necessary food, for their winter and summer clothing, and for a shelter which is capable of warding off harm from them due to rains, cold and heat and which gives them privacy from the public eye.[7]

Closely associated with *zakat* is an institution known as the *waqf* (pl.: *awqaf*). Awqaf are trusts or institutions allowing people to bequeath funds or properties for charitable purposes. These funds or properties are established in perpetuity, meaning that they cannot revert to personal profit-making status. People may donate to them only after they have fulfilled their legal obligations, meaning that they have provided for their families' maintenance and legal inheritance shares. Beyond that they may donate money or property for charitable purposes such as schools, hospitals, mosques, defense, the support of particular individuals and their descendents, or even as small an offering as a neighborhood fountain. Business interests can also be dedicated to the support of such concerns. Although there is a wide variety of opinions regarding details of the *awqaf* trusts in Islamic law, there is general agreement that, ideally, these trusts are to be administered by impartial people, such as judges free of government control. Although there is no requirement to establish this kind of charitable trust, many people do, because of the overwhelming consensus in Islam that contributing to social well-being in this way is an honorable thing to do.

WHEN WORK DOES NOT WORK: UNEMPLOYMENT, EXPLOITATION, AND ALTERNATIVES TO PROPER WORK

As discussed above, the Islamic ideal is a society in which the basic needs of all people are met. The intense concern in Islam with charity is a reflection of this ideal, as we saw. We also saw that exploitation of any kind is strictly prohibited

---

[7]From his *al-Muhalla* (6:156), cited by Fazlur Rahman in "Islam and [the] Problem of Economic Justice," 33.

in Islam. The charging of interest, gambling, and participating in economic practices in which one side has a distinct advantage over the other are all prohibited
in Islam. The overall goal, then, is to develop and preserve an atmosphere in
which all people, even the poor and marginalized, are able to provide for their
own needs. Charity is a responsibility when, for whatever reasons, people are not
able to provide for themselves. But it is assumed that, ideally, people should be
allowed to bear responsibility for themselves.

This is evident in one of Islam's most outstanding innovations: allowing
women to own and dispose of property as they see fit. Prior to the coming of
Islam in the Arabian peninsula, women were treated as the property of men,
first their fathers and then their husbands. They had no independent economic
rights whatsoever and, as a result, were utterly dependent upon men for survival. That is the reason that poor people often were driven to despair at the
birth of girls. The Qur'an considered that situation tragic and prescribed
correctives. We saw above that the practice of female infanticide was forbidden and that the Qur'an chastises those who express displeasure at the birth of
a girl:

> When one of them is given the good news of [the birth of] a girl, his face
> darkens as he suppresses his unhappiness. He hides from people because of the
> evil the good news meant to him [and wonders] whether to keep her in dis-
> grace or push her into the earth. Indeed, evil is what they judge. (16:59–60;
> cf. 43:18)

It insists on the equality of all human beings before God, including women and
the poor and dispossessed.

Accordingly, the Qur'an initiated measures designed to guarantee the freedom and dignity of women, by requiring that they be allowed economic independence. In pre-Islamic Arabia, marriage, such as it was, consisted of men
buying women from their families. The "bride price" (*mahr*, dower or dowry)
was negotiated by the men and paid by the prospective groom to the bride's
family. The Qur'an intervened in this practice and insisted that the dower be
given as a gift by the prospective groom to the bride herself, to do with as she
will. As the Qur'an says, "And for what you receive from them, give them their
due, as fixed, and there shall be no sin for you in anything you mutually agree
upon once it is fixed" (4:25). In addition, whatever inheritance a woman brings
to the marriage remains her personal property, in accordance with a Qur'anic
verse interpreted as guaranteeing women the right to own and dispose of property: "Men shall have a share of what they have earned and women a share of
what they have earned" (4:33).

Furthermore, the Qur'an insists that women be included in the family's inheritance shares: "And those of you who die and leave behind wives shall bequeath to their wives provision for a year without being turned out" (2:241). As
codified in law, the wife actually receives a share of inheritance determined according to the number and sex of the survivors. The wife receives one-quarter
of the husband's estate if there are no other descendents, and one-eighth if there
are. The Qur'an also stipulates that daughters must be included in inheritance
shares:

For men there is a share of what parents and near relatives leave, and for women there is a share of what parents and near relatives leave, whether it is a little or a lot, a fixed share. And when relatives and orphans and the poor are present at the division, give them from it and speak to them judicious words. And let those who fear, if they leave behind them their own weak children, for them, fear God and say the appropriate word. . . . God commands you concerning your children: A male shall have as much as the share of two females, but if there are females [only], more than two, then they get two-thirds of what is left, and if there is one, she shall have the half. (4:8–12)

The disproportion between females' and males' shares is a reflection of the historical context in which the Qur'an was revealed. Daughters were expected to marry and be supported by their husbands. Sons, on the other hand, were expected to marry and support not only their nuclear families but their extended families as well. But the principle of women's economic independence was established, clearly reflecting the Qur'an's position that the right to property and the dignity of work are at the core of a properly functioning society.

It is interesting to note that the term often used in the Qur'an for "dower" is not the standard term, *mahr,* but rather a term that means "wages," *ujur.* The verse cited above, for example—"And for what you receive from them, give them their due, as fixed, and there shall be no sin for you in anything you mutually agree upon once it is fixed" (4:25)—could just as accurately be translated "give them their wages, as fixed" (cf. 5:6; 33:51; 60:11). In fact, the Qur'an uses the same term, *ujur,* to describe the payment women must receive for carrying out their maternal duties. In the chapter entitled "Divorce," the Qur'an specifies that, when a couple has exhausted efforts to reconcile and has decided that divorce is the best course of action, if the woman is pregnant, the husband must provide for her until the baby is born. It then requires that if the woman decides to nurse the child, she must receive her *ujur,* wages (65:7). The significance of this terminology is that even women whose work it is to take care of the home and children are not considered unemployed. Their work is valuable. In order to guarantee recognition of that fact, in addition to providing wives a degree of economic independence, the Qur'an uses the term for "wages" rather than a term such as "maintenance" or "gift."

Similarly, the Qur'an prescribes economic freedom for slaves. In the society in which Islam was revealed, slavery was an integral part. Islam intervened in this system, insisting on the equality of all human beings in the sight of God. But prohibiting slavery altogether would have required a complete change of the economic and social structure of Arabian society. Therefore, rather than outlawing slavery outright, the Qur'an established the principle of human dignity and, based on that principle, recommended the freeing of slaves as an act of piety:

We have surely created the human being in difficulties.
Does he think that no one has power over him?
He says, "I have spent a great deal of money."
Does he think that no one sees him?

. . . And We have indicated to him two ways.
But he did not attempt the high road.
And what indicates the high road?
Freeing a slave
Or feeding on a day of hunger
an orphaned member of the family
or a poor person in trouble. (90:5–17; cf. 58:3)

In this way, the Qur'an establishes an ideal that believers must strive to achieve. A pious society is one in which slaves are set free. The Qur'an emphasizes this point by further recommending that any slave who would like to be emancipated should be allowed to purchase his freedom: "And those of your slaves who desire [a written decree of freedom], write it for them if you know of good in them and give them out of the wealth God has given you" (24:34). Not only were slaves to be granted freedom if they were able to support themselves, then, but owners were to advance them funds to purchase their freedom, if possible. They could purchase freedom by working for it, gradually paying the agreed upon sum, or by using the wealth they have managed to accumulate, since Islamic law allowed slaves to own property and manage it as they saw fit. When they were freed, their property went along with them. In fact, owners had the responsibility to make sure slaves were capable of managing their own property before setting them free. In early Islamic law, minors were not allowed to be freed until they were capable of taking care of their own property and business concerns.[8] Although this kind of slavery is a thing of the past, this concern for the responsible management of one's property again reflects the importance that the Qur'an places on economic freedom and independence for all human beings.

The fact that the Qur'an does not require the immediate cessation of slavery reflects its concern with the well-being of those who cannot manage for themselves. As noted above, economic exploitation is strictly prohibited in the Qur'an's legislation concerning business practices. All those who enter into economic relationships must be on equal footing; none may be placed at a disadvantage by the nature of the transaction itself. But the Qur'an is equally adamant that those who are already economically disadvantaged must be cared for. In the case of slaves, they must not be mistreated or turned out before they are capable of supporting themselves. Women must be allowed to inherit and maintain their own property. And the poor and needy are to be cared for by means of obligatory and voluntary charity. Since even "women's work"—maintaining a household and tending to children—is considered valuable work in Islam, deserving of wages, clearly the Qur'an does not envision a society in which unemployment persists. Where it does occur, it must be corrected, given the emphasis on human dignity through economic independence.

---

[8]See, for example, Imam Malik ibn Anas, *Al-Muwatta of Imam Malik ibn Anas: The First Formulation of Islamic Law*. Translated by Aisha Abdurrahman Bewley (London and New York: Kegan Paul International, 1989), 321-322.

UNCONVENTIONAL WORK:
WORKING FOR GOD

There is no clergy in the Christian sense in Islam, no class of people who act as intermediaries between God and human beings. Nor is the study of Scripture an end in itself in Islam. One encounters God in revelation, but not only in revelation; the Qur'an reminds people that God's signs are everywhere. In fact, the same term is used for verses of the Qur'an, *ayat,* as for the signs of God evident all around us, in all aspects of creation. The study of Scripture and other sources, such as oral literature and history, is a means toward an end: understanding the will of God for humanity and determining how best to implement the divine will in our daily lives. That is the overall meaning of *islam,* submission to the will of God. It is clear, moreover, that overall the divine will is that human beings serve God by acting as his deputies or stewards, doing what we were created to do: "establish justice," re-creating in society the equality all human beings share in the eyes of their creator. All those who participate in this effort, from the most humble to the most powerful, are working for God in the most general sense.

However, circumstances vary from region to region and throughout time. The Qur'an gives some specific legislation, such as the prohibitions of murder and usury, which are undoubtedly applicable in all times and places. But the majority of the Qur'an's teaching is of a more general character, establishing guidelines and ideals toward which humans must strive. The Qur'an therefore sets up a kind of creative tension between the eternal truths and standards it presents and the ever-changing circumstances in which we must find ways to apply those truths and achieve those standards. As President Khatami of Iran recently expressed it:

> [R]eligion transcends the specific civilizations that it gives rise to. . . . When conditions and times change, new questions arise that in turn require new answers—and hence a new civilization. Religion . . . sheds light on questions of eternity, charting a general and timeless path for humanity, giving direction to life despite its ever-changing circumstances. Religion guides human talents to their plateau, instilling in people a sense of duty in different historical conditions. . . . In this view, the core of religion possesses such dynamism that in any age it can provide answers to questions and a fulfillment of needs.[9]

We saw (in Volume I) an example of this dynamism in legislation concerning polygyny. The Qur'an clearly establishes a model of the marriage relationship, ideally a partnership between equals, devoted to one another, their families, and to the cause of God. However, in some circumstances, marriage to more than one woman may be more effective in establishing social well-being than strict monogamy. We also saw that divorce is highly discouraged in Islam but, in some cases, it may be in the best interests of all concerned. In order to determine adequately how best to implement the will of God, therefore, it

---

[9]Mohammad Khatami, *Islam, Liberty and Development* (Binghamton, NY: Binghamton University Institute of Global Cultural Studies, 1998), 59–60.

is necessary to have a clear and detailed understanding of the circumstances in which one lives. Not only is it necessary to understand the nature of the guidance given in revelation, and in fact the Qur'an refers to itself as guidance for people, but it is also necessary to understand the circumstances for which the guidance is needed. By analogy, it is necessary to know the properties of the medicine, but it is also essential to understand the illness before prescribing the cure.

As a result, scholarship of all kinds is highly regarded in Islam. The earliest specialists who developed in Islam were those who memorized the Qur'an as it was delivered, so that it would be available for future generations. After the Qur'an was committed to writing, memorization was still respected, as it is today, but other levels of important scholarship also developed. It became clear that careful understanding of the actual language of the Qur'an—Arabic, in the dialect used by Prophet Muhammad—was also necessary for understanding the message. Further, scholars took upon themselves the responsibility to gather as much information as possible about the circumstances in which the message was revealed; after all, the Qur'an was delivered over a period of some twenty-two years and much of it was contextualized in the specific circumstances of the young Muslim community's life. Mention is made in the Qur'an, for example, of specific people in Mecca, the birthplace of the Prophet; readers not familiar with those people and their character would be at a loss to understand the significance of those references. At the same time, scholars collected reports (*ahadith*; sing.: *hadith*) of the Prophet's words or deeds that were not contained in the Qur'an itself. Although these reports are not of the same level as the Qur'an, they are nonetheless essential components of divine guidance, for the Qur'an describes the Prophet as the best example of how to serve God. Another level of scholarship developed as these reports were scrutinized for accuracy, based on such factors as the proximity of the reporter to the source, the character of the reporter, and the availability or lack thereof of confirming reports. Scholars of this kind are called *'ulama* (sing.: *'alim*), specialists in religious knowledge.

An even more specialized kind of religious knowledge developed with the spread of Islam: that concerned with application of revelation to specific circumstances, or codification of revealed guidance for implementation on a daily basis. This kind of knowledge is called *fiqh,* often called the "queen" of religious sciences; its practitioners are called *fuqaha'* (sing.: *faqih*), legal specialists.

Judges and other legal authorities are generally chosen from among the *fuqaha'*. In the earliest days of Islam, judges (qadis) were originally political appointees of the caliph. They were assigned to the various cities of the empire and instructed to arbitrate disputes, allowing local custom to prevail except in cases in which it conflicted with Islamic teaching. The appointee was to use his own judgment to determine whether or not this was the case. But within two centuries of the Prophet's death, Islamic scholarship had developed to the extent that only properly trained legal scholars were authorized to make such judgments. And that proper training was rigorous. As described by legal scholar al-Shafi'i (d. 820 C.E.), it required, in addition to general good character:

knowledge of the commands of the Book of God [the Qur'an]: its prescribed duties and its ethical discipline, its abrogating and abrogated [communications], its general and particular [rules], and its [right] guidance. Its [ambiguous] communications should be interpreted by the Sunna of the Prophet; if no Sunna is found, then by the consensus [*ijma'*] of the Muslims; if no consensus is possible, then by analogical deduction.[10]

In other words, legal training requires knowledge of the general principles and the specific rules of the Qur'an and an understanding of the extent to which they are applicable, as well as a thorough knowledge of the collections of authenticated hadith materials, and the decisions concerning what is legal and illegal made unanimously by the pious ancestors. Legal scholars must therefore be honorable, highly proficient in the Arabic language of the sources, including its rules of grammar, thoroughly familiar with the legal sources, astute in logic, and careful to survey all the sources before determining an opinion.

All Muslims are required to know their basic responsibilities and prohibitions. As al-Shafi'i put it, they must know:

that the daily prayers are five, that men owe it to God to fast the month of Ramadan, to make the pilgrimage to the [Sacred] House whenever they are able, and to [pay] the legal alms in their estate; that [God] has prohibited usury, adultery, homicide, theft, [the drinking of] wine, and [everything] of that sort which He has obligated men to comprehend, to perform, to pay in their property, and to abstain from [because] He has forbidden it to them.[11]

This type of knowledge is necessary in any walk of life. It is an individual duty (*fard 'ayni*). But specialized religious knowledge is not an individual duty, incumbent upon all Muslims. It is considered obligatory only that at least some people pursue the specialized knowledge of the religious scholars and legal scholars. This type of knowledge is necessary for the proper functioning of the Muslim community in any time or place, but it is necessary for only enough people to do it so that the community receives proper guidance. It is thus known as a collective duty (*fard kifayah*) incumbent upon each local Muslim community as a whole. As such, those who carry out this responsibility deserve support of the community. This support is often given through local *waqf* donations to the schools and mosques that sustain these scholars, but it is common for people also to donate directly to the support of religious and legal scholars. When states choose judges from among the *fuqaha'*, to serve in the courts overseeing religious law, they receive state support, as well.

Religious scholars hold a slightly different position in Shi'i Islam (roughly 15 percent of the Muslim population worldwide). In Sunni Islam, anyone can be chosen as prayer leader at a mosque and thus be referred to as an "imam." When a scholar achieves acceptance as a person of great piety and learning, he may also be called "imam." But in Shi'i Islam, only those believed to be descendents of

---

[10]Majid Khadduri, *Islamic Jurisprudence: Shafi'i's Risala* (Baltimore: Johns Hopkins Press, 1961), 306.

[11]Khadduri, 81.

Prophet Muhammad are called "imam." Most Shi'is believe the heritage must be traced through the Prophet's daughter Fatima and her husband (and the Prophet's cousin) 'Ali. Shi'i imams are believed to possess a special kind of knowledge that is not achievable through study alone, and that is infallible. There is some disagreement among various schools of Shi'i thought as to the identity of the imams, but the majority believe that there are no imams in the present age. The pursuit of religious scholarship, therefore, is that much more important for guiding the community. As Iran's president Khatami has said:

> All throughout Shiism's history the clergy have played a crucial role in awakening people to social pathologies, inciting them to fight injustice, awakening their religious identity. . . . With their incessant calls to social justice throughout the history of Islam, populist religious leaders have served as society's most astute pathologists and healers.[12]

Shi'i Muslims therefore have a highly developed program of religious scholarship. Like Sunni religious scholars, they are accorded a great deal of respect and supported through charitable foundations and ongoing donations.

With all the respect paid to religious scholarship, however, both Sunnis and Shi'is believe it is a means toward an end, rather than an end in itself. Religious scholars bear the responsibility to help guide the community in its efforts to fulfill the will of God. The effort is ongoing, however, because circumstances develop and change and because human beings—except for the infallible imams of Shi'i Islam—are believed to be capable of error. Therefore, the Muslim community must produce scholars to continue the process of understanding the divine will. As Sunni scholar Falzur Rahman put it:

> The process of questioning and changing a tradition—in the interests of preserving or restoring its normative quality in the case of its normative elements—can continue indefinitely; . . . there is no fixed or privileged point at which the predetermining effective history is immune from such questioning and then being consciously confirmed or consciously changed.[13]

This orientation toward the ongoing need for religious scholarship is echoed in the comments of President Khatami:

> For those without formal religious training, heeding the prescriptions of the [religious scholars] is necessary in practical matters, but in the realm of thought, no thinker can blindly follow the clergy, however outstanding they are—unless religious leaders are among the Infallibles. . . . Their ideas must be subject to critique.[14]

Human beings, even religious scholars, make mistakes interpreting the religious sources for practical application. Even if they were infallible, circumstances change, resulting in different understandings and the need for revised

---

[12]Khatami, 72.

[13]Fazur Rahman, *Islam and Modernity: Transformation of an Intellectual Tradition* (Chicago and London: University of Chicago Press, 1982), 11.

[14]Khatami, 40.

interpretations. For these reasons, continuous study of the religious sources of law is necessary in Islam. Thus, the purpose of studying religious sources goes beyond the study itself; its purpose is to be able to put the teachings into practice. Correct knowledge in and of itself in Islam is only a partial goal. The overall goal in Islam is correct practice. Prayer, charity, fasting, and pilgrimage are essential components of correct practice, but they are not sufficient to fulfill the will of God. Fulfilling the will of God, *islam,* is the effort to direct every action toward creating a just social order. As noted above, all those who participate in that effort are doing the work of God.

COMMENTARIES

Judaism on Islam

by JACOB NEUSNER

Since God worked in Creation and since Adam and Eve were to till the Garden of Eden, Islam and Judaism as represented by Scripture concur that work is no punishment. But Judaism does maintain that the human condition, the struggle to earn a living—that does not represent how God had intended matters to be. Judaism concurs with the Islamic conviction that everything is created for a purpose (*khalifah*). Whether or not the sense of divine vocation assigned to each of us has its counterpart in Judaism is not equivalently clear. That is because, in Judaism, there is an explicit doctrine that favors work of one kind over all other kinds: study of the Torah excels. That is why Judaism cannot concur about accumulation of wealth in general and trade in particular. These are deemed means to the end of the support of disciples of sages in their studies. Judaism in its classical statement would organize the whole of society to that end. Islam has a more worldly view of matters, with which modern and contemporary Judaic religious systems certainly concur.

Judaism and Islam certainly agree on the prohibition of interest, defined by Judaism as any form of payment for waiting for the repayment of a loan. So too, Judaism takes the same view as Islam as to gamblers, denying them the right to testify in courts of law:

> And these are those who are invalid [to serve as witnesses or judges]:
> (1) he who plays dice; (2) he who loans money on interest; (3) those who race pigeons; (4) and those who do business in the produce of the Seventh Year.
> Mishnah-tractate Sanhedrin 3:3A–B

In this way Judaism expresses its disapproval of the same kinds of activities that Islam rejects in its legislation. So too when it comes to purchasing grain and reselling it at a higher price without receiving the goods, this speculation in grain futures is rejected as usurious, as in the following:

> What is interest, and what is increase [which is tantamount to taking interest]?
> What is interest?
> He who lends a sela [which is four denars] for [a return of] five denars,

two seahs of wheat for [a return of] three—because he bites [off too much].

And what is increase?

He who increases [profits] [in commerce] in kind.

How so?

[If] one purchases from another wheat at a price of a golden denar [25 denars] for a kor, which [was then] the prevailing price, and [then wheat] went up to thirty denars.

[If] he said to him, "Give me my wheat, for I want to sell it and buy wine with the proceeds"—

[and] he said to him, "Lo, your wheat is reckoned against me for thirty denars, and lo, you have [a claim of] wine on me"—

but he has no wine.

Mishnah Baba Mesia 5:1

In these and other ways, the two religions intersect on fundamental matters of conduct in the market. It will not surprise, therefore, that in many other details the two systems overlap. For example, in a partnership one must share both the risks and the rewards. Any other arrangement is usurious, just as Professor Sonn says.

The two religions agree on the primacy of philanthropy, which Judaism calls *sedaqah,* the word standing for both "righteousness" and "charity." It is an absolute obligation to help the poor, not a matter of discretion or personal preference but a religious duty. Judaism takes the view that *sedaqah* should be carried out anonymously if possible, and it further maintains that the highest form of *sedaqah* is to give the poor person not a fish but a fishhook.

Christianity on Islam

by BRUCE CHILTON

In its evidently higher valuation of work as compared to Judaism, the Qur'an can only seem even more perplexing to Christianity than the Mishnah is. That perplexity is somewhat heightened by the present exposition, since the link of primordial disobedience to work is said to be made "only in oral tradition (hadith)." Presumably, that means here that it is not to be taken seriously, so that work is a thoroughly good thing.

But then, we are told with equal emphasis a bit later: "In fact, in oral tradition (hadith), we find the opinion that engaging in honest trade is a moral duty." On the face of it, "oral tradition" is treated with a certain ambivalence, although on the whole a positive perspective on work, labor, and commerce is manifest. Still, it is clear that the play between Qur'an and hadith could do with some further explication: in the exposition, hadith is sometimes downplayed, sometimes privileged. In somewhat the same way, the disproportion between females' and males' shares is written off as "a reflection of the historical context in which the Qur'an was revealed." If there were some method for determining what the balance between revelation and history is in a particular case, it would be good to know what that might be.

As matters stand, a degree of picking and choosing within the tradition as a whole seems to be indulged. In the history of Christianity, a cognate controversy has attended the relationship between the Scriptures and later tradition, between the Old and New Testaments, and the evaluation of what should be attributed most directly to Christ (whether on the basis of attribution to the historical Jesus or on theological grounds). The exposition of the authoritative statements of Christianity within the present project is designed to address just that controversy in its many dimensions. Finding one's terms of reference within the study of Islam seems difficult, unless one buys into the historical account of revelation that the Qur'an itself sets out.

The prohibition of usury, on the other hand, seems straightforward, and might invite comparison with the practice of communal possessions within Christianity (discussed in "Christianity on Judaism"). But it then turns out that the foundations of what looks similar are quite different. Christian communism in Acts does not prohibit private property, but engages in communal living as the Holy Spirit's sign of the world that is coming, while the Qur'an's prohibition of *riba'* is for here and now.

Yet where it concerns a basic care for those who are most vulnerable to human injustice, the provisions of the Qur'an are remarkably similar to the injunctions in the Letter of James. Still, even that source, precisely when it seems to bring Christianity most into interface with Islam, goes its own way when the issue is motivation (James 1:27):

> Religion, pure and undefiled, with God and the Father, is this: to visit orphans and widows in their oppression, to keep oneself unstained from the world.

The effectuation of justice cannot await the world's being made just, any more than a commitment to love can await the perfection of the self (James 2:8–13). To approach the world, Christianity intentionally steps out of the world, and shows no patience with waiting for a consensus prior to transformation. Even Paul's collection for the community of Christians in Jerusalem was not merely an attempt to alleviate poverty, but part of what he called "the offering of the nations," the Zecharian program that linked Paul with Jesus and Peter in a strategy of eschatological transformation (Romans 15:16; also see "Christianity on Judaism").

Under the category of "Unconventional Work," the issue of ordained Christians is raised, but in the peculiar assertion that, in Islam, "there is no clergy in the Christian sense." But the exposition then goes on to speak of the expertise of the *'alim, faqih,* and *imam* in a way precisely analogous to the Christian *presbuteros* ("elder," taken up from the Hebrew *zaken*). When the Letter of James uses this term (5:14–15), it is to represent skill in the traditions of Israel and of Jesus, and to focus the faithful community's practice of prayer. These qualities could also extend to the administration of the communal wealth of a congregation, which led to the designations of "deacons" (from *diakonos,* servant) and "overseers" (from *episkopos* in Greek, *mebaqqer* in Hebrew). Where Christianity departs from Islam is not over the structural issue of whether there are clergy, but in the systemic evaluation of what clergy are to do. The term itself derives from the Greek term *kleros* (meaning "portion" and "lot"), and refers to the part that a person designated for ministry might have (Acts 1:17, 26). In Christianity, that apostolic service includes the announcement and effectuation of global change.

Hinduism on Islam
by BRIAN K. SMITH

Islam, like Hinduism, does not conceive of work per se as "punishment"; in both traditions it is just assumed that humans have both a need and a duty to work. Both assume also that work is integral to the purpose and meaning of life. For Islam, that purpose is to act as God's assistants in recreating "the equality all human beings share in the eyes of God." For Hinduism, the purpose of work is to participate in the ongoing order of things, where everything and everyone has an appointed place and assigned function in the cosmic whole. For Islam, the end is to "establish justice" and thus conform to the will of God; for Hinduism, the end is to maintain order and thus play one's part in the cosmic unfolding of things.

Different kinds of work, and different kinds of workers, are also both assumed and legitimated in both religions. In Islam, the goal "is not a uniform humanity . . . but a just society." Most Hindus would, I think, ascribe to such a sentiment. The question concerns the definition of "justice." Traditionally, Hinduism would not conceive of justice as in any way involving "equality." In Hinduism, as in Islam, exploitation and mistreatment of others is abhorred, but "justice" is wrapped up in a system that presumes the automatic workings of a just moral system in the form of the law of karma. Ultimately, justice is operating apart from the human manipulations of it, although that does not preclude the development of Hindu law and its agents who see to the more immediate situation.

The fact that much of the Qur'an's teachings on work evolved out of the mercantile context of its time has shaped both the specifics and the metaphors that tradition uses in relation to the subject. Hinduism's metaphorical language has evolved out of the religious and ritual context; the reverberations in Islam between moral "good" and material "goods" are absent here. But in Hinduism, no less than in Islam, there is (for most classes, in the proper stage of life) no shame in making a "good living" (within the boundaries of permissible occupations). The accumulation of honestly begotten wealth (one of the meanings of the Hindu term *artha,* one of the "goals of life" in this religion) is a religiously valid pursuit for both traditions.

Finally, both Islam and Hinduism place a high premium on charity—but do so out of very different considerations. The community orientation of Islam guides its emphasis on charity: giving to the poor helps to redistribute wealth, correct social injustices, and move the community closer to the ideal of equality and justice. In Hinduism, the object of charity (in two senses) is different. The object in the sense of the proper recipient of charity is usually not "the poor" but the religious (who are, nevertheless, sometimes materially poor too).

And the object in the sense of the purpose of charity is less any kind of redistribution of wealth and more a kind of transformation of it: material goods, when given to a proper recipient, can be changed into spiritual merit. Generally speaking, whereas charity in Islam appears to have primarily a social purpose, in Hinduism it serves the individual's quest to gain personal virtue.

Buddhism on Islam

by CHARLES HALLISEY

As with Judaism and Christianity, the general purposes of work in Islam are strikingly different from what we see in Buddhism. Work in Islam, as a kind of divine service, teaches us about our relationship to God. Obviously, no such conception is possible with Buddhism, a tradition that has been quite resolute in its disinterest in a Creator God. At the same time, the practicalities of work, the virtues that make up good work such as humaneness, honesty, steadfastness, fairness, and generosity, are remarkably similar in the two traditions. Moreover, both traditions show a marked appreciation of wealth, and encourage its accumulation, and neither sees poverty as a moral virtue. Both traditions also encourage the use of surplus wealth in charity, although Islam clearly has a stronger emphasis on correcting the conditions of social injustice than was generally the case in premodern Buddhism.

This kind of comparison presents us with a real challenge: how do we explain the practical similarities between these two traditions that are so different in their theological worldview? At one level, we could say that there is no moral tradition that sees deceitfulness, sloth, and selfishness as human virtues and that this is a witness to the fact that we belong to a *human* community, for all our cultural and religious differences. In our contemporary world, where cultural and religious difference is so much a source of conflict, it is important to remind ourselves that there is considerable commonality between human communities and we should allow this commonality to inform our visions of a global ethic. At another level, we could say that the commonalities between Islam and Buddhism stem from their presence in the world among mercantile communities. Both the Islamic world and the Buddhist world historically represented vast world systems of trade, and the virtues that they highlighted were precisely those virtues that would be highly valued by merchants no matter what their religious affiliation.

SUMMARY

Islamic teaching assumes that human beings must work to sustain themselves. The need to struggle is part of the overall picture of creation in Islam and the Qur'an presents itself as a guide for people in all their efforts. But our role is a positive one; human beings were created to serve as God's stewards on earth. Our job is to re-create in society the equality all human beings share in the eyes of God. In short, human beings were entrusted by God at creation with the task of "establish[ing] justice," as the Qur'an puts it. All efforts to fulfill this trust (*amanah*) are known as *jihad*. And all work we do to fulfill our responsibilities qualifies. That includes our careers, provided the purpose of our effort is to support the people who are dependent upon us, that we earn our living in honorable ways (meaning that our work involves no exploitation and that we do not deal in prohibited activities or substances such as prostitution, drugs, or alcohol), and that we are generous with any excess capital we earn.

GLOSSARY

'alim   Islamic religious scholar

amanah   the responsibility humans were entrusted with at creation; the purpose of human existence

ayah   verse of the Qur'an; sign of God

faqih   Islamic legal scholar

fard 'ayni   individual responsibility; duty all Muslims must fulfill

fard kifayah   communal responsibility; duty encumbent upon society as a whole but not necessarily upon each individual

fiqh   Islamic legal knowledge

hadith   oral tradition; extra-Qur'anic report of words or deeds of Prophet Muhammad

'ibadah   "servitude"; ideal relationship of believers to God

ijma'   "consensus" of Muslim scholars concerning a legal opinion

'ilm   Islamic religious knowledge

jihad   "effort" to fulfill the divine will

khalifah   "successor" of Prophet Muhammad in political rule; more generally, "steward" or "vicegerent" of God; humans' role on earth

khilafah   "stewardship"—human responsibility on earth

mahr   "dower"; bridal gift

riba   financial interest rate or usurious interest rate

sadaqah   "charity"

ujur   "wages"

waqf   charitable endowment

zakat   alms; charity required of all Muslims on an annual basis

DISCUSSION QUESTIONS

1. What does the concept *khilafah* (stewardship) mean in Islam?
2. Does the Qur'an have a negative attitude toward the accumulation of wealth?
3. What is the purpose of wealth in the Qur'an?

4. What kinds of economic activities are Muslims not allowed to undertake?

5. Explain why *zakat* is an essential Islamic value.

6. When were women given the right to own property in Islam?

INFOTRAC

If you would like additional information related to the material discussed here, you can visit our Web site: http://www.wadsworth.com

4

Hinduism

BY BRIAN K. SMITH

WHY MUST WE WORK?

Over the long course of the history of Hinduism, the notion "work" has
had different connotations at different times, and has taken on different
meanings and significances within different historical and religious contexts. The question of "why must we work?" also entails the definitional question of "what is 'work'?" and the answers to both of these queries have changed
over time in Hinduism.

In the earliest period of the history of the Hindu tradition—an era that begins with the entry of the Indo-European or Aryan peoples into India in the second millennium B.C.E.—the concept of work was inextricably bound up in the
religion of that period. Vedic religion revolved entirely around the performance
and ideology of the fire sacrifice, an extremely intricate and complex ritual centering on the offering of oblations dedicated to one or another of the many gods
of the pantheon into fire. The original meaning of the term *karma* is "work" in
the sense "ritual action or labor," that is, correctly and precisely executed activity that will have a salutary effect on the participants of the ritual and, indeed,
on the universe as a whole. With this definition of "work" in mind, we can turn
to the question of "why must we work?" as it is understood in this context and
period of the history of Hinduism.

The philosophy underlying Vedic ritualism assumed that the universe was, in
the beginning, created by a god (Purusa, the Cosmic Man, or Prajapati, the
"Lord of Creatures"), but that this work was defective. The creator "emits"
from himself the creation, but in this cosmogonic move from primordial unity
to multiplicity and diversity the cosmogonic product is characterized by discon-
nection, confusion, and disarray. The parts of time, too, are in origin created dis-
connected and "disjointed": "When Prajapati had emitted the creatures, his
joints became disjointed. Now Prajapati is the year, and his joints are the two
junctures of day and night, of the waxing and waning lunar half-months, and of
the beginnings of the seasons. He was unable to rise with his joints disjointed"
(Satapatha Brahmana 1.6.3.35).

The point of such Vedic myths of origins is to represent God's cosmogonic activity as faulty; creation here is not cosmos. The universe, as it was in the
beginning, is in need of repair. And it is precisely the work of ritual activity (carried
out by both the gods and human beings) that is designed to "fix" the universe.

How, then, to answer the question "why must we work?" in this period? We must "work," that is, perform ritual sacrifices, in order to continually "heal" a world that was created faulty and perpetually tends toward its "natural" state of chaos. The ritual was conceived as a connective, reparative activity. "With the Agnihotra [the twice-daily sacrifice performed at dawn and dusk] they healed that joint [which is] the two junctures of night and day, and joined it together. With the new and full moon sacrifices, they healed that joint [which is] between the waxing and waning lunar half-months, and joined it together. And with the Caturmasyas [performed quarterly at the beginning of the seasons] they healed that joint [which is] the beginning of the seasons, and joined it together" (Satapatha Brahmana 1.6.3.36).

Ritual labor was not only supposed to have such cosmological powers, but also was the means by which a human, born also in the natural state of defectiveness, was constructed into a proper human being. Rituals beginning with the *samskaras,* rites of passage performed at critical junctures in the life of a youth, had as their purpose to repair the imperfections of birth. Ritual work thus also consisted of the construction of a religiously viable self, and while Vedic fire sacrifices tended to be eclipsed by other forms of religious practice in later Hinduism, the performance of the *samskaras* have continued to the present day and are done for much the same reason. Work was performed to construct an identity and "world" or status for the sacrificer. "Man is born into a world made by himself" (Satapatha Brahmana 6.2.2.7); that is, one's identity or stature in this world was the product of the sacrifices one offers.

Finally, in the Vedic period ritual work was also the means for creating a desirable afterlife for oneself. "Born out of the sacrifice, the sacrificer frees himself from death. The sacrifice becomes his self" (Satapatha Brahmana 1.3.2.1). A "divine" or "heavenly" self is "born out of the sacrifice"; that is, it is the product of one's ritual resume, of the "work" one has done throughout one's lifetime. "The sacrifice becomes the sacrificer's self in yonder world," it is said. "And truly, the sacrificer who, knowing this, performs that [sacrifice] comes into existence [there] with a whole body" (Satapatha Brahmana 11.1.8.6). Or again, another text declares that the sacrificer "is united in the other world with what he has sacrificed" (Taittiriya Samhita 3.3.8.5), his ritual accomplishments on earth being the precise measure of his divine self in heaven.

The notion that one's own *ritual* acts (for in Vedic times, these were the only acts that really mattered) had consequences—in the future as well as the present—is one of the possible sources for a post-Vedic doctrine that was to have huge implications for the religious worldview of all subsequent Indian traditions. This was the doctrine that stated that *all* actions produced fruit, good or bad, that determined the quality of one's life. This causal and moral "law of karma" first appears in Hindu texts called the Upanishads, which date to the middle of the first century B.C.E., and also features as a prominent doctrine in the new religions that arose in India at this time, Buddhism and Jainism. From this time forward, the nature of one's work—and the attitude with which it was performed—was believed to have determinative consequences over one's future, both in this lifetime and in future rebirths.

In its earliest appearances, this theory of karma and rebirth after death is regarded as a "secret" doctrine, to be revealed by a teacher only to his well-prepared student. Furthermore, the source of karma is located in desire, which begins a causal chain—from desire comes resolve, from resolve comes action, and from action comes karmic reaction:

> "Yajnavalkya," said [Artabhaga, the student], "when the voice of a dead man goes into fire, his breath into wind, his eye into the sun, his mind into the moon, his hearing into the quarters of heaven, his body into the earth, his soul into space, the hairs of his head into plants, the hairs of his body into trees, and his blood and semen are placed in water, what then becomes of this person?" "Artabhaga, my dear, take my hand. We two only will know of this. This is not for us two [to speak of] in public." The two went away and deliberated. What they said was karma. What they praised was karma. Verily, one becomes good by good action, bad by bad action. . . . According as one acts, according as one conducts himself, so does he become. The doer of good becomes good. The doer of evil becomes evil. One becomes virtuous by virtuous action, bad by bad action. But people say: "A person is made [not of acts, but] of desires only." [In reply to this I say:] As is his desire, such is his resolve; as is his resolve, such the action he performs; what action [karma] he performs, that he procures for himself.[1]

This new concept of a "law of karma"—whereby good acts result in good results, bad in bad—extends the Vedic notion of consequential action from the confines of the ritual to the whole of life. And just as in the Vedic period one's future life is the product of one's "work" (as defined in that context), here too one's rebirth is directly correlated to actions performed in this life. One text posits an exact, and sometimes amusing, correlation between evil deeds and the consequences visited upon the evildoer subsequently. The passage begins by noting that "Some evil-hearted men undergo a reverse transformation of their form because of evil practices here (in this life), and some because of those committed in a former life."

> A man who steals gold has mangled fingernails; a man who drinks liquor has discolored teeth; a priest-killer suffers from consumption; and a man who violates his guru's marriage-bed has a diseased skin. A slanderer has a putrid nose; an informer, a putrid mouth; a man who steals grain lacks a part of his body, but an adulterator of grain has a superfluity (of parts of his body). A thief of food has indigestion; a thief of words is a mute; a man who steals clothing has white leprosy; and a horse-thief is lame. A man who steals lamps becomes blind, and a man who extinguishes lamps, one-eyed; a sadist is always sick, and an adulterer is rheumatic. Thus, because of the particular effects of their past actions, men who are despised by good people are born idiotic, mute, blind, deaf, and deformed.[2]

---

[1]Brhadaranyaka Upanishad 3.2.12; 4.4.5. In Robert Ernest Hume, translator, *The Thirteen Principal Upanishads*, 2nd ed. (London: Oxford University Press, 1931; reprint 1975). Unless noted, all other citations from the Upanishads are from this translation.

[2]Manusmriti (hereafter Manu) 11.48–54. In *The Laws of Manu*, translated by Wendy Doniger with Brian K. Smith (London: Penguin Books, 1991), 278–279. All subsequent quotations from this text are taken from this translation.

In the Upanishads, where the doctrines of karma and rebirth first appear, it is not only the fear that evil action will produce unpleasant rebirths that concerns the sages. Reversing the earlier notion that it was work (in the sense of ritual action) that was the most important duty of human beings, the Upanishadic philosophers and mystics argued that work or karma (in the sense of all action) was the cause of perpetual and potentially unending rebirth. Karma thus went from being the religious solution (cosmologically, as well as personally) in the Vedic period to being the principal problem itself in post-Vedic Hinduism. Since the middle of the first millennium B.C.E., Hindu traditions have all faced the same predicament: How can one free oneself from the endless cycle of karma and rebirth? How can one escape the suffering that pervades the world known as samsara (the wheel of continual and repeated birth, life, death, and rebirth)?

Beginning also in the Upanishads was the notion that there was an alternative to karma and rebirth and the wheel of samsara. This state of "release," "freedom," or "liberation" from karma and rebirth was called *moksha*. To obtain this liberation one needed to stop karma, to cease "working" and desiring. Such ideas and doctrines were put forward by various groups of world renouncers—some of whom gravitated to heterodox traditions such as Buddhism and Jainism, and some of whom remained in the Hindu fold (and whose views are represented in the Upanishads). In all cases, the pessimism surrounding the value of worldly life that accompanies the doctrines of karma, rebirth, and samsara were counterbalanced by alternatives, methods that were designed to obtain for the practitioner a release from the wheel of phenomenal existence.

Chief among these methods was the attempt to eliminate the production of karma by eliminating desire and minimizing activity. The latter was in part accomplished by renouncing the world of work and social activity and wandering about homeless, practicing asceticism. All desires are to be overcome, and to this end renunciation of the life of a householder is required:

> On knowing him (the true self), one becomes an ascetic. Desiring him only as their home, mendicants wander forth. Verily, because they know this, the ancients desired not offspring, saying: "What shall we do with offspring, we whose is this Soul, this world?" They, verily, rising above the desire for sons and the desire for wealth and the desire for worlds, lived the life of a mendicant. For the desire for sons is the desire for wealth, and the desire for wealth is the desire for worlds; for both these are desires.
>
> (Brhadaranyaka Upanishad 4.4.22)

Another strategy for eliminating karma was the development of the discipline called yoga. Yoga was intended to calm the mind and body, obtain equanimity and tranquility, by ceasing to act ("curbing his movements," as the text below states) and focusing the mind:

> When he keeps his body straight, with the three sections erect, and draws the senses together with the mind into his heart, a wise man shall cross all the frightful rivers. . . . Compressing his breaths in here and curbing his move-

ments, a man should exhale through one nostril when his breath is exhausted. A wise man should keep his mind vigilantly under control, just as he would that wagon yoked to unruly horses.[3]

In the next few centuries following the production of the early Upanishads and the rise of the heterodox religions of world renunciation, a reaction against this pessimistic view of the world of activity arose in certain quarters of the Hindu tradition. A new configuration, centering on the concept of religious duty, or dharma, and especially revalorizing the significance of the householder, is evident in texts that date to the second or third centuries B.C.E. Under such a view, work was understood to be both necessary and religiously valid. While the problem of karma and rebirth carried over into this and all other subsequent traditions of Hinduism, the solution to such a problem was no longer to be found in fleeing from one's responsibilities in the social and familial worlds. One's duty or "work" in this new sense—very much including carrying out one's proper occupation in this world of social activity—was now a necessary precursor and prerequisite to the search for final liberation.

One of the most important texts produced in this period was the Bhagavad Gita. The text is composed in the form of a dialogue between a warrior named Arjuna, who is unable to perform his proper duty due to his confusion about right and wrong, and his charioteer, advisor, friend, and God, Krishna. In a clear contestation of certain earlier teachings concerning the desirability of abandoning action and work, Krishna teaches Arjuna that such teachings are not only false but impossible; what is necessary is not to cease working, but to work with the proper attitude of detachment:

> A man cannot escape the force
> of action by abstaining from actions;
> he does not attain success
> just by renunciation.
> No one exists for even an instant
> without performing action;
> however unwilling, every being is forced
> to act by the qualities of nature.
> When his senses are controlled
> but he keeps recalling
> sense objects with his mind,
> he is a self-deluded hypocrite.
> When he controls his senses
> with his mind and engages in the discipline
> of action with his faculties of action,
> detachment sets him apart.
> Perform necessary action;
> it is more powerful than inaction;

---

[3]Svetesvatara Upanishad 2.8–9. In Patrick Olivelle, translator, *Upanishads: A New Translation* (New York: Oxford University Press, 1996).

without action you even fail
to sustain your own body.
Action imprisons the world
unless it is done as sacrifice;
freed from attachment, Arjuna,
perform action as sacrifice![4]

The Gita thus teaches a method for acting without producing karmic "fruits" that will need to be reaped later in this lifetime or in future lifetimes. It is through detached, "sacrificial" action that one is saved from karma and rebirth. One must do one's proper duty, but one should act like God acts, without ego, desire, or greed. For if God did not do his job the universe would collapse:

Whatever a leader does,
the ordinary people also do.
He sets the standard
for the world to follow.
In the three worlds,
there is nothing I must do,
nothing unattained to be attained,
yet I engage in action.
What if I did not engage
relentlessly in action?
Men retrace my path
at every turn, Arjuna.
These worlds would collapse
if I did not perform action;
I would create disorder in society,
living beings would be destroyed.
As the ignorant act with attachment
to actions, Arjuna,
so wise men should act with detachment
to preserve the world.
No wise man disturbs the understanding
of ignorant men attached to action;
he should inspire them,
performing all actions with discipline.
Actions are all effected
by the qualities of nature;
but deluded by individuality,
the self thinks, "I am the actor.". . .
Surrender all actions to me,
and fix your reason on your inner self;

---

[4]Bhagavad Gita 3.4–9. This and all subsequent citations from this text are taken from Barbara Stoler Miller, translator, *The Bhagavad-Gita: Krishna's Counsel in Time of War* (New York: Bantam Books, 1986).

without hope or possessiveness,
your fever subdued, fight the battle!

(Bhagavad Gita 3.21–27, 30)

Here we have the culmination of centuries of thinking, in different ways, about the question "why must we work?": we must work because it is our duty to do so and because we should imitate God who works in order to preserve and maintain the universe and all creatures in it. Work becomes here the supreme obligation of human beings and the best way to live in conformity to the ways of God. But clearly also is the necessity to work in a particular kind of way— disciplined, wise, unattached, and in a devotional manner through which all actions are surrendered to God.

Thus it is that both the definition of and the rationale for "work" has shifted over the course of the centuries as various Hindu traditions have sequentially unfolded. While we have thus far concentrated on the different meanings of "work" in their largest philosophical and religious contexts, in all periods work has had a more common meaning as well—an occupation or job. Already in the earliest texts of Hinduism, the Vedas, and continuing through the texts on dharma or duty, the tradition has specified, sometimes in great detail, the proper occupations for Hindus of different sorts, and the kinds of jobs that should be avoided if possible.

HOW OUGHT WE TO WORK? KINDS OF WORK TO BE PREFERRED OR AVOIDED

Hinduism since its origin has understood society to be made up of different kinds of people performing different kinds of necessary economic and social functions. The Hindu tradition understands differences between people as intrinsic to who they are by birth (for they have been born who they are by virtue of their past karma). People are born into different social groups (classes and castes) that have different occupational niches in society, and an individual should adopt the occupation of his group—for clearly that is the job for which he or she is, by birth, most suited. As several texts declare, it is better to do the job assigned to you and your group poorly than to do a job assigned to another well.

The earliest and basic form this ideology took was a system of four classes: Brahmin priests, Kshatriyas (warriors and rulers), Vaishyas (commoners, including agriculturalists, pastoralists, and merchants), and Shudras (servants). Each of these four classes was assigned specific roles and functions and was, under ordinary circumstances, prohibited from the occupations appropriate to other classes. The "naturalness" of this arrangement—or even its divine sanction—was asserted in part by integrating the origins of the social classes within stories of the origins of the cosmos itself. The social classes and their assigned roles are thus represented as a natural part of the world around us, and as part of the way things were made in the very beginning.

The most famous of the texts in which the social classes are depicted as part of the original creation is Rig Veda 10.90, which tells of the origins of the universe as stemming from a primordial sacrifice of God, here called the "Cosmic Man." From that sacrifice and dismemberment the various elements of the cosmos came into being: the worlds, the sun and moon, the seasons, the various types of supernatural beings, the animals, and so forth. And also, we learn, the social classes originated then, brought forth from the parts of the body of the Creator God: "When they divided the Cosmic Man, into how many parts did they apportion him? What do they call his mouth, his two arms and thighs and feet? His mouth became the Brahmin; his arms were made into the Kshatriya; his thighs the Vaishya; and from his feet the Shudras were born" (Rig Veda 10.90.11–12).

Note here how the occupations assigned to the four classes are correlated with the body parts of the deity from which they supposedly originated. The Brahmins who, as priests, make their living in part by reciting holy verses and ritual spells, come from the mouth of the Cosmic Man. Furthermore, because the priests were created from the mouth they are to be henceforth and forever regarded as the purest class: "A man is said to be purer above the navel; therefore the Self-existent one said that his mouth was the purest part of him. The priest is the Lord of this whole creation, according to the law, because he was born of the highest part of the body" (Manu 1.92–93). The warrior class stems from the deity's strong arms; from the "thighs" (which could also imply the stomach and genital region) comes the Vaishya, who is charged with jobs having to do with fecundity, fertility, material growth and prosperity, and so on; and the servant class is born from the feet, the lowest and most polluted or "base" part of the body, but also the "base" in the sense of the basis upon which all other classes stand and depend.

A somewhat later text, drawing upon the cosmogony cited above, enunciates in more specific terms the inborn duties the creator allocated to each of the social classes:

> But to protect this whole creation, the lustrous one made separate innate activities for those born of his mouth, arms, thighs, and feet. For priests, he ordained teaching and learning, sacrificing for themselves and sacrificing for others, giving and receiving. Protecting his subjects, giving, having sacrifices performed, studying, and remaining unaddicted to the sensory objects are, in summary, for a ruler. Protecting his livestock, giving, having sacrifices performed, studying, trading, lending money, and farming the land are for a commoner. The Lord assigned only one activity to a servant: serving these (other) classes without resentment.
>
> (Manu 1.87–91)

And as another text makes clear, the Brahmin alone is capable of teaching (the sacred Veda) as well as learning it, sacrificing for others as well as having sacrifices performed for himself, and receiving gifts as well as giving them. These are the "six innate activities of the high-born priest," three of which are also specified to be his proper means for making money. The ruler and commoner, prohibited from making money through religious occupations, have their own and unique means of earning a living as well as their religious duties to give gifts to Brahmins, recite the Veda, and offer sacrifices:

> Priests who remain within the womb of the Veda and are steadfast in carrying out their own innate activities should make a living properly by six innate activities, in order, the six innate activities of a high-born priest: teaching (the Veda), reciting (the Veda), sacrificing for themselves, sacrificing for others, teaching, and receiving gifts from a pure man. Three duties of a priest are denied to a ruler: teaching, sacrificing for others, and, third, receiving gifts. And these are also denied to a commoner; this is a fixed rule. For Manu the Lord of Creatures has said that these duties are not for those two (classes). As a means of livelihood, bearing weapons and missiles is for a ruler, while trade, (tending) livestock, and farming are for a commoner. But their duty (as opposed to their livelihood) is giving, reciting (the Veda), and sacrificing. Teaching the Veda, for a priest, protecting, for a ruler, and trading, for a commoner, are pre-eminent among their own innate activities.
>
> (Manu 10.74–80)

Such is the basic outline of the caste system—four principal classes, each with their own assigned occupation, hierarchically ranked. At the top is the class whose job concerns the religious sphere; the Brahmin priest is, according to the texts (not uncoincidentally composed by members of this class), "a great deity whether or not he is learned, just as fire is a great deity whether or not it is brought to the altar. . . . Thus priests should be revered in every way, even if they engage in all kinds of undesirable actions, for this is the supreme deity" (Manu 9.317, 319). The Kshatriyas are to be rulers and warriors and engage in the activities appropriate to their birth. By doing so, they will go to heaven after death:

> When a king who protects his subjects is challenged by kings who are his equal or stronger or weaker, he should remember the duties of rulers and not turn away from battle. Not turning away from battle, protecting subjects, and obedience to priests are the ultimate source of what is best for kings. Kings who try to kill one another in battle and fight to their utmost ability, never averting their faces, go to heaven.
>
> (Manu 7.87–89)

As for the commoners, they are to pursue occupations concerned with wealth and prosperity—tending livestock, trade, and agriculture—and should do so happily:

> When a commoner has undergone the transformative rituals and has married a wife, he should constantly dedicate himself to making a living and tending livestock. For when the Lord of Creatures emitted livestock he gave them over to the commoner, and he gave all creatures over to the priest and king. A commoner must never express the wish, "I would rather not tend livestock," nor should they ever be tended by anyone else when a commoner is willing. He should know the high or low value of gems, pearls, coral, metals,

woven cloth, perfumes, and spices. He should know how to sow seeds, and recognize the virtues and faults of a field, and he should know how to use all sorts of weights and measures; and the worth or worthlessness of merchandise, the good and bad qualities of countries, the profit and loss from trades, and the way to raise livestock. And he should know the wages of hired servants, the various languages of men, the way to preserve goods, and buying and selling. He should make the utmost effort to increase his goods by means in keeping with his duty, and take pains to give food to all creatures.

(Manu 9.326–333)

The servant's duty and occupation are straightforward: serve humbly members of the higher classes and hope for a better rebirth: "If (a servant) is unpolluted, obedient to his superiors, gentle in his speech, without a sense of 'I', and always dependent on the priests and the other (higher classes), he attains a superior birth (in the next life)" (Manu 9.335).

While members of each class thus have their own "innate activities" and duties specific to their birth to perform, there are also and in general proper and improper ways of making money. One text, for example, lists "seven ways of getting property in accordance with the law" and "ten ways of making a living":

There are seven ways of getting property in accordance with the law: inheriting, finding, buying, conquering, investing, working, and accepting from good people. (Imparting) knowledge, handicrafts, working for wages, service, tending livestock, marketing, farming, being supported, begging for alms, and lending money are ten ways of making a living.

(Manu 10.115–116)

Some of these methods of making money are appropriate or inappropriate depending on one's class, but the purpose of the list seems to be to provide a comprehensive survey of the kinds of work allowable. Conversely, the following list enumerates occupations thought to be contemptible for one reason or another (because they are impure, involved in violence, criminal, etc.); members of these walks of life should thus be excluded from the religious rituals of the high-born classes:

Doctors, priests who attend on idols, people who sell meat, and people who support themselves by trade are to be excluded from offerings to the gods and ancestors; so, too . . . a usurer, a menial servant of the village or of the king . . . a herdsman . . . a traveling bard . . . an arsonist or poisoner . . . a man who sells Soma (a plant used in sacrifice), a seafarer, a panegyrist, an oil-vendor . . . a gambler . . . a seller of spices, a man who makes bows and arrows . . . a man who lives by shooting dice . . . a trainer of elephants, oxen, horses or camels, an astrologer, a breeder of birds, and an instructor in the martial arts; . . . a housebuilder, a messenger, and a (professional) tree-planter, a man who keeps sporting dogs, a falconer . . . a man who makes a living off servants . . . a farmer . . . a man who keeps sheep or buffaloes . . . and a man who carries out dead bodies—all these are to be strenuously excluded.

(Manu 3.152–166)

Finally, there are the occupations of those who live beyond the pale, the out-
casts and "aliens" who are "excluded from the world" of proper Indian society.
These castes are below even the servants, for the latter at least were supposedly
born from the feet of the creator god; but they too have their own, if despica-
ble, "innate activities":

> All those castes who are excluded from the world of those who were born
> from the mouth, arms, thighs, and feet (of the primordial Man) are tradition-
> ally regarded as aliens, whether they speak barbarian languages or Aryan lan-
> guages. Those who are traditionally regarded as outcasts (born) of the
> twice-born and as born of degradation should make their living by their innate
> activities, which are reviled by the twice-born: for (the caste called) "Chario-
> teers," the management of horses and chariots; for the caste of "Remaining-
> with-the-Mother," medical healing; for the "Videhan" caste, doing things for
> women; and for the "Magadhan" caste, trade; for the "Hunters," killing fish;
> for the "Unfit," carpentry; for the "Fatty," "Andhran," "Notorious," and
> "Diver-bird," the slaughter of animals that live in the wilderness; for those of
> the "Carver," "Dreaded," and "Tribal" castes, catching and killing animals that
> live in holes; for those of the "Shame on you!" caste, leather-working; for
> those of the "Reed-worker" caste, playing the drum. These (castes) should live
> near mounds, trees, and cremation-grounds, in mountains and in groves, rec-
> ognizable and making a living by their own innate activities.
>
> (Manu 10.45–50)

WHY MUST WE HELP OTHERS?
PRIVATE GAIN AND PUBLIC BENEFIT

Regardless of one's caste or occupation, a married man in what is called the
"householder" stage of life has as one of his religious obligations the pursuit of
artha—"private gain" understood as material prosperity, self-interest, political
advantage, and, in general, getting ahead in the world. Making a good living (as
long as one is following an acceptable occupation) and taking care of one's family is thus recognized by Hinduism as an important and indeed religiously binding goal of life. *Artha* is listed as one of the three "ends of life" in Hindu texts,
the other two being the pursuit of religious duty (*dharma*) and the pursuit of pleasure (*kama*). And while following the dictates of religious duty is obviously of
great importance for one's spiritual well-being, and the pursuit of pleasure and
"creature comforts" lead to a certain kind of happiness, in some texts it is said
that *artha* is in fact the most important of these ends of life: "Of the three ends
of human life, material gain is truly the most important. . . . For the realization
of religious duty and pleasure depend on material gain" (Artha Sastra 1.7).

Both pleasure and religion depend on the householder's ability to finance
these enterprises. As for religious duty, the householder's ritual obligations require the wherewithal to carry them out properly. As the following text indicates, the householder's daily life is filled not only with more or less costly (and

time-consuming) sacrificial rituals (the support, as it were, of the invisible community) but also with the support of various members of his household and the social community. Given the host of beings who depend on the householder, it is no wonder that other texts regard the householder as the best of all stages of life and the one on which members of all other stages of life depend:

> A householder should perform every day a domestic sacrifice on the nuptial fire or on the fire brought in at time of the partition of ancestral property. He should (additionally) perform a Vedic sacrifice on the sacred fires. . . . Having offered oblations to the sacred fire . . . he should go to his lord (i.e., his boss or patron) for securing the means of maintenance and progress. Thereafter, having bathed, he should worship the gods and also offer libations of water to the ancestral spirits. . . . Offering of the food oblation, offering with the utterance *svadha*, performance of Vedic sacrifices, study of the sacred texts, and honoring the guests—these constitute the five great daily sacrifices dedicated respectively to the spirits, the ancestors, the gods, the Brahman, and men. He should offer the food oblation to the spirits (by throwing it in the air) out of the remnant of food offered to the gods. He should also cast food on the ground for dogs, untouchables, and crows. Food, as also water, should be offered by the householder to the ancestral spirits and men day after day. He should continuously carry on his study. He should never cook for himself only. Children, married daughters living in the father's house, old relatives, pregnant women, sick persons, and girls, and also guests and servants—only having fed these should the householder and his wife eat the food that has remained.[5]

If the householder has the obligation to work hard and amass wealth, he also has the duty to give away large portions of his wealth in the form of sacrificial offerings and gifts of food and other goods. Such gifts are to be given not only to members of his own family, however, but to a variety of community members who depend upon the generosity of the householder. Here we have the ancient Indian version of "public charity."

Charity, indeed, is one of the most important of the virtues and duties of the householder; through such gift-giving he wins great merit. But in order to do so, the householder must give in the proper spirit and with the right attitude. Charity is divisible into three kinds, and ranked in descending order:

> Given in due time and place
> to a fit recipient
> who can give no advantage,
> charity is remembered as lucid.
> But charity given reluctantly,
> to secure some service in return
> or to gain a future reward,
> is remembered as passionate.

---

[5]From the Yajnavalkya Smriti, translated in Ainslie T. Embree, *Sources of Indian Tradition*, *Vol. One: From the Beginning to 1800*, 2nd ed. (New York: Columbia University Press, 1988), 227–228.

> Charity given out of place and time
> to an unfit recipient,
> ungraciously and with contempt,
> is remembered for its dark inertia.
>
> (Bhagavad Gita 17.20–22)

As this statement indicates, the giver, even with the right attitude, must also make sure he gives to a worthy recipient for it to be beneficial. In the following text we read of the types of Brahmin who "beg in accordance with the law," "dispossessed men" who should be given alms "in proportion to their learning":

> A man who wants descendants; one who wants to perform sacrifices; a traveler; a man who has given away all his property for the Veda; (one who begs) for the sake of his guru, his father, his mother, or for the sake of his livelihood as a student of the Veda; and man consumed with illness—these nine priests should be known as Vedic graduates who beg in accordance with the law, and a gift should be given to these dispossessed men in proportion to their learning. Food, together with a sacrificial gift, should be given to these priests.
>
> (Manu 11.1–3)

In another passage, several types of people are mentioned to whom the householder should give—a guest, a beggar, and a student of the Veda practicing chastity. But he should also give on a daily basis to Brahmin priests who are knowledgeable about "the true meaning of Veda." Such a gift is regarded as a sacrificial offering offered into the "fire which is the mouth of a priest." Should this gift be offered to an unworthy Brahmin, however, it is as if it were offered into a fire that had already gone out and "become dead ashes":

> When he has performed this ritual of the propitiatory offering, he should first feed a guest and, in accordance to the rules, give alms to a beggar and to a chaste student of the Veda. By giving alms, the twice-born householder wins a reward of merit which is the same as the reward for merit won by giving a cow to the guru in accordance with the rule. He should present alms, or even just a vessel of water that has first been ritually prepared, to a priest who knows the true meaning of the Veda. The offerings that ignorant men make to the gods and ancestors are lost if the donors give them by mistake to priests who have become dead ashes. An offering offered in the fire which is the mouth of a priest rich in learning and inner heat rescues (the sacrificer) from an unfortunate fate and a great offence.
>
> (Manu 3.94–98)

If the householder should be careful about the type of Brahmin priest to whom he offers gifts, conversely Brahmins should be wary about from whom they accept such gifts. While charity to Brahmins is encouraged or even mandated, from the Brahmin's point of view receiving such gifts is highly dangerous and ultimately undesirable, for by accepting the gift one has also taken a bit of the giver's very being and thus potentially corrupted one's own purity:

The food of a king takes away brilliant energy; the food of a servant (takes away) the splendor of the Veda; the food of a goldsmith, longevity; that of a leather-worker, fame. The food of a manual laborer kills off the progeny (of the man who eats it); that of a washerman (saps his) strength; the food of the hordes or of whores cuts him off from (all desirable) worlds. The food of a doctor is pus, the food of a woman who runs after men is semen, the food of a money-lender is excrement, and the food of an arms-dealer is dirt.

(Manu 4.218–220)

The danger of accepting gifts is particularly high for a Brahmin who is unlearned in the sacred lore encapsulated in the Veda and who is greedy (who "loves to accept" gifts), for he "sinks down together with that one (who gives)":

Even if he is eligible to accept (gifts), he should avoid becoming addicted to that; for his brilliant energy that comes from the Veda is quickly extinguished through accepting (such gifts). If he does not know the rules regarding the law for accepting material objects, a wise man should not accept (gifts), even if he is fainting from hunger. An ignorant man who goes about accepting gold, land, a horse, a cow, food, clothing, sesame seeds, and clarified butter is reduced to ashes, as if he were wood. Gold and food burn up his longevity, land and a cow his very body, a horse his eyesight, clothing his skin, clarified butter his brilliant energy, and sesame seeds his progeny. But a twice-born man who loves to accept (gifts), sinks down together with that one (who gives), as if in water with a boat made of stone. An ignorant man should therefore be afraid to accept gifts from just anyone; for an ignorant man is sunk even by a very small (gift), like a cow in mud.

(Manu 4.186–191)

While charity to Brahmins is thus simultaneously expected and problematic (especially for the Brahmin), another kind of giving is seemingly more straightforward. The householder, as we have seen above, has also a daily obligation to feed and honor "guests," an activity equated to one of the five "great" and daily sacrifices, the "sacrifice to men." The honoring of guests is one of the most important methods in Hinduism for practicing altruism and charity as a householder, and "No guest should reside in his house without being honored, to the best of his ability" (Manu 4.29). The practice of offering hospitality to guests is laid out in the texts in some detail, as is the definition of who counts as a "guest." The rewards of this act of charity are listed, as are the punishments for its neglect:

He should offer a guest, as soon as he arrives, a seat, some water, and food that has first been ritually prepared and perfectly cooked, to the best of his ability. If a priest stays (as a guest) and is not honored, (when he departs) he takes away all the (credit for) good deeds even of someone who lives by gleaning (corn) and gathering (single grains), even of someone who makes regular offerings in five fires. Grass (laid down for a resting place), space (to rest), water, and pleasant conversation—these four things never run out in the house of good people. A priest who stays even one night is traditionally regarded as a guest. . . . A convivial priest who lives in the same village should not be regarded as a guest, even when he comes to a house where there are a wife and (sacrificial) fires. Stupid householders who live off other people's cooked food become because of that, after death, the livestock of those who have given them food. A guest who comes with the setting sun in the evening should not be turned away by the householder who is a sacrificer; whether he arrives at a convenient time or an inconvenient time, he should not be allowed to stay in his house without eating. (The householder) should not himself eat anything that he does not feed to his guest. The revering of guests wins wealth, a good reputation, long life, and heaven. . . . If even commoners and servants have arrived at the house as guests, in a show of his mercy he may feed them along with his dependents. Others, too, such as friends who have come to the house in the spirit of good will, he may feed with natural food along with his wife, to the best of his ability. He may without hesitation feed newlywed women, right after the guests. The fool who eats first, without giving anything to these people, does not know that because he is eating he himself is devoured by dogs and vultures.

(Manu 3.99–106, 112–115)

In general, the duty of the householder to help others in the form of gift-giving, charity, and hospitality is elevated to a very high place indeed among the religious obligations and virtues of members of that stage of life. The generous man is on a par, or even superior to, a man learned in the sacred Veda, and, in a system that assumes future karmic rewards for acts of present virtue, the incentives for gifts of all sorts are many:

The gods considered the case of the miser who knows the Veda by heart and that of the liberal money-lender and decided that the food of both was equal. The Lord of Creatures came to them and said, "Do not make equal what is unequal; that (food) of the liberal man is purified by his faith, while that of the other is destroyed by lack of faith." . . . (A man) should always fulfill the duty of giving gifts involving offerings and rewards, placing them in the proper receptacles with a contented disposition, to the best of his ability. Whatever he may be asked for he should give without resentment; for the receptacle for it that will appear will save him in all ways. A man who gives water obtains satiation; a giver of food, incorruptible happiness; a bestower of sesame seeds, sight. The giver of land himself gets land; the giver of gold, long life; one who gives a house, the finest dwellings; the giver of silver, superb beauty; a man who gives clothing, the world of the moon; a man who gives a horse, the world of the Divine Horsemen; (a giver) of a draught ox (obtains) prosperous good fortune; a giver of a cow, the summit of the chestnut horse (i.e., the highest world of the sun); a man who bestows a carriage or a bed (obtains) a wife; the bestower of safety, sovereignty; the giver of grain, perpetual comfort; the giver of the Veda, identity with the power of ultimate reality. . . . In whatever manner he presents whatever gift, he is honored in return by obtaining that very gift in that manner. Both he who receives with honor and he who gives with honor go to heaven; in the opposite case, to hell.

(Manu 4.224–225; 227–232; 234–235)

WHEN WORK DOES NOT WORK: UNEMPLOYMENT, EXPLOITATION, AND ALTERNATIVES TO PROPER WORK

As we have seen, Hindu texts generally insist that one should do the work assigned to one's own caste: "Your own duty done imperfectly is better than another man's done well. It is better to die in one's own duty; another man's duty is perilous" (Bhagavad Gita 3.35). Staying within the occupational guidelines of one's class and "doing one's own duty" are the bulwarks of the caste system; conversely, "rejection of one's own innate activity" is listed as one of the causes for the "confusion of class" said to be the sign of a chaotic and dangerously disorganized society: "Through sexual misconduct between classes, through (carnal) knowledge of women who should not be known, and through rejection of one's own innate activity, (sons) of confused class are born" (Manu 10.24). Commoners and servants, in particular, who reject their duties for "alternative work" threaten the well-being of the entire universe; thus a king must be careful to make sure these classes pursue the work appropriate to them: "(The king) should make the commoner and the servant carry out their own innate activities diligently; for if the two of them should slip from their own innate activities, they would shake this universe into chaos" (Manu 8.418). Indeed, as it is made graphically clear in another passage, those who turn their backs on the work proper to their caste, who "slip from their own innate activities," are doomed to horrible rebirths after death:

> But those classes who slip from their own innate activities when they are not in extremity pass through evil transmigrations and then become the menial servants of aliens. A priest who has slipped from his own duty becomes a "comet-mouthed" ghost who eats vomit; a ruler (who has turned his back on the work prescribed to his class) becomes a "false-stinking" ghost who eats impure things and corpses. A commoner who has slipped from his own duty becomes a ghost "who sees by an eye in his anus," eating pus; a servant (who has so slipped) becomes a "moth-eater" (ghost).
>
> (Manu 12.70–72)

Even in times when members of the higher classes are down on their luck they should, if possible, be allowed to "carry out their own innate activities," as the following text recommends. This passage begins with a statement regarding the ordinary state of affairs—under usual circumstances, a king should see to it that a commoner and servant pursue work proper to them. But the text then turns to the obligations a Brahmin priest has to those of the higher, "twice-born" classes who find themselves "starved for a livelihood." They should not, under any circumstances, be put to work as slaves. On the other hand, members of the lowest class are slaves for life, even if they are set free:

> (The king) should make a commoner engage in trade, lend money, farm the land, or keep livestock; and (he should make) the servant the slave of the twice-born. A priest should out of mercy support both a ruler and a commoner if they are starved for a livelihood, and have them carry out their own

innate activities. But if a priest, out of greed and a sense of power, makes twice-born men who have undergone the transformative rituals do the work of slaves against their will, the king should make him pay a fine. . . . He may, however, make a servant do the work of a slave, whether he is bought or not bought; for the Self-existent one created him to be the slave of the priest. Even if he is set free by his master, a servant is not set free from slavery; for since that is innate in him, who can take it from him?

(Manu 8.410–414)

Despite insisting that people engage in the work assigned to their class, Hindu texts also make allowances for the possibility that an individual, in times of crisis and desperation, will not be able to pursue his or her proper occupation. Under such circumstances, the ordinary prescribed duty gives way to what the texts call "emergency duty," a kind of escape clause that allows for alternative forms of making a living. It is in such times of emergency—then, and then only—that alternatives to one's proper work are permitted, and even these alternatives are fairly strictly regimented. We have seen above how even in such cases of emergency Brahmins, rulers, and commoners should not be made slaves, and there are other restrictions on what members of the upper classes can do to make a living even when under severe distress.

Generally speaking, however, the rule is that members of the higher castes can, in times of emergency, adopt the occupations of those lower than themselves, for under the ideology of caste hierarchy the higher classes "encompass" within themselves the lower. Adopting the livelihood of one's superiors, however, is strictly forbidden. A member of the ruling and warrior class, for instance, "should never be so proud as to assume the livelihood of his betters (i.e., the Brahmin priests)," and members of the servant class who take on the occupations of their superiors should be punished and banished from the kingdom:

If man of the lowest caste should, through greed, make his living by the innate activities of his superiors, the king should confiscate his wealth and banish him immediately. One's own duty, (even) without any good qualities, is better than someone else's duty well done; for a man who makes his living by someone else's duty immediately falls from (his own) caste.

(Manu 10.95–97)

Despite such warnings, however, the texts do allow for members of the higher classes adopting the livelihoods of those below them, in times of "emergency." Thus, for example, "A priest who cannot make a living by his own innate activity just described (i.e., teaching the Veda, etc.) may make his living by fulfilling the duty of ruler, for he is the very next lower class" (Manu 10.81). And if he cannot make a living as a ruler, he may dip lower to the level of the commoner. But if he should pursue that class's assigned occupations, the Brahmin should try to avoid farming, for the violence connected with that line of work can do serious damage to his purity, which depends, in part, on a nonviolent lifestyle:

And if (this question) should arise: "What if he (a Brahmin) cannot make a living by either of these two (livelihoods, i.e., his own and that of the

ruler)?", he may make his living by farming and tending livestock, the livelihood of the commoner. But a priest or ruler (note here that a ruler can, in
times of distress, also take up the work of the commoner) who makes a living
by the livelihood of a commoner should try hard to avoid farming which
generally causes violence and is dependent on others. Some people think,
"Farming is a virtuous trade," but as a livelihood it is despised by good people, for the wooden (plough) with the iron mouth injures the earth and the
creatures that live in the earth.

(Manu 10.82–84)

Furthermore, if a Brahmin or Kshatriya take up another occupation assigned to
the commoner caste, that of trade, they must also be careful as to what substances
they sell. For one of the hazards of adopting an occupation other than that of
your own class is that you might fall rather quickly into the status of the lower
caste whose job you assume:

But if, for insufficient means of livelihood, a man gives up the duty in which
his is skilled, to increase his wealth he may sell the merchandise that commoners sell, with the following exceptions. . . . (What follows is a long list of
items it is forbidden to sell). By (selling) meat, lac, or salt, a priest immediately falls; by selling milk, he becomes a servant in three days. But by will-
ingly selling other (forbidden) merchandise, a priest assumes the nature of a
commoner here on earth in seven nights.

(Manu 10.85–94)

Brahmins, in particular, must be very careful as to how they make a living
even in the worst of economic circumstances. "By (making a living from) crafts
or business or from cows, horses, and carts . . . (or) by farming the land, by
serving a king . . . families (of Brahmins) . . . quickly perish" (Manu 3.64–65).
And in the following, the author begins with the ideal livelihood of a priest,
entailing professions that cause no or little harm to living beings and that are
not overly concerned with amassing wealth. Other occupations are allowable
too in times of distress, but are ranked in descending order of desirability. At
the bottom is "the dog's way of life," servitude, which should be avoided by a
Brahmin at all costs:

A priest should make his living by taking up a profession which causes no
harm, or very little harm, to living beings—except in extremity. He may accumulate some wealth through pursuit of the innate activities that are proper
for him and not contemptible, but without any undue bodily stress and only
for the purpose of attaining a minimal subsistence. He may make a living by
(pursuing the occupations called) "lawful," "immortal," "mortal," "deadly,"
or also the one called "simultaneously good and unlawful," but not by the
one called "the dog's way of life." (Subsisting by merely) gleaning (corn) and
gathering (single grains) should be known as the "lawful" (way of life); (living
off) unsolicited gifts would be the "immortal" (way of life); begging for alms
is the "mortal" (way of life); farming the land is traditionally known as the
"deadly" mode of life. Trade is the "simultaneously good and unlawful" (way

of life), but one may make a living even in this way (in times of emergency). Servility is called "the dog's way of life," and therefore one should avoid it.

(Manu 4.2–6)

If a Brahmin can, under certain circumstances, practice the occupations of the ruler and commoner, and if a ruler can in times of emergency adopt the livelihood of the commoner, the commoner, faced with a similar crisis can make a living as a servant, "but he must not commit actions that (he) should not do, and he should stop when he can" (Manu 10.98). A servant should not under any circumstances do the work of his betters, and should also not "amass wealth, even if he has the ability, for a servant who has amassed wealth annoys priests" (Manu 10.129). Rather, a member of this class should ideally take service with a commoner or ruler or, even more preferably, with a priest from whose example the servant benefits:

> But if a servant is searching for a means of livelihood he may make himself useful to a ruler, it is said; or a servant may try to make a living by making himself useful to a wealthy commoner. But he should make himself useful to priests, either for the sake of (winning) heaven (after death) or for the sake of both (heaven in the afterlife and a good reputation in this life). . . . Serving priests alone is recommended as the best innate activity of a servant; for whatever he does other than this bears no fruit for him. . . . But servants who want to carry out duties, who know duty, and who emulate the duties of good men, without reciting Vedic verses, are not defiled but praised. For the more a servant undertakes the behavior of good men, without resentment, the more he gains this world and the next, blameless.
>
> (Manu 10.121–123, 127–128)

For Brahmins who wish to protect their purity even in periods of economic hardship and distress, other options are available. We have seen above how a Brahmin can keep himself alive by living off of wild and cultivated plants (gleaning corn and gathering grains), accepting gifts, and begging. The lawbooks make distinctions among these emergency modes of subsistence; accepting gifts is the worst, although the nature of the gift is more or less corrupting:

> Among accepting gifts (from despicable men), sacrificing for them, or teaching them, accepting gifts is the worst and most despised for a priest (even) after his death. Sacrificing and teaching are always done for men who have undergone the transformative rituals, but gifts are accepted even from a servant of the lowest birth. The error of sacrificing or teaching (despicable men) is dispelled by chanting (the Veda) and making offerings into the fire, but the one that arises from accepting gifts (from them is dispelled only) by discarding (the gift) and by inner heat. A priest who cannot make a living should even glean (ears of corn) and gather (single grains) from any (field) whatsoever; gleaning is better than accepting gifts, and gathering is preferable even to that. If priests who are Vedic graduates are fainting (with hunger) for want of base metals or money, they should ask the king, and if he does not wish to give anything he should be rejected. (Accepting) an untilled field is not as much of

a fault as (accepting) a tilled one; a cow, a goat, a sheep, gold, grain, and cooked food—each (is less of a fault to accept) than the one that follows it.

(Manu 10.109–114)

But while begging and accepting gifts can be corrupting for a Brahmin householder, even in times of emergency, they are one of the standard forms by which others, who are pursuing the religious life, keep body and soul together. These individuals, who live on the margins or altogether outside of social and economic life, have taken work that transcends the occupations of the castes and classes. They are working for salvation or "working for God."

UNCONVENTIONAL WORK: WORKING FOR GOD

When it comes to the conventional understanding of work, it is members of the householder stage of life who pursue the occupations appropriate to the class or caste. But there are also three other stages of life delineated within Hinduism. And within all three of these other stages of life what counts as "work" is quite different from the pursuit of a livelihood.

The first stage of life in the ideal structure laid out in Hindu texts is that of a student. A young boy is given over to a teacher or guru with whom he lives and serves for a period of many years while studying the sacred Veda under the teacher's guidance. The lifestyle assigned to this stage of life is one of austerity, asceticism, and discipline. Not only should the student remain chaste for the duration of this period, but he should also observe a variety of other kinds of restraints and avoidances:

The chaste student of the Veda who lives with his guru should obey these restraints, completely restraining the cluster of his sensory powers to increase his own inner heat. . . . He should avoid honey, meat, perfume, garlands, spices, women, anything that has gone sour, and violence to creatures that have the breath of life; anointing (his body with oil), putting make-up on his eyes, wearing shoes, and carrying an umbrella; desire, anger, and greed; dancing, singing, and playing musical instruments; gambling, group arguments, gossip, telling lies, looking at women or touching them, and striking another person. He should always sleep alone and never shed his semen, for by shedding his semen out of lust he breaks his vow.

(Manu 2.175–180)

Another text gives a slightly different list of observances, vows, and practices, but similarly emphasizes the importance of an austere life dedicated to self-restraint, the cultivation of virtue, and obedience to the teacher:

Now (follow) the rules for the studentship. He shall obey his teacher, except when ordered to commit crimes which cause loss of caste. He shall do what is serviceable to his teacher, he shall not contradict him. He shall always occupy a couch or seat lower than that of his teacher. He shall not eat food offered at a sacrifice to the gods or the ancestors, nor pungent condiments, salt, honey, or meat. He shall not sleep in the daytime. He shall not use perfumes. He shall preserve chastity. He shall not embellish himself by using ointments and the like. He shall not wash his body with hot water for pleasure. But, if it is soiled by unclean things, he shall clean it with earth or water, in a place where he is not seen by a guru. Let him not sport in the water whilst bathing; let him swim motionless like a stick. . . . Let him not look at dancing. Let him not go to assemblies for gambling, etc., nor to crowds assembled at festivals. Let him not be addicted to gossiping. Let him be discreet. Let him not do anything for his own pleasure in places which his teacher frequents. Let him talk with women so much only as his purpose requires. Let him be forgiving. Let him restrain his organs from seeking illicit objects. Let him be untired in fulfilling his duties; modest; possessed of self-command; energetic; free from anger; and free from envy.[6]

In this stage of life, the student does not perform conventional labor, nor is he paid for his asceticism, study, and service to the teacher. In ancient India (and to a large extent continuing into modern India), those pursuing the religious life are supported by those occupied in more conventional forms of work. Among the other duties laid out for those in the student stage of life is begging for a living—or, more precisely, begging and then turning over all that is given to the teacher. We have seen above how the householder has an obligation to give to those who come around begging for religious purposes, and one such type of solicitor would be the religious student. But just as the householder should take care to give only to those who are worthy of his gifts, so too should the student of the Veda beg only from householders who lead righteous lives. Begging, for the religious student and others who legitimately live by such a means, is said to be the equivalent of fasting:

> He should fetch a pot of water, flowers, cowdung, clay, and sacrificial grass, as much as are needed, and go begging every day. A chaste student of the Veda, purified, should beg every day from the houses of people who do not fail to perform Vedic sacrifices and who are approved of for carrying out their own innate activities. He should not beg from his guru's family nor from the relatives of his mother or father, but if he cannot get to the houses of others he should avoid each of these more than the one that precedes it. And if there are none of the people mentioned above, he should beg from the whole village, purified and restrained in his speech, but he should avoid those who have been indicted. . . . When he is under the vow (of a chaste student) he should make his living by begging, nor should he eat the food of just one person; when begging is the livelihood of a person under a vow it is traditionally regarded as equal to fasting.

(Manu 2.182–185, 188)

---

[6]From the Apastamba Dharma Sutra, in Ainslie T. Embree (editor), *The Hindu Tradition: Readings in Oriental Thought* (New York: Vintage Books, 1972), 84–86.

Members of two other stages of life also make their living in unconventional ways. After finishing the life of a student and having married and raised a family as a householder, a man may enter the third stage of life as what is called a "forest-dweller." This stage of life, too, is characterized by ascetic practices and gradual detachment from the world, including the renunciation of cultivated food (he should live on wild food that grows in the jungle) and, indeed, the renunciation of "all possessions":

> After he has lived in the householder's stage of life in accordance with the rules in this way, a twice-born Vedic graduate should live in the forest, properly restrained and with his sensory powers conquered. But when a householder sees that he is wrinkled and gray, and (when he sees) the children of his children, then he should take himself to the wilderness. Renouncing all food cultivated in the village and all possessions, he should hand his wife over to his sons and go to the forest—or take her along. . . . He should eat vegetables that grow on land or in water, flowers, roots, and fruits, the products of pure trees, and the oils from fruits. . . . He should not eat anything grown from land tilled with a plough, even if someone has thrown it out, nor roots and fruits grown in a village, even if he is in distress (from hunger).
>
> (Manu 6.1–3, 13, 16)

Subsistence on gathered food that grows naturally and spontaneously in the wild is apparently supplemented by food obtained by begging, for in this stage of life, too, begging is allowed as a legitimate form of survival. The begged food, however, should be only enough for "bare subsistence" and should be obtained from the right donors:

> He should get food for bare subsistence by begging from priests who are ascetics themselves, from householders, and from other twice-born forest-dwellers. Or a man who lives in the forest may get (food) from a village, receiving it in the hollow of a leaf or in his hand or in a broken clay dish, and eat (only) eight mouthfuls of it. To perfect himself, a priest who lives in the forest must follow these and other preparations for consecration, as well as the various revealed canonical texts of the Upanishads, and those that sages and priestly householders have followed, to increase learning and inner heat and to clean the body.
>
> (Manu 6.27–30)

The final stage of life is that of the world-renouncer who continues and furthers the ascetic practices of the forest-dweller: "And when he has spent the third part of his lifespan in the forests in this way, he may abandon all attachments and wander as an ascetic for the fourth part of his lifespan" (Manu 6.33). In this stage, even more than the others in which alternative modes of survival are allowed, the wandering hermit should live entirely detached from the things of this world, alone and without companionship, perfectly content and equaniminous. He should beg but once a day, and not be "addicted to food" or hope for lots of alms, nor be disappointed should he receive nothing. He should "work" for only as much as will sustain his life:

He should always go all alone, with no companion, to achieve success; realizing that success is for the man who is alone, he neither deserts nor is deserted. The hermit should have no fire and no home, but should go to a village to get food, silent, indifferent, unwavering and deep in concentration. A skull-bowl, the roots of trees, poor clothing, no companionship, and equanimity to everything—this is the distinguishing mark of one who is Freed. He should not welcome dying, nor should he welcome living, but wait for the right time as a servant waits for orders. . . . He should live here on earth seated in ecstatic contemplation of the soul, indifferent, without any carnal desires, with the soul as his only companion and happiness as his goal. . . . He should go begging once a day and not be eager to get a great quantity, for an ascetic who is addicted to food becomes attached to sensory objects, too. . . . He should not be sad when he does not get anything nor delighted when he gets something, but take only what will daily sustain his vital breath, transcending any attachment to material things.

(Manu 6.42–45, 49, 55, 57)

The Hindu tradition validates work of all sorts, seeing all occupations as necessary, albeit more or less desirable. Those living in the world as householders should pursue the work proper to both their class or caste and their stage of life, and should, according to the texts, do their best to succeed in the profession assigned to them. But Hinduism also accepts the notion that work of all kinds, in the sense of karma, binds one to a series of perpetual rebirths. This religious tradition has thus also embraced alternative "occupations" and unconventional forms of "work" that are designed to gradually wean an individual from all worldly attachments. There are, as it is said in one text, two kinds of "Vedic activity"; that is, there are two principal forms of life recommended by the sacred texts. Both are religiously legitimate, and both will result in spiritual rewards:

There are two kinds of Vedic activity: the one that brings about engagement (in worldly action) and the rise of happiness, and the one that brings about disengagement (from worldly action) and the supreme good. The activity of engagement is said to be driven by desire in this world and the world beyond; but the activity of disengagement is said to be free of desire and motivated by knowledge. The man who is thoroughly dedicated to the activity of engagement becomes equal to the gods; but the man who is dedicated to disengagement passes beyond the five elements.

(Manu 12.88–90)

COMMENTARIES

Judaism on Hinduism

by JACOB NEUSNER

The Hebrew word *abodah,* work or labor, shares with the Vedic word for work, *karma,* the same meaning: "ritual action or labor." That is, the priests in the Temple conduct the *abodah,* the heavy labor, of the Temple offerings. By extension, *abodat haqqodesh,* holy labor, is one way of referring to the activity of public prayer. But a different word pertains to creation, and certainly there is no intersection at the mythic level between Scripture's story of Creation and the counterpart story in Hindu texts. While the details intersect, the systems of belief do not. For example, the Hindu belief that people are born to their tasks by virtue of their past karma denies what Judaism takes for granted, which is that people can make choices as to their vocation. No one would imagine that one's existence in a prior life accounts for his or her situation in this world. On the contrary, an absolute given is that people can choose to study the Torah (to take an obvious example), whatever their circumstance, whatever their age. Even family circumstance plays no role, as this account of the origins as to study of Torah of a principal sage of the first century C.E. indicates:

> How did R. Aqiba begin [his Torah-study]?
>
> They say: He was forty years old and had never repeated a tradition. One time he was standing at the mouth of a well. He thought to himself, "Who carved out this stone?"
>
> They told him, "It is the water that is perpetually falling on it every day."
>
> They said to him, "Aqiba, do you not read Scripture? *The water wears away stones* (Job 4:19)."
>
> On the spot R. Aqiba constructed in his own regard an argument *a fortiori:* now if something soft can [Goldin:] wear down something hard, words of Torah, which are as hard as iron, how much the more so should wear down my heart, which is made of flesh and blood."
>
> On the spot he repented [and undertook] to study the Torah.
>
> He and his son went into study session before a children's teacher, saying to him, "My lord, teach me Torah."
>
> R. Aqiba took hold of one end of the tablet, and his son took hold of the other end. The teacher wrote out for him *Alef Bet* and he learned it, *Alef Tav* and he learned it, *the Torah of the Priests* [the books of Leviticus and Numbers] and he learned it. He went on learning until he had learned the entire Torah.
>
> He went and entered study-sessions before R. Eliezer and before R. Joshua. He said to them, "My lords, open up for me the reasoning of the Mishnah."
>
> When they had stated one passage of law, he went and sat by himself and said, "Why is this *alef* written? why is this *bet* written? Why is this statement made?" He went and asked them and, in point of fact, [Goldin:] reduced them to silence.
>
> Fathers According to Rabbi Nathan VI:V.1

What emerges clearly is that every Israelite is challenged to make a decision to study the Torah, and nothing in one's present circumstance needs to stand in the way. On the other hand, Judaism and Hinduism concur on physicians and butchers and the like: "Most ass-drivers are evil, most camel drivers are decent, most sailors are saintly, the best among physicians is going to Gehenna, and the best of butchers is a partner of Amalek" (M. Qiddushin 4:14). The real point of difference between Judaism and Hinduism, it is clear, comes at the end: Judaism thinks people have choices, and caste status does not have to dictate the kind of work one does or does not do. Hinduism, as we have seen, emphasizes remaining within the work assigned to one's own caste.

Christianity on Hinduism
by BRUCE CHILTON

The discussion of the portrayal of spiritual sacrifice in 1 Peter 2, in "Christianity on Judaism," has also prepared the way for a response to the treatment from the perspective of Hinduism. The definition of *karma* as "ritual action or labor" makes it clear that it is a category comparable to sacrifice within Christian tradition, although the activities have different ends (as well as means). The aim of offering is not the repair of cosmogony (although that may be an ancillary result of spiritual sacrifice), but the creation of what 1 Peter 2:4–5 styles a Temple built of "living stones," of which Christ was the first, the engine of spiritual sacrifice.

The constructive result of sacrifice is therefore an axiom shared by Hinduism and Christianity, and that results in a peculiar sense of affinity between the two religions. During a recent stay in Delhi, the sight of individual worshippers burning incense before the shrines and reciting praises and prayers under their breaths became a familiar one to me. More than any public liturgy, seeing them made me feel as at home as when I have happened upon crosses at the roadside in Catholic France and Germany, or joined Protestants in informal hymn-singing in England and America. In all those cases, the integration of individual within society, and society within the act of worship, is palpable and—for practitioners—reassuring.

Indeed, this sense of integration with the present world seems stronger in Hinduism than in Christianity. The gathering of "living stones" does not change their status here, or condition a rebirth into this world, as the later development of the karmic principle would have it. Rebirth is also a Christian metaphor, as when the readers of 1 Peter are urged to long for spiritual milk, as infants just born (1 Peter 2:2), and certain theologians—most famously, Origen—have toyed with the theoretical thought that God's power includes the capacity to make a world like ours all over again. But the conditions one endures in this life are not a function of personal responsibility. Just that theory is put to Jesus in John's Gospel, when he is asked, "Rabbi, who sinned, this person or his parents, so that he was born blind?" (John 9:2). In a rich answer, redolent of the Johannine technique of framing Jesus' speech to articulate a coherent theology, a key correction is introduced (v. 3): "Neither this person sinned, nor his parents, but so that the deeds of God might be manifested in him." Just as clearly as the disciples' question opens the door to a retributive explanation for a person's difficulty, Jesus slams that door. The aim of Christianity falls more on the side of transcending current relations than integrating them within an understanding of divine will. It is a persistently restless religion, even as its skepticism about the value of work releases a considerable degree of energy for such skepticism.

The portrayal of the Cosmic Man in Rig Veda 10.90, as apportioned to the classes (Brahmin, Kshatriya, Vaishya, and Shudras), makes a nice contrast to Paul's depiction of the body of Christ (1 Corinthians 12:12–31). To be sure, the metaphor of a corporate body was a feature of Stoic thought long prior to Paul. It is in his adaptation of the idea that his presentation is distinctive, and eloquent of the Christian theology that was then emerging. An implicit hierarchy is embedded in the metaphor, and in fact post-Pauline authors fully exploit the notion of the headship of Christ over his "body" (see Colossians 1:18; Ephesians 4:15–16). Paul, however, gets himself into a famous tangle by trying to repress any development of that implication. He imagines the absurdity of one body part declaring itself autonomous of the rest (1 Corinthians 12:14–21), and then argues rather more successfully (vv. 22–26) that all members of a body suffer or rejoice together.

The reason Paul strains his own metaphor is that he wants to take it in a new direction, in which hierarchy is dissolved in the notion of equality in Christ, Jew or Greek, slave or free, on the basis that all were baptized of Spirit and drink of the same Spirit in Eucharist (1 Corinthians 12:12–13). There is certainly an integrative aspect of this argument, which Paul harnesses as best he can to encourage the good order of those he is addressing (vv. 28–31; falling back into hierarchical thinking in order to do so!). But the more emphatic character of this line of thought is its discomfort with a directly organic metaphor for the reality emerging by means of an adherence to Christ, because this world cannot contain the reality that is being unveiled.

Islam on Hinduism

by TAMARA SONN

Contrary to the Vedic view, Islam does not see the universe as defective, in need of repair. It is as God created it and everything in it is a sign of God's power and wisdom. Rituals are therefore not for the sake of the universe, but for our sake: to remind us of our proper roles in life as God's servants. Nor is the individual in need of repair; we only need to remind ourselves of God's centrality to our lives so that we may remain focused on our goal of fulfilling the divine will. There is a sense in which Islam and Vedic religion agree, however. Both hold that one's deeds in the present life determine one's status in the next life. But there are two important differences between Vedic religion and Islam on this point. In Islam, there is only one "next life," one's eternal reward or punishment. There are no multiple rebirths. More important, the deeds for which one will be rewarded or punished are not ritual. The Qur'an teaches that the ritual sacrifice itself does not reach God, only the piety of the one participating in the ritual (Qur'an 22:35). Thus, Islam agrees with the Upanishadic view that all actions—not just rituals—influence the status of the believer in the next life. But the contrast emerges again with the Upanishadic goal of eventually being able to end work and live a life disengaged from the world. In Islam, daily life is a means toward an end—working toward fulfillment of the divine will and thus earning eternal reward. The highly motivated Muslim, therefore, seeks to remain engaged in this struggle as long as possible. Furthermore, unlike Indian religion, in Islam there is no place for religious distinctions by birth. Although it is recognized that each person has different roles and capacities, Islam teaches that we are all equally morally responsible for our choices. This again reflects the fact that in Islam, rituals are not the source of moral reward; our properly intended efforts to contribute to social justice are.

Buddhism on Hinduism

by CHARLES HALLISEY

Comparisons between Buddhism and Hinduism are of a different order than comparisons between Buddhism and the three Abrahamic religions also covered in this volume. This is because Hinduism and Buddhism have, in part, a common history. Buddhism developed in India as a distinct religious tradition at about the same time as the Vedic tradition developed into the patterns of classical Hinduism, and each tradition interacted with, shaped, and left an imprint on the other. Comparison of historically related traditions is thus more than a means of opening our eyes to what is distinctive in each tradition. It helps to identify real family resemblances between the two traditions, displaying significant aspects of each tradition that are grounded in a particular, but common historical context. Even though Buddhism continued to develop into a very internally diverse tradition as it spread across Asia, it never lost the basic contours of thought and action that it assumed in India.

In other words, comparisons between Buddhism and Hinduism that highlight their similarities can help us to see just how *Indian* Buddhist values and aspirations really are. For example, one can easily see that both Hinduism and Buddhism connect the value of conventional work to the production of surplus wealth that can be used for charity, and especially for the support of those pursuing religious lives—with Hinduism, students and ascetics; with Buddhism, monks. Similarly, the notion that work will have a salutary effect on the doer and on others, a notion that can be traced back to Vedic conceptions of the sacrifice that structured Hindu understandings of work, has a deep resonance in Buddhist attitudes toward work.

Such comparisons help us to see important continuities in the midst of sharp differences. The basic notion of work in the Hindu tradition as activity that is connective and reparative, designed to "fix" the universe, is very similar to Buddhist appreciations of work as an antidote to greed, something that is capable of fixing an inherent flaw in human beings. The difference between Hinduism and Buddhism in this regard is that Hinduism sees work as fundamentally a cosmological activity, while Buddhism radically "ethicized" the Hindu pattern and projected it onto the domain of a person's interior life.

Comparisons between Buddhism and Hinduism also bring to light some of the critiques that Buddhists historically made of Hindu values and aspirations. Most notably, Buddhists rejected the moral and practical implications that Hindus saw in human difference, which they institutionalized in the caste system. Buddhists rejected the idea of different groups, each with their own assigned occupation and hierarchically ranked, in favor of a more universalist ethics in which human difference was deemphasized before human sameness. For Buddhists, it was the moral intentions behind work that mattered more than the outward forms of different kinds of work. This universalist ethical vision of Buddhism, similar in its basic thrust to those found in Christianity and Islam, was a crucial element in Buddhism's appeal to men and women across Asia.

SUMMARY

Hinduism delineates different kinds of appropriate work at different times in its history and for the different types of people that make up the social order structured by the caste system. Early conceptions of "work" or *karma* were wholly defined as ritual activity. Later, the concept of *karma* was expanded to include all forms of action and was tied to the theory of rebirth determined by one's *karma*. Shortly thereafter, Hinduism developed the central idea that one's proper and religiously validated work was correlated to one's birth in a particular class or caste and to one's stage of life. But while Hinduism affirms the (hierarchically differentiated) value of work and activity of many different sorts, it also maintains that all actions result in *karma* and rebirth and has provided different methods for obtaining liberation from the world of ordinary work.

GLOSSARY

Artha "private gain" or "material or political advantage," "self-interest," "getting ahead in the world"; one of the "ends of life" in Hinduism, especially appropriate to the householder

Aryan literally "noble one," the name the early Indo-European invaders of India gave to themselves

Bhagavad Gita a key text of Hinduism that synthesizes some of the strands of the tradition around the concept of bhakti

Bhakti literally "participation" in the divine being, or more commonly translated as "devotion" to God

Brahmins "priests" or religious specialists, the highest of the classes or castes in the traditional Hindu social order

Dharma a multivalent word that in Hinduism usually refers to "religious duty," determined by one's caste and stage of life

Guru religious teacher

Kama "sensual pleasure," one of the "ends of life" in Hinduism

Karma "work," originally in the sense of "ritual activity" and later generalized to include all acts. In all senses of the word, karma refers also to actions that create the causes for experiences (pleasant and unpleasant) in the future.

Krishna one of the chief deities of the Hindu pantheon and the central figure in the Bhagavad Gita

Kshatriyas the warrior class of the traditional Hindu social order

Moksha "freedom" or "liberation" from samsara, the ultimate goal of Hinduism

Prajapati "lord of Creatures," a name for the creator god in Vedism

Purusa "cosmic Man," one name for the creator god of the Vedic pantheon

Rig Veda the oldest text of the ancient Indian Vedas, which are regarded as sacred scripture by most Hindus

Samsara the wheel of continual birth, life, death, and rebirth. Samsara in Hinduism and Buddhism is also characterized in general by suffering.

Samskaras the term for the rites of passage in Hinduism

Shudras "servants," the lowest class or caste in the traditional Hindu social order

Svadha a ritual utterance in some Hindu ceremonies

Upanishads ancient texts in Hinduism that deal with philosophy and metaphysics

Vaishyas the commoners (merchants, agriculturalists, traders, etc.) of the traditional Hindu social order

Veda collective term for a group of ancient Indian texts regarded by most Hindus as sacred scripture

Vedism the earliest form of the Hindu tradition in India. The religion centered on the performance and ideology surrounding the fire sacrifice.

Yajnavalkya a religious teacher who figures prominently in some of the Upanishads

DISCUSSION QUESTIONS

1. How and why has the concept of "work" changed over the course of the history of Hinduism? How are some of those changes reflected in the different meanings of the word "karma"?

2. Discuss the concepts of rebirth and liberation from the cycle of rebirth in relation to the Hindu conception of work.

3. What does the Bhagavad Gita say about the nature and consequences of work? What method does it provide for doing one's "duty" and still obtaining salvation?

4. Discuss the relation between the Hindu conception of one's "proper work" or "duty" (dharma) and the class or caste one is born into and the stage of life one is in.

5. What kinds of work and which occupations should be avoided according to Hinduism?

6. What kinds of "work" do those living the life of world-renunciation pursue?

 **INFOTRAC**

If you would like additional information related to the material discussed here, you can visit our Web site: http://www.wadsworth.com

5

Buddhism

BY CHARLES HALLISEY

WHY MUST WE WORK?

You can take the word *why* in the question "why must we work?" in two quite different ways. One way directs our attention to something inherent in human life, something about us that prompts us to work. Seen this way, work is an ordinary part of life. Obviously this ordinary part of life can be valued differently too. If work is considered with falling in love, play, language, art, and eating, on the one hand, it appears as a vital aspect of life, but when it is considered with violence, cruelty, and exploitation, it appears more as a bane to life itself. The second way of taking the question directs our attention to the results of work, results that are wanted because they contribute to human well-being. There are different kinds of results from work, from material products and wages to personal characteristics that work cultivates. In this sense, work is a means to other ends, and not an end in and of itself, as the first way of taking the question suggests that it is.

In the course of more than 2,500 years, men and women in the different Buddhist communities around the world have given close attention to both ways of thinking about work, and they have formulated a wide variety of answers to the question of "why must we work?" Considering some of these answers is valuable for our understanding of Buddhism because they remind us that Buddhists have been concerned about this-worldly activity, even as they have been alert to what transcends the world—the experience of enlightenment, for example—although, generally students of Buddhism have been drawn more to the latter because of its comparative distinctiveness. While some of these answers can seem inconsistent with each other, the variety itself is not surprising in view of the historical diversity of the Buddhist world. What is somewhat surprising, however, is that frequently each way of answering the question is posed as a counterpoint to the other. This is the first thing that we can learn from Buddhist discussions about work: there is a value to reflecting not only on how work can be both an end and a means to an end, but also on how these two ways of thinking about work interrelate with each other.

When Buddhists regard work as inherent in life as it is ordinarily lived, they often see it as an end that masquerades as a means. This is because Buddhists often perceive work as an expression of desire and greed, just as sex and eating frequently are. Although work might seem to be the means to satisfying a particular want, Buddhists have been acutely aware of the manner in which individual wants are just symptoms of the disease of desire. As Prayudh Payutto, a contemporary Thai monk, puts it, desire "has many faces and takes many forms. It may be wanting your life to evolve in a certain way, such as wanting to be rich, have status, or be a god so you may have everything you desire, or wanting to escape from undesirable conditions of boredom, hopelessness, or suicidal tendencies."[1] Work, in other words, is a fundamental way that beings seek happiness, by struggling to satisfy particular needs that appear to be necessary for happiness, but insofar as work does not really provide a means to satisfy desire itself, work is unable to be a means to anything other than more desire.[2] To quote Prayudh Payutto again:

> In a fundamental way, struggling and seeking to respond to various needs is symptomatic of craving [i.e., desire]. This also includes being bored with what you have or who you are, along with experiencing despair and depression, which are conditions that become unbearable because there is nothing present that responds to growing needs. What becomes abundantly clear is that [desire] does not allow human beings to be at peace.[3]

Work, however, can also be a way of restraining desire and greed, a way of checking our propensities to harm ourselves and others in the pursuit of our desires. This is because the world of work is an arena in which we can and sometimes must cultivate virtues like perseverance, energeticness, creativity, and self-discipline, all of which are necessary to check our desires and eradicate desire itself.

Work is, in short, both an expression of and an antidote to greed.

How work originates in desire and greed is explained in "The Discourse on What Is Primary" (*Aggañña sutta*), a canonical text recording one of the Buddha's sermons. "The Discourse on What Is Primary" gives a charter myth about the origins of human social life;[4] this text is best known among Theravāda Buddhists in Sri Lanka and Southeast Asia. It traces the evolution of the entire natural world as well as the broad contours of human life—sexuality, politics, work, social relations—to actions prompted by greed. This etiology indicates that greed is part and parcel of all of the structures of human life.

---

[1]Phra Prayudh Payutto, *Buddhadhamma: Natural Laws and Values for Life* (Albany: State University of New York Press, 1995), 122.

[2]"Modern economics and Buddhism both agree that mankind has unlimited wants. As the Buddha said, 'there is no river like craving.' Rivers can sometimes fill their banks, but the wants of human beings can never be fulfilled. Even if money were to fall from the skies like rain, man's sensual desires would not be satisfied." (Prayudh Payutto, *Buddhist Economics* [Bangkok: Buddhadhamma Foundation, 1994], 31).

[3]Payutto, *Buddhadhamma*, 131.

[4]See, for a translation and interpretation of this important text, Steven Collins, "The Discourse on What Is Primary (Aggañña-sutta): An Annotated Translation," *Journal of Indian Philosophy* 21 (1993), 301–393.

"The Discourse on What Is Primary" tells us first that at the beginning of the universe,

> there is nothing but water, (all) is darkness, (just) deep darkness. It is not pos-
> sible to discern the moon or sun, the twinkling stars, night or day, months or
> half-months, seasons or years, men or women. Beings just have the name
> "beings." Then (on one such occasion) an earth-essence spread out on the
> waters. It appeared in the same way as (does) the spreading out (of skin) on
> top of boiled milk-rice as it cools down. It had colour, smell and taste; its
> colour was like sweet ghee or cream, its taste like fine clear honey. Then a
> certain being, greedy by nature, thinking "what can this be?" tasted the
> earth-essence with his finger. As he tasted the earth-essence with his finger he
> was pleased, and craving came upon him. Other beings imitated that being,
> tasting the earth-essence with their fingers. They too were pleased, and crav-
> ing came upon them. Then these beings started to eat the earth-essence tak-
> ing (big) mouthfuls of it with their hands.[5]

It is important to draw our attention to some foundational points that might be overlooked too easily because of their mythological garb in this passage. First, notice how greed grows: one being, "greedy by nature," eats. Although "he" is pleased, "he" is not satisfied, and instead wants more. The important point here is that desire cannot be quenched, the way thirst can; it is worth recalling here Payutto's comment that desire "does not allow human beings to be at peace."[6] Desire only generates more desire, and when work is motivated by desire, it be- comes a never-ending treadmill. Second, notice how greed spreads: other be- ings—who the sermon does not describe as "greedy by nature"—imitate the first being's actions, and they in turn become greedy themselves. The important point here is that actions are never neutral. Action not only expresses inner states, it generates them, and thus human beings have to be careful about what they do. This is because actions always transform our character, although there is oppor- tunity here, too, because this means that wholesome actions can change our characters for the better just as much as unwholesome actions change them for the worse. This opportunity provides much of the rationale for the Buddhist re- ligious life. Note too that as greed grows and spreads, it apparently intensifies: the beings first dipped their fingers in the earth-essence, but subsequently they gobble it by the handful. Third, consider again that greed spreads through imi- tation. Another important point in the notion of imitation is that the actions of most individuals are inevitably shaped by others. Since this is the case, reflection on the importance of work in human life leads us to consider not only what it does for an individual, but what impact it has on others.

As the sermon continues, we learn that the eating of the earth-essence had two effects, one on the natural world in which the beings lived, the other on the bodies of the beings themselves; the point is made in mythological terms in "The Discourse on What Is Primary," but the truth of the point can be seen when we

---

[5]Collins, "Discourse on What Is Primary," 342.

[6]Payutto, *Buddhadhamma*, 131.

reflect on how our modern consumer culture has transformed both the natural world and our understanding of human nature. As the beings gobbled up the earth-essence, a light that had previously emanated from the beings' bodies disappeared, and was replaced by the light of the sun and the moon, which were, in turn, joined by the stars. With the appearance of the sun and the moon, day and night appeared, and then seasons and years. As the beings ate more and more of this earth-essence, physical differences also appeared among them. Some became attractive, others were not, and with these differences conceit and arrogance appeared. Gradually, the earth-essence was replaced by plants on which these beings subsisted, and ultimately rice appeared:

> [T]here appeared for those beings rice, growing without cultivation; it was without powder, (already) husked, sweet-smelling and ready to eat. Whatever they gathered in the evening for their evening meal, in the morning had grown back ripe again; whatever they had gathered in the morning for their morning meal, in the evening had grown ripe again: (the work of) harvesting was unknown. Those beings, monks, spent a long time eating the rice which grew without cultivation, living on it as their food. According to how much these beings ate, so to an even greater degree did their bodies become hard, and good and bad looks become known. The female parts appeared in a woman, and the male parts in a man; the woman looked at the man with intense, excessive longing, as did the man at the woman. As they were looking at each other with intense longing passion arose in them, and burning came upon their bodies; because of this burning, they had sex.[7]

The basic theme of this passage is that greed begets more greed, but note too how the passage is tragic in its portrayal of human work. It names each step in the production of food—planting, harvesting, husking, and cooking the rice—even as it says that once none of these activities were necessary in order to eat. In other words, work as it is now known among humans only became necessary with the appearance of greed among beings. There is a critical eye at work here: work exists because of greed. Before there was greed, work was unnecessary as a means of survival. Equally important is the emphasis on unintended consequences in the sermon: the beings engage in actions quite innocently, thinking that they will accomplish one thing without anticipating the real results of their actions. We see here the fundamental Buddhist principle that the actions of ordinary people are frequently ineffective because they are thoroughly conditioned by ignorance.

As we shall see in the last section of this chapter, a basic question that has animated much of Buddhist thought and practice is whether it is possible to return, through spiritual cultivation, to this state before greed. The answer generally is yes, even if it is admitted that only a few will have the capabilities to do so. These few will be drawn to the Buddhist monastic life, a social institution that replicates the conditions of the world before greed appeared and allows those who enter the monastic community an opportunity to check their own innate dispositions toward greed. Although we will return to the monastic life as a form of

---

[7]Collins, "Discourse on What Is Primary," 343.

unconventional work later in this chapter, it is worth noting in the present context that the life of a monk or nun is thought to be a state without ordinary labor.

Returning to the story of "The Discourse on What Is Primary," we see that with the appearance of sexuality, the beings' desire and greed in turn intensified and became more focused. Moral disapproval also appeared with the appearance of sexuality. When beings saw others having sex, the sermon tells us, they chased them away by throwing dirt and other things at them. Note, however, how throughout this account the natural world changes as morality devolves; as moral ambiguities and wrongs emerge from desire and greed, the natural world becomes less hospitable and survival requires more effort on the part of beings. In other words, the necessity of work is a sign of moral degradation; we shall see in the third section that many Buddhists think the converse is true too—present prosperity is a sign of past moral cultivation. The devolution of morality continues in this account with the appearance of delusion in the midst of sexuality:

> Since those beings were excessively intoxicated at that period of time [by sex], they took to building houses to conceal it. Then a certain being, lazy by nature, thought "Well! Why am I troubling myself gathering rice for my evening meal in the evening, and (again) for my morning meal in the morning? Why shouldn't I gather it just once, for both evening and morning?" And he did so. Then another being came up to him and said "Come, being, let's go to gather rice." There's no need! I've gathered rice just once for both evening and morning. The (second) being thought "that seems (a) good (idea), my friend," and imitated him by gathering rice just once for two days. . . . Because these beings took to eating rice which they had stored up, powder and husk then covered the grain, cutting without regeneration and harvesting became known; and the rice stood in clumps.[8]

We see again the role of imitation in the spread of greed, although the account does, admittedly, seem to reverse much of what might be assumed about the necessity of work in human life. Work is not an intentional activity in which human desires are conditioned and checked only by natural and social limits, a notion that is common in the modern West. The methods of growing, harvesting, and storing rice are not the result of hungry humans adapting to the life cycle of rice within the natural environment. Instead the life cycle of rice is a response to the greedy actions of humans who take more than they need. The basic activity that the beings engage in here—gathering food with an eye to the future and storing it—surprisingly finds no approval in this sermon, although it does find approval in other sermons of the Buddha found in the Pali canon.[9] Here, collecting food for future use is not attributed to either prudence or efficiency, but to some innate laziness in one being (perhaps an association with sexual lassitude is intended). As we have seen already, the first being's actions are then imitated by others and we can presume, as before, that an inner state fol-

---

[8]Collins, "Discourse on What Is Primary," 344.

[9]One sermon says that a householder should put aside one-fourth of his or her assets, to be saved in case of need in a time of adversity; D III.188.

lows from these imitated actions. According to this account, then, it is because of work, ironically, that laziness is found among humans.

The account continues with the creation of private property. The beings notice that "the rice now stands in clumps. Let us now divide up the rice and set up boundary lines."[10] They do so, and with the creation of private property, thievery develops, and then accusations, false denials, and punishments all follow. In the end, the beings choose a king to administer justice.

A major theme of "The Discourse on What Is Primary" is that "what was thought improper at that time is nowadays thought proper."[11] We can see that, for this sermon, this is true for work in a number of ways. First, work itself is now thought proper, but the sermon makes it clear that it stems from greed and laziness, all human characteristics that are wrong and unwholesome. Second, the cooperation that humans engage in, when they are working together, while often admired and encouraged now, is portrayed here as merely the imitation of bad behavior. And third, "putting aside for a rainy day" is displayed as stemming more from greed than from prudence or industry.

Many contemporary Buddhist writers are alert to the ways that the structures of economic activity in the modern world are the result of and the condition for greed, and their comments are often reminiscent of the critical judgments of the "The Discourse on What Is Primary" insofar as it showed how work motivated by greed inevitably is harmful to oneself, others, and the natural world. For example, notice how Prayudh Payutto, who was quoted above, applies insights similar to those found in the "The Discourse on What Is Primary" to our contemporary economy:

> One way to evaluate the ethical quality of economic activity is to look at the effects it has on three levels: on the individual consumer, on society and on the environment. Let us return to the example of the bottle of whiskey and the Chinese dinner. It is obvious that, though their market prices may be the same, their economic costs are not equal. The bottle of whiskey may damage the consumer's health, forcing him to spend money on medical treatment. The distillery which produced the whiskey may have released foul-smelling fumes into the air. This pollution has economic repercussions, forcing the government to spend resources on cleaning the environment. Moreover, one who drinks and suffers from a hangover on the job will work less efficiently, or he might get drunk and crash his car, incurring more economic costs. Then there are detrimental social effects: drinking can contribute to crime, which has very high costs for society.
>
> Although ethical questions, they all have economic ramifications. They imply the necessity of looking at economic costs on a much wider scale than at present—not just in terms of market prices. There is now a trend toward including environmental costs in economic calculations. Some economists even include them in the cost of a finished product. But this is not enough.

---

[10]Collins, "Discourse on What Is Primary," 345.

[11]Collins, "Discourse on What Is Primary," 344.

In the case of the bottle of whiskey, apart from the environmental costs, there are also the social, moral, and health costs—inefficient production, auto accidents, liver disease, crime—all of which have economic implications.

A second way to evaluate the ethical quality of economic activity is to determine which kind of desire is at its root.[12] The most unethical economic activities are those that feed [greed (*tanhā*)] while undermining well-being. Trade in tobacco, drugs, and prostitution are examples of detrimental economic activities geared solely toward satisfying a craving for pleasure.

The more people are driven by [greed] the more they destroy their true well-being. This principle applies not only to the obvious vices, but to all economic activities. Thus, in decisions dealing with consumption, production, and the use of technology, we must learn how to distinguish between the two kinds of desire and make our choices wisely.[13]

Buddhadasa, another contemporary Thai Buddhist thinker, demythologizes the account of origins of human social life found in "The Discourse on What Is Primary," but still preserves its basic themes by translating them into images of human prehistory:

When humans first evolved and inhabited the forests and jungles, they had no granaries or storehouses. . . . They ate only what was necessary to survive, and day by day they gathered whatever food they needed. No one person or group stockpiled a surplus of anything, so . . . social problems . . . did not yet exist.

According to Buddhist scriptures, our problems began when someone got the idea of stockpiling grains and other food, causing shortages for others. Once people began to hoard supplies, problems of unequal distribution and access arose. The problems multiplied over time. Leaders of groups of people would be in charge of stockpiling supplies for the group. Fighting among the groups became inevitable. Even when primitive humans inhabited forests, some people or groups began to take more than they needed for themselves. To maintain control over society and to limit [human dispositions toward evil], laws and moral systems developed.[14]

It would be misleading, however, to leave the impression that Buddhist thought does not value the material products of work or that it is suspicious of

---

[12]Payutto distinguishes between greed, or *tanhā*, which is a desire for pleasure objects, and desire for well-being (*chanda*): "Tanhā and chanda both lead to saitisfaction, but of different kinds. Using the example of eating, people who are driven by tanhā will seek to satisfy the blind craving for sensual pleasure which, in this case, is the desire for pleasant taste. Here, satisfaction results from experiencing the flavor of the food. But when guided by chanda, desires are directed to realizing well-being. We are not compelled to overeat or to eat the kinds of foods that will make us sick simply because they taste good. Instead, we eat to satisfy hunger and nourish the body. Here satisfaction results from the assurance of well-being provided by the act of eating." (Payutto, *Buddhist Economics*, 35.)

[13]Payutto, *Buddhist Economics*, 37–38.

[14]Buddhadasa, *Me and Mine*, edited and with an Introduction by Donald Swearer (Albany: State University of New York, 1989), 174.

them as only being the objects of greed. Buddhadasa acknowledges that "we all have a natural right to take as much as we need, but not more,"[15] an indication that we must work to get what we need. Payutto's distinction between two kinds of desire, between desire for pleasure (*tanhā*) and desire for well-being (*chanda*), directs our attention to the material results of work that are valued because they contribute to human well-being, both for oneself and for others. The Buddha explained in one sermon that there were five reasons for seeking possessions:

A householder makes himself happy, pleases himself and preserves his happiness well with possessions earned by industry and energy, collected by the strength of his arms, earned by the sweat of his brow, obtained morally in a lawful way; with the same, he makes his parents happy, pleases them and preserves their happiness well; he also makes his wife and children, his servants and workers happy, pleases them and preserves their happiness well. This is the first reason for seeking possessions.

With possessions that are earned by industry and energy, collected by the strength of his arms, earned by the sweat of his brow, obtained morally in a lawful way, he makes his friends and colleagues happy, pleases them, and preserves their happiness well. This is the second reason.

With possessions that are earned by industry and energy, collected by the strength of his arms, earned by the sweat of his brow, obtained morally in a lawful way, he is able to protect these possessions from misfortune, such as fire and water, kings and thieves, enemies and heirs, and thus keep himself in well-being. This is the third reason.

With possessions that are earned by industry and energy, collected by the strength of his arms, earned by the sweat of his brow, obtained morally in a lawful way, he is able to give offerings to relatives, guests, ancestors, kings, and gods. This is the fourth reason.

With possessions that are earned by industry and energy, collected by the strength of his arms, earned by the sweat of his brow, obtained morally in a lawful way, he is able to give offerings to ascetics and brahmins who abstain from pride and laziness, who bear all things in patience and gentleness, who discipline themselves, who calm themselves, who each extinguish greed. These offerings result in heaven, have happiness as their fruit, lead to heaven. This is the fifth reason.[16]

We see a number of important points here that we will explore in greater detail in subsequent sections of this chapter. First, notice that the way that possessions are earned defines their value. Possessions are only valuable when they are earned in a moral and legal way; we will consider this further in the next section, which looks at kinds of work to be preferred or avoided. We shall also see in that section that the qualities of the ascetics and Brahmins—abstention from pride and laziness, bearing all things in patience and gentleness, self-discipline, calming themselves, and the extinction of greed—are all personal

---

[15]Buddhadasa, *Me and Mine,* 175.

[16]A III.45–46.

characteristics that are integral to every form of proper work. Second, notice that the possessions that are the result of work contribute to the well-being and happiness of others. We will explore this aspect of Buddhist understandings of work in the third section on private gain and public benefit; this section also will take up how miserliness can prevent work from working. Third, notice how giving away the results of work in the present is productive for well-being in the future. How work benefits oneself in the present and in the future will also be considered in the third section, under the rubric of private gain and public benefit, and it is sufficient to note here that this obviously suggests that wealth in the present is the result both of self-effort now and giving wealth away in the past. As Nāgārjuna, an Indian Buddhist philosopher from the second century C.E., said in *The Precious Garland,* a letter on proper behavior that was written to a king:

> You get pleasure in this life from enjoying your wealth.
> Pleasure in the next life comes from giving it away.[17]
> If you do not give away to supplicants
> the wealth you obtained through previous giving,
> then due to your greed and lack of gratitude,
> you will not obtain that wealth again.[18]

HOW OUGHT WE TO WORK? KINDS OF WORK TO BE PREFERRED OR AVOIDED

We need to approach the question of what kinds of work are to be preferred or avoided in two ways. First, we can ask which kinds of work are to be preferred or avoided, understanding by this that we are asking about different occupations. In the terms of the Buddha's sermon that gave five reasons for seeking possessions, we can say that we are interested in knowing which kinds of work are both moral and legal. Second, we can ask about which ways of working are to be preferred or avoided, understanding by this that we are asking about the manner in which we actually do our work. Work can be done with enthusiasm or with resentment, carefully or carelessly. In other words, when we take the question in this second way, we are interested in the style of life that a person brings to work. This can include, in the terms of the sermon just quoted, not only industry and energy, effort, the inner spirit that evinces itself in sweat on the brow, but also concern for others, gentleness, and restraint of one's own desires. Thus, being a merchant, for example, is preferable to being a professional murderer, but to say this is not sufficient. It is preferable that, if one is a merchant, that one is a scrupulous and industrious merchant who includes the needs of others in one's decision making.

---

[17]Nāgārjuna, *The Precious Garland,* translated by John Dunne and Sara McClintock (Boston, Wisdom, 1997), 59.

[18]Nāgārjuna, *The Precious Garland,* 58.

Choices about livelihood can be guided generally by a principle about all action provided by Nāgārjuna in *The Precious Garland:*

> What harms others are faults;
> what helps them are good qualities . . . .[19]

Nāgārjuna suggests, in a manner reminiscent of "The Discourse on What Is Primary," that inner moral qualities and outer actions are mutually constitutive, reminding us again that action not only expresses inner states, it generates them; thus human beings have to be careful about what they do, because all actions, including work, transform our characters. He also gives us a straightforward answer to the first concern of this section: what kinds of work are to be preferred and avoided. Those kinds of work that hurt others are to be avoided, while those that help others are to be preferred. The latter category is more inclusive than the former, because it includes not only those kinds of work that directly help someone else, but also those kinds of work that produce wealth that can bring happiness to others, as we saw in the Buddha's sermon on five reasons for seeking possessions.

Given the inclusive nature of the kinds of work to be preferred, it is perhaps not surprising that Buddhists have generally given more attention to specifying the kinds of work to be avoided. A deeper reason may be at work here, however. It is the case cross-culturally that more ethical reflection and argument are devoted to actions that cause harm to others than to those that benefit others, and Buddhists are not an exception to this deep human disposition. Americans argue more about the death penalty, for example, than about individual acts of charity; while they may admire extraordinary acts of generosity, they do not feel the same necessity to justify them as they seem to do when an action inflicts harm on another.

A good idea of what kinds of work are to be avoided is found in the Noble Eightfold Path, a schema of practice that leads to the cessation of suffering and which is the last of the Four Noble Truths taught by the Buddha in his First Sermon. The Noble Eightfold Path "is a way of life to be followed, practised and developed by each individual. It is self-discipline in body, word and mind, self-development and self-purification. . . . It is a Path leading to the realization of Ultimate Reality, to complete freedom, happiness and peace through moral, spiritual and intellectual perfection" and it has been said that "practically the whole teaching of the Buddha, to which he devoted himself during 45 years, deals in some way or other with this Path."[20] As its name indicates, the Noble Eightfold Path consists of eight elements that can be divided into three groups, each distinguished according to its general aim: some are dedicated to moral development, others to mental cultivation, while the remaining ones are concerned with the cultivation of wisdom. Work, or as it is called, "right livelihood," is one of the elements of this path "to complete freedom, happiness and peace":

---

[19]Nāgārjuna, *The Precious Garland,* 67.

[20]Walpola Rahula, *What the Buddha Taught* (New York: Grove Press, 1974), 49–50, 45.

Ethical Conduct:
  Right Speech
  Right Action
  Right Livelihood

Mental Cultivation:
  Right Effort
  Right Mindfulness
  Right Concentration

Wisdom:
  Right Thought
  Right Understanding[21]

Payutto explains that right livelihood "is not determined by the amount of material wealth it produces, but rather by the well-being it generates. Many livelihoods that produce a surplus of wealth simply cater to desires rather than providing for any true need."[22] Payutto gives us two markers that help us to identify which kinds of work are to be preferred: first, work should produce well-being and second, it should be a means to gaining some necessity for life. The contemporary Sri Lankan monk, Walpola Rahula, adds a third when he explains what "right livelihood" means in language that echoes Nāgārjuna's general principle about action that we saw above:

> Right livelihood means that one should abstain from making one's living through a profession that brings harm to others, such as trading in arms and lethal weapons, intoxicating drinks, poisons, killing animals, cheating, etc., and should live by a profession which is honourable, blameless and innocent of harm to others.[23]

A short discussion of the Buddha's names similar "trades [that] ought not to be plied by a lay-disciple": "trade in weapons, trade in human beings, trade in flesh,[24] trade in spirits and trade in poisons."[25]

One could go on listing other kinds of work that ought to be avoided, but the general principle is obvious: one should not engage in any kind of work that requires one to harm others. The broader significance of the notion of right livelihood becomes clearer when work is considered as part of the ethical components of the Noble Eightfold Path. According to Joseph Goldstein, a contemporary American Buddhist teacher, right speech, right action, and right livelihood "have to do with how we relate to the world; how we relate to our environment, to other people. They are a prescription for putting us into har-

---

[21]For an introduction to the other elements of the Noble Eightfold Path, see Walpola Rahula, *What the Buddha Taught*, 47-49.

[22]Payutto, *Buddhist Economics*, 63.

[23]Walpola Rahula, *What the Buddha Taught*, 47.

[24]The commentary explains that such a person breeds and sells animals, like pigs and deer.

[25]E. M. Hare, *Gradual Sayings III* (London: Pali Text Society, 1988), 153.

mony with our surroundings, for establishing a proper ecology of mind so that we're not in discord with others or with nature around us."[26]

Work also establishes "a proper ecology of mind" that puts us in harmony with ourselves, creating the personal characteristics that allow us to pursue our aims successfully. This can be seen in the *Mangala sutta,* a small text that is extremely popular among Buddhists in Sri Lanka and Southeast Asia, which praises those "spheres of work that are said to bring no conflict" as a good omen, something auspicious. Its commentary explains that

> such spheres of work as agriculture, cattle-keeping, commerce, etc., which owing to [their promoting] punctuality, seemly action, industriousness, excellence of energy in rising [early], and freedom from malpractices, are devoid of any such unprofitableness as dilatoriness, unseemly action, inaction, tardy action, and the like. These are called a good omen, since, when thus exercised either through one's own shrewdness or through that of one's wife and children or one's bondsmen and servants, they are a cause for the obtaining of increased riches here and now. And this is said by the Blessed One [i.e., the Buddha]

> > One seemly in his acts, responsible,
> > Who rises [early], will augment his fortune.[27]

and

> > Who's habit is to sleep by day,
> > And who is seen to rise by night,
> > And constantly gets drunk with wine,
> > Is all unfit to keep a house.
> > "Too cold! Too hot! Too late!" they say;
> > And opportunities pass by
> > the tyros who thus shirk the task.
> > But he that heeds no more than straws
> > Both cold and heat, doing men's work,
> > Need never fail in happiness.[28]

and again

> > So when a man saves up his wealth,
> > Emulating the honey-bee,
> > His riches will accumulate,
> > Just as an ant-hill is built up.[29]

This passage praises work that brings no conflict because of the personal characteristics that it inculcates, but notice how its praise of personal virtue

---

[26]*Radiant Mind: Essential Buddhist Teachings and Texts,* edited by Jean Smith (New York: Riverhead Books, 1999), 94.

[27]Sn 187.

[28]D III.185.

[29]D III.188. The whole passage is from Ñanamoli, translator, *Minor Readings and Illustrator* (London: Pali Text Society, 1991), 151.

shades into acknowledgment of the desirability of the material rewards that result from a proper style of working. These personal characteristics of diligence and energy are repeatedly praised in Buddhist texts. For example, the Buddha explains that "a woman [is] capable at her work" when

> [w]hatever her husband's home industries, whether in wool or cotton, therein she is deft and tireless; gifted with an inquiring turn of mind into all such undertakings, she is able to arrange and carry them out. In this way a woman is capable at her work.[30]

The exact same language is used by the Buddha to describe the personal characteristics that can be "to [the] advantage and for [the] happiness [of male householders] here on earth, for [their] advantage and happiness in the world to come":

> By whatsoever activity a [man] makes his living, whether by the plough, by trading or by cattle-herding, by archery or [as a servant of the king], or by any of the crafts—he is deft and tireless; gifted with an inquiring turn of mind into ways and means, he is able to arrange and carry out his job.[31]

The commentary on the *Mangala sutta* also makes it clear that these personal characteristics were considered to be crucial to the successful pursuit of the Buddhist religious life itself. Explaining why diligence is a good omen, the commentary says:

> Diligence . . . should be understood as the habit of never being without mindfulness of profitable ideals, which, as to meaning, is the converse of the negligence stated as follows: "There is carelessness, inattentiveness, heedlessness, hanging back, unzealousness, uninterestedness. . . ."[32] This [diligence] is called a good omen since it is a cause for achieving the various kinds of what is profitable and since it is a cause for reaching the Deathless [i.e., nirvana]. And the Master's [i.e., the Buddha's] message to be recalled here is that in such passages as follows "When [a monk abides] diligent, ardent [and self-controlled], his . . ."[33] and "The way of deathlessness is diligence."[34]

In some respects, however, the personal characteristics of diligence, perseverance, zealousness—just hard work, in general—are morally neutral. That is, they can serve the pursuit of greed and desire, just as much as they can serve the pursuit of more lofty aims. We still need to consider, however, just how it is that work serves as an antidote to greed.

---

[30]E. M. Hare, *Gradual Sayings IV* (Oxford: Pali Text Society, 1989), 179.

[31]Hare, *Gradual Sayings IV,* 188.

[32]Quoting Vbh 350.

[33]Quoting M I.350.

[34]Quoting Dh 21. The whole passage is from Ñanamoli, translator, *Minor Readings and Illustrator,* 155–156.

WHY MUST WE HELP OTHERS?
PRIVATE GAIN AND PUBLIC BENEFIT

Work can serve as an antidote to greed if it is done with an eye to how it benefits others. Thus, it is important for us to extend the concern of the previous section by considering another crucial element in the kinds of work that are preferred in Buddhism. We shall see that the best kind of work is not that which benefits only others, however, but that which benefits oneself and others. This is in keeping with Buddhist moral practice more generally. "The most basic point to be made about Buddhist social ethics is that in keeping with the Buddhist doctrine of dependent co-arising, individual betterment and perfection on the one hand and the social good on the other are fundamentally interrelated and interdependent."[35]

The implications of this point are far-ranging. For one thing, it suggests that it is in one's self-interest to be altruistic. It is common for many of us, however, to see benefits for others, or public benefit, as being the opposite of concern for oneself, or private gain. The Buddhist traditions, while recognizing that this is how men and women ordinarily think and live, have insisted that they are not necessarily antithetical, and have instead affirmed that private gain and public benefit are only truly achieved when concern for self and concern for others are blended. Work, then, is an activity that should benefit others as well as oneself. Shinichi Inoue, a Japanese bank president, explains this by contrasting the values of Buddhist economics with what he see as the values of Western economics:

> Economics, as developed by Adam Smith, was predicated on "self-benefit," and led people being more concerned with enriching themselves without giving much, if any, thought to how they might benefit their fellow men. During Smith's day, the major contribution to the economy of colonial powers such as England or Spain came from the resources taken from other, poorer regions. In contrast, the earlier Buddhist societies, such as India during the time of the Buddha, about 2,500 years ago, or Japan during the lifetime of Prince Shotoku (574–622), operated with a radically different social approach. In these societies, where the density of population was high, human relations were more interwoven and, for good or bad, how other people thought or reacted mattered a great deal. In the world of business, earning the trust of others and looking for mutually beneficial transactions were a priority. Although the phrase "benefiting oneself and others" comes from *Jodo Wasan*—a text by the medieval Buddhist priest Shinran (1173–1263), who was the founder of the Jodo Shinshu sect of Pure Land Buddhism—in fact, the idea of mutually beneficial activities is a basic undercurrent that sustains all Buddhist societies.[36]

---

[35]Prayudh Payutto (a.k.a. Rajavaramuni), "Foundations of Buddhist Social Ethics," in *Ethics, Wealth, and Salvation,* edited by Russell Sizemore and Donald Swearer (Columbia: University of South Carolina Press, 1990), 31.

[36]Shinichi Inoue, *Putting Buddhism to Work: A New Approach to Management and Business* (Tokyo: Kodansha International, 1997), 68.

Inoue is making a fundamental point here: attention to public benefit is a necessary part of private gain. Inoue reminds us that part of public benefit is the manner in which work is pursued, and avoiding harm to others is an important part of public benefit, but this does not exhaust the connection between private gain and public benefit. The use of the products of work is obviously part of public benefit too. This point was emphasized by the Buddha himself on an occasion when a king told him about a wealthy man who had died without leaving a will that instructed how his estate should be divided. The king ordered that this man's wealth be brought to his palace, so that he might take it for himself, and when this was done, the king also learned how the man had acquired such wealth. He was cheap, both to himself and to others. He ate the meanest of foods—leftovers of the coarsest grains—and wore the most uncomfortable clothes. The Buddha, when he heard this story, responded in a manner that recalls what he said in the sermon about reasons for seeking wealth that we considered in the first section of this chapter:

> A man who is not good but who has acquired a great fortune cheers and pleases [with his possessions] neither himself nor his parents, nor his wife and children, nor his servants, craftsmen, and workers, nor his friends and colleagues; nor does he give to ascetics and brahmins any offering stimulating spiritual growth, productive of future bliss, fruitful in happiness, conducive to celestial attainment. Those riches of his, not being rightly utilized, are either confiscated by kings or by robbers, or are burnt by fire, or are carried away by flood, or are appropriated by heirs for whom he has no affection. That being so, o king, riches that are not rightly utilized run to waste, not to enjoyment.[37]

The Buddha's response gives us an added insight into our initial question about why we must work: work is a means to happiness, and its products should be used to make ourselves and others happy. Moreover, gifts to ascetics and Brahmins would have produced future happy states for this rich man too. His miserliness toward all around him only wasted his efforts and his money.

It is important to note that the gifts to ascetics, such as Buddhist monks, and other religious professionals, such as Hindu priests (Brahmins), are not, strictly speaking, a form of charity. They are alms given to individuals who are worthy of gifts. These individuals, who themselves are engaged in serious religious pursuits, are "fields of merit." The agricultural metaphor reminds us that generosity, like a seed, produces the most fruit in a fertile field, namely noble and accomplished recipients.

Gifts to such noble and accomplished recipients produce happy states for the giver in the future through the workings of karma. Buddhist thought traditionally accepted that all beings experienced multiple lives, and the conditions of rebirth for each individual were defined by karma. Karma is a law of moral cause and effect, which teaches us that if one does a good action, then a good result follows, while if one does a bad action, a bad result will follow. Generosity is a

---

[37]Caroline Rhys Davids, translator, *Kindred Sayings I* (Oxford: Pali Text Society, 1989), 115, translation modified.

supremely good action in Buddhist ethics, and work produces the surplus material resources that allow one to be generous to others, and thus to produce future good for oneself. In the workings of karma in rebirth, we can see the blending of private gain and public benefit in the most fundamental and systematic way.

We should not lose sight of the significance of the Buddha's comments for life in the present. They remind us that work can be harmful in and of itself (e.g., the selling of weapons), that work can be harmful if it is used to pursue harmful ends (e.g., a merchant who earns money honestly but uses his money to purchase weapons to hurt others), and that work can be harmful if the wealth that results from it is only hoarded and not put to good use for oneself and for others.

Work then provides the means to combat greed because it produces surplus resources that can be given away. This generosity, in turn, helps to develop the detachment toward one's own possessions. This is obviously a necessary virtue if one is to be generous to others, but it also helps to develop an inner strength that allows one to check desire. As Payutto says,

> While wealth as a resource for achieving social good can help create favorable circumstances for realizing individual perfection, ultimately it is mental maturity and wisdom, not wealth, that brings about its realization. Wealth mistreated and abused not only obstructs individual development, but can also be detrimental to the social good. . . . A life that is free—one that is not overly reliant on material things—is a life that is not deluded by them. This demands a clear knowledge of the benefits and limitations of material possessions. Without such wisdom, we invest all our happiness in material things, even though they can never lead to higher qualities of mind. In fact as long as we remain attached to them, possessions will hinder even simple peace of mind.[38]

The act of giving to others thus produces a benefit for oneself in the present, because it contributes to detachment, a necessary character trait if one is ever to become free from greed.

The Buddha's response to the king is quite revealing about how he saw public benefit. He criticized the miser for not bringing happiness to other people that he met in face-to-face encounters. In this respect, the Buddha saw the others who could be benefited by work in very concrete and particular ways: they were mothers and fathers, wives and children, friends, ascetics. It is important to note that he did not speak of public benefit in terms of an impersonal society of anonymous individuals. Some contemporary Buddhists have appropriated the modern notion of "society" and utilized it in their ethical reflections. For example, Buddhadasa, the Thai monk whom we encountered above, has developed an idea of Buddhist socialism which has emphasized that private gain cannot be at the expense of public benefit. He says that the Buddha's truth

> teaches us to be content with what we have, that is to accumulate and own just enough to take care of our material needs. Accordingly, it places great emphasis on being generous with what we have. A true Buddhist community,

[38]Payutto, *Buddhist Economics*, 68.

even of lay people, would be content with the basic necessities of life. Whatever a person did not really need would be left available for the use of the entire community.

Let me give an example. A person of great wealth (Sanskrit *sresthi*) in the
Buddhist tradition differs greatly from the capitalist of today. Outside of Buddhism, sresthi has the same meaning as [capitalist]—one who keeps accumu-
lating material wealth far beyond what he actually needs. In the Buddhist
tradition, however, the status of sresthi was measured by the number of *rong
than* that person had. A *rong than* was an almshouse, a communal place where
those in need could find what they lacked materially. The more *rang than* one
had, the wealthier one was considered to be.[39]

WHEN WORK DOES NOT WORK:
UNEMPLOYMENT, EXPLOITATION,
AND ALTERNATIVES TO PROPER WORK

Buddhadasa's comments show how public benefit and private gain are thoroughly intertwined. The *sresthi* is judged by others as personally successful by his
generosity to the community. Buddhadasa brings us to the next topic in this
chapter, what happens when work does not work?" by specifying that the actions of the *sresthi* are aimed at assisting those in need. There is a public responsibility when work does not work for some, but with the connection between
private gain and public benefit in mind, we also need to consider what are the
personal costs of unsuccessful work.

Before looking at the personal costs of unsuccessful work, we should briefly
note that exploitation of workers by employers is obviously to be deplored, as
harm done to another because of greed. This reminds us that the social structures and institutions that organize work are often contaminated by greed, and
Buddhist texts frequently admonish employers to treat their workers honorably.
Employers are to assign work according to capability, supply workers with food
and wages, tend to them in sickness, share with them "unusual delicacies," and
give them time for relaxation.[40]

But work does fail all too often in that it does not provide the material resources for the necessities of life. The opportunities for work not working are so
ordinary and so many that Buddhist texts advise that one should prepare for lean
times. One text suggests that an individual should divide his resources into four
parts: one part should be used for immediate necessities and enjoyment, two
parts should be reinvested in work activities, and the fourth part should be set
aside "so there'll be wherewithal in times of need."[41]

For many people, failure in work comes, often through no fault of their own,
but Buddhist texts do not single out the failure of work as being qualitatively dif-

---

[39]Buddhadasa, *Me and Mine,* 172.

[40]D III.191.

[41]D III.188.

ferent from success in work. Instead, a sense of equanimity and detachment, such as one gains from giving away one's possessions, is encouraged as living "the even life":

What is the even life? Here a person, while experiencing both gain and loss in wealth, continues his business serenely, not unduly elated or depressed. He thinks: "Thus my income, after deducting the loss, will stand (at so much) and my outgoings will not exceed my income." Just as one who carries scales, or his apprentice, knows, on holding up the balance, that neither by so much it has dipped down or by so much it has tilted up; even so, a person experiencing both gain and loss continues his business serenely, neither unduly elated nor unduly depressed, but realizes that after allowing for the loss his income will stand at so much and his outgoings not exceed his income.[42]

> Up and alert about his task and toil,
> A careful man, he minds his wealth and lives
> The even life; and he is virtuous,
> Believing, kind and bountiful; he clears
> The onward Way to faring well hereafter.[43]

This passage, while noting the importance of diligence and industry and the association of work with generosity, adds yet another personal characteristic to the style of work to be preferred: equanimity and contentment in the face of success and failure. This equanimity seems to presuppose that one still has the means to provide oneself with the basic necessities of life, but there are times, of course, when individuals are unable to acquire those necessities and must depend on the largesse of others.

Poverty is not a virtuous state in Buddhism, but a state of suffering that leads to further suffering and harm, as we see in the following conversation between the Buddha and some monks:

"Monks, is poverty a woeful thing . . . ?"
"Surely, Lord."
"And when a man is poor, needy, in straits, he gets into debt; and that is woeful too?"
"Surely, Lord."
"And when he gets into debt, he borrows; and is that woeful too?"
"Surely, Lord."
"And when the bill falls due, he pays not and they press him; is that woeful too?"
"Surely, Lord."
"And when pressed, he pays not and they beset him; is that woeful too?"
"Surely, Lord."
And when beset, he pays not and they bind him; is that woeful too?"
"Surely, Lord."

---

[42]E. M Hare, *Gradual Sayings IV,* 189.

[43]Hare, *Gradual Sayings IV,* 191.

"Thus, monks, poverty, debt, borrowing, being pressed, beset and bound are all woes. . . ."[44]

When men and women respond to the suffering of those who are needy through the failure of work, they do so out of sympathy and compassion, very important Buddhist virtues, but such aid is not really an absolute responsibility. Moreover, such acts of charity, while admired, are not thought to produce the same karmic rewards as generosity to accomplished individuals does. A medieval text from Sri Lanka suggests that the reward for giving to the needy is immediate insofar as it can be seen on their faces:

A liberal donor sees some poor person come begging [and then sees him] gleeful because of obtaining his request; what fruit is greater than that? As for the poor person, obtaining his gift and pleased to attain his desire, his face is lustrous as a full-blown lotus and fairer [than before]. The giver, seeing [that fairer face] and obtaining extraordinary comfort, enjoys [it]; this fruit is enough even if there be no [fruit] in the next world.[45]

Clearly, this passage assumes the same intertwining of private gain and public benefit that we saw shaping Buddhist understandings of work in the previous section.

UNCONVENTIONAL WORK: WORKING FOR GOD

Sociologically, Buddhist communities have traditionally been divided between those in lay society and those in the monastic order. In a conventional sense, the world of work is fundamentally an affair of laypeople. As we have already noted, through the surpluses created by their labors, laypeople support monks and nuns and thereby earn merit that creates happy conditions for them in the future. In this final section, in which we will look at monastic life as a form of unconventional work, we will return to a number of the themes that have been taken up already in previous sections, most notably, the connection between greed and work and the manner in which the monastic order replicates the state before greed that once existed among humans and the role that personal characteristics cultivated in work, such as diligence and discipline, play in the spiritual formation of a monk.

Buddhadasa has written that human progress is, in fact, a movement backwards to a state before greed:

The highest form of social service one could perform in these forward-thinking times would be to help people go backwards. In our desire to be progressive and get ahead, we have fallen away from the only real way to

---

[44]E. M. Hare, *Gradual Sayings III*, 249.

[45]Hazlewood, translator, *Saddhammopayana*, 111.

progress. Indeed we have lost our way to such an extent that all of humanity is now in grave danger. To push ahead in the same direction we have been going only invites catastrophe.

If we drive a car off the road into a ditch, we must back up and get onto the road so that we can go on driving. Modern societies are in a similar situation. We have lost the way of the *dhamma* (i.e., the Truth taught by the Buddha about the way things are) or the Way of God, both on an individual level and on a social level. We must back up, collectively and individually, and get ourselves turned in the right direction.[46]

For Buddhadasa, the Buddhist monastic order provides a model for how contemporary people might back up and return to the way of *dhamma*.

The Buddha prescribed the system of monastic discipline (vinaya) for the purpose of binding all persons together into an indissolvable group or aggregation. We know this truth from the word *sangha* itself. Sangha literally means an aggregation or group. It never refers simply to a single individual. When people live as an aggregation or group they need something to hold them together, a principle imbedded in the nature of things which will bind them all together. In the Buddhist community the vinaya embodies such a principle. Above all, it calls for moderation and balance. In particular, monks are enjoined not to take more than they need. To take in excess is to transgress the vinaya. For example, if a monk has more than three robes he commits an ecclesiastical offense. He is to have only one almsbowl, and modest living quarters. Monks are to be content with moderation in all aspects of life. . . .

A monk who consumes or acquires in excess will be overwhelmed by things and will not progress. . . . From another prospective, if each person does not take in excess there will be much left over. That excess will be shared with others, and they will not be in short supply. Excessive hoarding leads to scarcity, and scarcity leads to poverty. Therefore, not to take or consume in excess will lead to the elimination of poverty. Those who take or consume in excess will lead to the elimination of poverty. Those who take more than they need do so driven by greed. Greed, then, is at the heart of scarcity and poverty.[47]

We saw in the first section that greed is also at the heart of work. A further association between greed and work is suggested by a common prohibition of monks engaging in remunerative labor. Men and women enter the Buddhist monastic order "after putting aside the sickle and the flail."[48] Monks and nuns, their material needs met by donations from the laity, do not have to support themselves by working for a living, and work is rejected because it can encourage an attachment to material things—"I earned this, it's mine"—and because work requires involvement in and compromise with the world. Thus, to the

---

[46]Buddhadasa, *Me and Mine*, 167.

[47]Buddhadasa, *Me and Mine*, 197.

[48]M II.180.

degree that work expresses greed, it is something that is excluded from the monastic life.

We have also seen in this chapter that Buddhists have recognized that work inculcates personal characteristics that are highly desirable in any life. There are some kinds of work that, "owing to [their promoting] punctuality, seemly action, industriousness, excellence of energy in rising [early], and freedom from malpractices, are devoid of any such unprofitableness as dilatoriness, unseemly action, inaction, tardy action, and the like"[49] and are useful in the training of a monk. These activities have been adopted as part of a spiritual regime and not as work meant to produce material products. In East Asia, in particular, daily work is part of monastic training, such as preparing, raising, and preparing food and taking care of the necessities of the monastery.

In the following exchange between a new trainee and a head monk in a Japanese Zen monastery, we can see how work is imbedded not in structures of greed, but in structures of spiritual transformation. Notice too how work in this conversation is connected to right awareness or mindfulness in the Noble Eightfold Path and not to Right Livelihood:

> "Buddha," said the head monk, "had to go a long way before he found the final enlightenment. Later he told others about the road he followed so that they would be able to follow him. Buddha talked a lot about right awareness. Do you know what it is?"
>
> I tried to shift my weight, for my legs were already beginning to hurt again. "Look where you are going," I said.
>
> "Yes," the head monk said, "but you can't do that when you are asleep. When you are asleep anything can happen and you won't even know it. The temple may burn down and when you eventually wake up because your sleeping bag is getting burnt, it will be too late. Don't take me literally. The monastic training tries to wake us up, but when it is time to sleep you may sleep. But when you are not asleep, be awake. When you are cleaning vegetables, you really have to clean them. The idea is to throw the good pieces into the pot and the rotten pieces into the tin, not the other way around. Whatever you are doing, do it well, as well as you can, and be aware of what you are doing. Don't try to do two things at the same time, like pissing and cleaning your teeth. I have seen you do that. Perhaps you think you are saving time that way, but the result is no more than a mess in the lavatory and a mess in your mouth."[50]

This discussion shows that, in the largest context, Buddhists place work within a process of spiritual transformation, and its contribution to our transformation is as an antidote to greed.

---

[49]Ñanamoli, translator, *Minor Readings,* 155.

[50]Janwillem van de Wetering, *The Empty Mirror* (New York: St. Martin's Griffin, 1999), 42–43.

COMMENTARIES

Judaism on Buddhism

by JACOB NEUSNER

Buddhism encompasses two ways of thinking about work: an end that masquerades as a means and a way of restraining desire. Since we deal mainly with the classical statements of Judaism on work (and other topics), we miss the diversity that we might find were we to encompass the two thousand years of Judaism from the formative age to the present day. But it would be difficult to find in the authoritative writings of Judaism a view so negative as the one recorded by Professor Hallisey: "work is unable to be a means to anything other than more desire." So implacable a rejection of this world has no counterpart in Judaism. Then the virtues of work—perseverance, discipline—need not balance its negative side.

Where Buddhism and Judaism concur is that possessions that are ill-gotten are not valuable. This is expressed in different ways by Judaism. For example, one cannot perform a religious obligation with a stolen property.

> A stolen or dried-up palm branch is invalid.
> And one deriving from an asherah or an apostate town is invalid.
> A stolen or dried-up myrtle branch is invalid.
> And one deriving from an asherah or an apostate town is invalid.
> A stolen or dried-up willow branch is invalid.
> And one deriving from an asherah or an apostate town is invalid.
>
> Mishnah Sukkah 3:1–3

The context is set by the religious objects used in celebration of the festival of Tabernacles, listed in sequence. If these derive from an act of theft, the person who uses them does not carry out his religious duty. So too if they derive from idolatry ("asherah"), the same rule governs. So too, the sages of the classical age of Judaism concur on the virtue of generosity, though they would maintain, as we recall, that giving away one's possessions for the right purpose—support of disciples of sages in their Torah-study—defines the particulars of the action. In the practical law of Judaism that pertains, I cannot find a counterpart to the Buddhist conception of "a proper ecology of mind." The sages would concur, however, that some professions nurture virtue, others not.

Judaism does not make the case for helping others on the basis of self-interest or private gain. The proper motivation is to carry out God's will. Helping the poor is a critical component of what God wants us to do. But Judaism concurs that giving to those who are worthy of the gifts forms a great virtue, as in the story of how Aqiba sold Tarfon's land to support Torah-students: "He took him and showed him the scribes, Mishnah teachers, and people who were studying Torah, and the Torah that they had acquired." In this regard, Judaism and Buddhism stand together: alms given to worthy persons do not add up to charity in the conventional sense at all.

What we learn in the comparison of Judaism and Buddhism on work is how little the two great traditions intersect. Each pursues its own program, and only occasionally do they talk about the same thing. That makes all the more striking how much they concur when they do.

Christianity on Buddhism
by BRUCE CHILTON

Much as Hinduism appeals to the Catholic, sacrificial character of Christianity, so Buddhism has exerted a profound influence on its more Protestant, analytic side. Particularly, the insight that work can not accomplish the happiness that it seeks is resonant with the skepticism of thinkers during the nineteenth century, such as Henry David Thoreau and Ralph Waldo Emerson, who questioned the values of the Industrial Revolution and the concentration of capital, even as those forces were transforming the economic face of the United States. The problem of greed was certainly not invented during that period, but a genuinely theological critique of the acquisitive nature of capitalism became influential, and persists in a great deal of progressive thinking in the West, whether religious or deliberately nonreligious, to this day.

One of the ironies of the close of the twentieth century was that political critiques of capitalism assumed that religion as such was on the side of capital, and therefore eschewed the kind of theological support that might have made for greater influence. The century opened with the Christian movement called "the Social Gospel" in the mist of the ferment of progressive thinking, but closed with both the "Left" and the "Right" assuming that religion was on the side of the "Right." That distortion was caused both by the influence of Marx on one side and the influence of authoritarian ideas such as Fundamentalism and papal infallibility on the other side.

Forgetfulness seems to be a perennially human condition, as Buddhist sources emphasize. Within the Letter of James, the cause of that is that we see who we are as in a mirror within in God's word, God's law, and then persistently walk away from that mirror into ignorance about our true selves (James 1:23–24). Wisdom showers from the divine heights to us, providing us with an identity we then promptly forget (1:17–18). The means of recovering that identity within Christianity differ from Buddhism's. In James, forgetfulness may only be overcome by activity, not the activity of work per se, but the activity of pursuing the "law of freedom" (1:25). This law is nothing other than Jesus' Levitical principle of loving one's neighbor as oneself, which implies just the care for one's neighbor that the Torah requires in all its particulars (James 2:8-13).

The articulation of this principle in the Letter of James is reminiscent of Nāgārjuna's in *The Precious Garland* in its spiritual pragmatism. The truth that love does no harm as defined by the Torah was familiar to James from the Pauline tradition (Romans 13:8–10). But James then challenges that tradition (if not Paul himself) in the strong admonition not to rest content with being a hearer of the law: actually doing the law is the only remedy against forgetfulness (James 1:25). "So even faith, if it has no deeds, is by itself dead" (James

2:17) stands side by side in the New Testament with Paul's equally vehement assertion that "if you are led by the Spirit you are not under the law" (Galatians 5:18). It is certainly possible to read these principles as antitheses, and that has been common since the Reformation. But in fact each finds its sense in its evaluation of the movements of the Spirit. As the Letter of James later puts the matter, "Because just as the body apart from Spirit is dead, so also faith apart from deeds is dead" (2:26). Deeds of the law of freedom, defined by the commandment to love, amount to a spiritual transcendence of both self and regulation, in acts that mirror the gifts of God. With Buddhism, Christianity seeks for transformation, but it refuses to make greed or even awareness the horizon of its concern, because it sees the power of change outside of humanity, as well as within.

Islam on Buddhism

by TAMARA SONN

Like Buddhists, Muslims see work as an inherent part of life. But in Islam work is not an end in itself. It is a means to a variety of ends and is meritorious or not depending upon one's intentions in performing it. If one's goal is the acquisition of wealth or power, for example, the work is not meritorious. If, on the other hand, one's goal is to contribute to the well-being of one's family and society, the performance of the same tasks is meritorious. Nor is work in Islam the result of greed or a degenerate state of being, as some Buddhists consider it. Therefore, there is neither need for, nor benefit in, efforts to avoid work or to achieve a situation in which work is unnecessary. Thus, neither the acquisition of wealth nor private property is considered problematic in Islam. Some Muslims throughout history have advocated a socialist or even communist economic system in order to establish the just society called for by the Qur'an. However, the mainstream position is that Islam approves of private property and thus the acquisition of wealth under specific circumstances. First, as noted, the purpose for acquiring the wealth must be to support others and, second, the wealth must not be acquired by illegal means or at the expense of others. In this respect, Islam agrees with mainstream Buddhist thought.

Hinduism on Buddhism

by BRIAN K. SMITH

Buddhism and classical Hinduism share common origins in ancient India; both emerged out of the reformational trends stimulated by the appearance of world renunciatory ideologies in the middle centuries of the first millennium B.C.E. Both religions were formulated around the new doctrines of karma and rebirth, and both assume that ethical behavior results in "good karma" while evil activity eventually, but inevitably, brings suffering upon the actor: "Irreligious practices do not yield their fruits right away in this world, like a cow, but, turning back on him little by little, they sever the roots of the perpetrator. . . . A man thrives for a while through irreligion; he sees good fortune because of it and he

conquers enemies because of it; but finally he and his roots are annihilated"
(Manusmrti 4.172, 174).

Both Buddhism and Hinduism have also incorporated another of the principal doctrines of those world renunciatory ideologies: ahimsa, "not hurting" or
"nonviolence." This tenet guides much of Buddhist teachings on proper and improper work. Proper work is, among other things, what does not hurt oneself or
others; improper work is what does. In general, Hinduism agrees. Ahimsa is
listed as one of the "general duties" (together with charity, patience, honesty, and
others) incumbent upon all members of society. But together with such general
ethical precepts, Hinduism has also stressed the specific, particular duties appropriate to members of different castes. "Your own duty done imperfectly is better than another man's done well. It is better to die in one's own duty; another
man's duty is perilous" (Bhagavad Gita 3.35). Thus, morally bad action could
refer not only to harming others but also to doing "another man's duty," or step-
ping outside the boundaries that were set for you by the class and caste in which
you were born. One's "own duty" in fact can supersede one's "general duty";
for some (e.g., members of the warrior classes) that means that violence (ideally
conducted, however, with yogic discipline and without desire) will be both necessary and religiously approved. It is principally the "confusion of classes, by
means of which irreligion, that cuts away the roots, works for the destruction of
everything" (Manusmrti 8.353) that must be avoided in traditional Hinduism.

Buddhism in India (and, of course, outside of it to an even greater degree)
disregarded the caste system and its social and religious imperatives, which accounts for some of the differences in both emphasis and specifics between the
two religions on the question of what constitutes an "honest living." Both have,
however, offered similar alternatives to work in this world of karma, suffering,
and rebirth. The figure of the Buddhist monk is matched in Hinduism by the
world-renouncer; both have left the world of "work" to pursue an "occupation"
that seeks release from the bonds created and perpetuated by desire and action.

SUMMARY

Buddhists place work within a moral economy of appetites and desire and they
see the necessity of work in human life as the result of greed. At the same time,
Buddhists see work as an antidote to greed and a source of human well-being
when it helps us to transform our characters and when it contributes to the well-
being and happiness of others. Thus, work, for Buddhists, has to do with how
we relate to ourselves as imperfect beings, how we relate to other people, and
how we relate to the work around us.

GLOSSARY

Aggañña-sutta   "The Discourse on What Is Primary," an account in Pali, preserved by Theravāda Buddhists, that explains the origins of human social life

bodhisattva   a being who is cultivating the virtues and capabilities necessary to become a Buddha

Buddha   an awakened one who is able to freely aid others because of his true understanding of reality

chanda   [Pali] the acceptable desire for well-being; it is contrasted with tanhā, greed for pleasure

dhamma or dharma   the true nature of the world that was taught by the Buddha. The word dhamma refers to both reality itself and to the Buddha's teaching.

karma   [Sanskrit] a law of moral cause and effect by which good actions produce good results, especially good rebirths and bad actions produce undesirable results

Nāgārjuna   a second century Indian Buddhist philosopher, one of the most influential thinkers in the Buddhist tradition

samsara   [Sanskrit] the cycle of birth and death in which beings are reborn in varying conditions of well-being or torment

sangha   [Pali] the Buddhist monastic order

Soka Gakkai   a new Buddhist lay association which originated in Japan in this century, now found around the world

sresthi   [Sanskrit] a person of great wealth

tanhā   [Pali] the self-destructive greed for pleasure

Vinaya   the code of behavior for Buddhist monks

DISCUSSION QUESTIONS

1. How is it that work creates what Joseph Goldstein called (p. 131), "a proper ecology of mind" in us and what does this state of mind contribute to our well-being?

2. How do Buddhists connect self-interest and public benefit?

3. In what ways are the material rewards of work valued in Buddhist ethics? Why do Buddhists have some ambivalence about these material rewards?

4. What is the relationship between greed and work? What impact does greed have on our relationships with others?

5. Is work part of the Buddhist vision of the ideal human life?

6. Why is equanimity and detachment necessary for successful work?

☌ INFOTRAC

If you would like additional information related to the material discussed here, you can visit our Web site: http://www.wadsworth.com

APPENDIX

Where Do We Find the Authoritative Statements of the Religious Traditions?

When we represent the views of the religions treated here, we rely upon and cite at some length the classical and authoritative sources of those traditions. The writings on which we base our accounts are the ones that the generality of the faithful of the respective traditions acknowledge as authoritative. That is to say, whatever other writings groups of the faithful of those religious traditions may value, the ones on which we draw exercise authority for all of the faithful within the large and diverse religious tradition at hand.

We recognize that many diverse writings and viewpoints are encompassed by each tradition treated here. For all of them trace long histories, played out over vast spaces and many centuries. Surely over time people formed conflicting opinions on the basis of diverse experience. And in today's world, the faithful of Judaism, Christianity, Islam, Buddhism, and Hinduism divide into competing, often conflicting groups. Reform and Orthodox Jews differ on important religious questions, as do Protestant, Catholic, Orthodox, and Mormon Christians, Sunni and Shi'ite Muslims, Theravada and Mahayana Buddhists, and Vaishnava and Shaivite Hindus. Not only so, but individual practitioners of the great religious traditions accept the faith but also pick and choose and form their own ideals in dialogue with the received ones. But all those who practice (a) Judaism refer to the Torah, all who practice (a) Christianity build upon the Bible, all Muslims base themselves on the Qur'an and the Sunna of Prophet Muhammed, all Hindus acknowledge the authority of the Vedas, and all Buddhists see their authoritative texts as "Buddha-speech." So in portraying the Judaic, Christian, Muslim, Hindu, and Buddhist views on the issues we address, we refer specifically to documents or doctrines to which all of the faithful of Judaism, Christianity, Islam, Hinduism, and Buddhism, respectively, will refer and affirm. Whatever writings may find a hearing in the diverse systems of the families of

Judaism, Christianity, Islam, Hinduism, and Buddhism, the sources cited here will enjoy authoritative standing in their respective traditions. That is what we mean when we call them "classical."

JUDAISM

Like Christianity, Judaism begins in the writings of ancient Israel and appeals to the Hebrew Scriptures that the world knows as "the Old Testament" and Judaism calls "the Written Torah." But Judaism appeals also to oral traditions called "the Oral Torah." So, like Christianity, Judaism values additional writings. To state the matter in simple language: the New Testament is to the Old Testament as the Oral Torah is to the Written Torah. What is the meaning of this key word, "Torah"?

The word covers a number of matters. "The Torah" refers first of all to the Pentateuch, the Five Books of Moses, Genesis, Exodus, Leviticus, Numbers, and Deuteronomy. These are inscribed in a scroll, read aloud in synagogue worship, carefully protected as a holy object: "the Torah." So by "the Torah" Judaism means, the object, the holy scroll that sets forth the Pentateuch. But the Torah is comprised, further, by the remainder of the Hebrew Scriptures, the prophets and the writings. The prophets are the books of Joshua, Judges, Samuel, Kings, Isaiah, Jeremiah, and Ezekiel, as well as the twelve smaller collections. The writings encompass Psalms, Proverbs, Chronicles, Job, the Five Scrolls (Lamentations, Esther, Ruth, Song of Songs, a.k.a. Song of Solomon, and Qoheleth, a.k.a. Ecclesiastes). All together, if we take the first letters of the three words—Torah, Nebi'im, and Ketubim—the Torah (Pentateuch), Prophets (Hebrew: Nebi'im), and Writings (Hebrew: Ketubim) yield the Hebrew neologism for the Old Testament, TaNaKH.

But since Judaism, like Christianity, values further traditions as divinely revealed at Sinai, by "the Torah," more writings are encompassed. Specifically, classical Judaism, which took shape in the first seven centuries of the common era (= A.D.), by "the Oral Torah" means traditions revealed by God to Moses at Sinai—oral traditions right along with the Written Torah (Genesis through Deuteronomy). These other traditions were preserved orally, in a process of oral formulation and oral transmission, from Sinai through prophets and elders, masters and disciples, until they were finally reduced to written form in a set of documents that reached closure from ca. 200 to ca. 600 C.E. (= A.D.). All together, these documents are classified as "the Oral Torah," meaning the repositories of the oral tradition of Sinai.

What are the documents that initially comprise "the Oral Torah"? The first and most important of them is the Mishnah, a law code of a deeply philosophical character, closed at 200. The code quickly attracted commentators, who analyzed its contents and clarified and applied its rules. The work of the commentators was put together and written down. It reaches us in two Talmuds, that is, two distinct traditions of explanation of the Mishnah, the Talmud of the Land of Israel, which reached a conclusion at ca. 400 C.E. in what was then Roman-ruled Palestine, and the Talmud of Babylonia, finished at ca. 600 C.E. in Iranian-ruled Babylonia (approximately the area of central Iraq today).

Once the work of explaining the Mishnah got under way, the same approaches to the reading of the received tradition led the Judaic sages to provide the Hebrew Scriptures with compilations setting forth extensive explanation and amplification. This work of rereading Scripture in light of contemporary questions was called "Midrash," from the Hebrew word *darash,* meaning search. In the formative age of the Judaism based on the written and the oral traditions of Sinai, a number of compilations of readings of scriptural books were completed. In particular, books of the Written Torah that are read in synagogue services received systematic exposition. To the book of Genesis was attached Genesis Rabbah (the amplification of Genesis); so too to Leviticus, Leviticus Rabbah; to Exodus came a work amplifying the normative rules of Exodus, called Mekhilta Attributed to R. Ishmael; to Leviticus another legal commentary, Sifra; to Numbers and Deuteronomy legal commentaries called Sifré to Numbers and Sifré to Deuteronomy. Four of the Five Scrolls—Ruth, Esther, Song of Songs, and Lamentations—were systematically reread. In medieval times, other compilations addressed the books of the Written Torah neglected in the formative age.

These are the sources utilized in the account of Judaism's positions on the practical issues addressed in these pages. Most Judaic religious systems we know today—Reform, Orthodox, Conservative, Reconstructionist, New Age, and the like—value other writings in addition, but all share in common the Torah, oral and written, that took shape in ancient times, differing on its authority and its meaning. And, needless to say, other writings, authoritative for one Judaism or another, take up the same topics. But most Judaisms would concur on the pertinence of the sources cited here, even though each Judaic religious system will assign its own weight to the classical sources and will, further, add to the list of authoritative writings further documents of its own choosing. So "Judaism" here is represented by its formative and normative writings.

CHRISTIANITY

The Scriptures of Israel have always been valued within the Church, both in Hebrew and in the Greek translation used in the Mediterranean world. (The Greek rendering is called the "Septuagint," after the seventy translators who were said to have produced it.) Those were the only Scriptures of the Church in its primitive phase, when the New Testament was being composed. In their meetings of prayer and worship, followers of Jesus saw the Scriptures of Israel "fulfilled" by their faith: their conviction was that the same Spirit of God that was active in the prophets was, through Christ, available to them.

The New Testament was produced in primitive communities of Christians to prepare people for baptism, to order worship, to resolve disputes, to encourage faith, and like purposes. As a whole, it is a collective document of primitive Christianity. Its purpose is to call out and order true Israel in response to the triumphant news of Jesus' preaching, activity, death, and resurrection. The New Testament provides the means of accessing the Spirit spoken of in the Scriptures of Israel. Once the New Testament was formed, it was natural to refer to the Scriptures of Israel as the "Old Testament."

The Old Testament is classic for Christians, because it represents the ways in which God's Spirit might be known. At the same time, the New Testament is normative: it sets out how we actually appropriate the Spirit of God, which is also the spirit of Christ. That is why the Bible as a whole is accorded a place of absolute privilege in the Christian tradition: it is the literary source from which we know both how the Spirit of God has been known and how we can appropriate it.

Early Christianity (between the second and the fourth centuries C.E.) designates the period during which the Church founded theology on the basis of the Scriptures. Although Christians were under extreme—sometimes violent— pressure from the Roman Empire, Early Christianity was a time of unique creativity. From thinkers as different from one another as Bishop Irenaeus in France and Origen, the speculative teacher active first in Egypt and then in Palestine, a common Christian philosophy began to emerge. Early Christianity might also be called a "Catholic" phase, in the sense that it was a quest for a "general" or "universal" account of the phase, but that designation may lead to confusion with Roman Catholicism at a later stage, and is avoided here.

After the Roman Empire itself embraced Christianity in the fourth century, the Church was in a position to articulate its understanding of the faith formally by means of common standards. During this period of Orthodox Christianity, correct norms of worship, baptism, creeds, biblical texts, and doctrines were established. From Augustine in the West to Gregory of Nyssa in the East, Christianity for the first and only time in its history approached being truly ecumenical.

The collapse of Rome under the barbarian invasions in the West broke the unity of the Church. Although the East remained wedded to the forms of Orthodoxy (and does so to this day), the West developed its own structure of governance and its own theology, especially after Charlemagne was crowned as emperor of the Romans by Pope Leo III on Christmas day in 800 C.E.

To severe arguments regarding political jurisdiction, East and West added doctrinal divisions. The pope was condemned by a synod in Constantinople in 876 for failing to prevent a change in the wording of the Nicene Creed that had become accepted in the West. A papal legate in 1054 excommunicated the patriarch of Constantinople. But even those acts pale in comparison with what happened in 1204: European Crusaders on their way to Jerusalem sacked and pillaged Constantinople itself.

European Christianity flourished during the Middle Ages, and Scholastic theology was a result of that success. The Scholastics were organized on the basis of educational centers, Thomas Aquinas at the University of Paris during the thirteenth century being the best example. During the periods of Early Christianity and Orthodoxy, theologies as well as forms of discipline of worship were developed for the first time. Scholastic theology was rather in the position of systematizing these developments for the usage of the West. At the same time, Scholastic theologians also rose to the challenge of explaining Christian faith in the terms of the new philosophical movements they came into contact with.

The Reformation, between the sixteenth and the eighteenth centuries, challenged the very idea of a single system of Christianity. Martin Luther imagined that each region might settle on its own form of religion, while in England the settlement was on a national basis and in Jean Calvin's Geneva the elders of the city made that determination. But in all its variety, the Reformation insisted that the Bible and worship should be put into the language of the people, and that their governance should be consistent with their faith.

From the eighteenth century until the present, Christianity in its modern form has been wrestling with the consequences of the rise of rationalism and science. The results have been diverse and surprising. They include Protestant Fundamentalism, a claim that the Bible articulates certain "fundamentals" that govern human existence, and the Roman Catholic idea of papal infallibility, the claim that the pope may speak the truth of the Church without error. In both cases, the attempt is made to establish an axiom of reason that reason itself may not challenge. But modern Christianity also includes a vigorous acceptance of the primacy of individual judgment in the life of communities: examples include the Confessing Church in Germany, which opposed the Third Reich, and the current movement of Liberation Theology in Central and South America.

Today, Christians may use many combinations of the sort of sources named here to articulate their beliefs, and the resulting pattern is likely to be as distinctive as what has been produced in the past.

ISLAM

The absolute foundation of Islam is the Qur'an (which used to be spelled phonetically as "Koran"), Islam's sacred Scripture. The Qur'an is believed to be the literal word of God, revealed through Prophet Muhammad, in the early seventh century C.E. in Arabia. (The Arabic word *qur'an* means "recitation.") Muhammad is called the prophet of Islam, but he is not considered its founder. In fact, he is called the last prophet of Islam, the "seal of the prophets" (Qur'an, Sura [chapter] 33:40). He is believed to be the one chosen by God to deliver the full and final message of God to humanity. Islam's beginnings are believed to be primordial; the Qur'an tells of a sacred trust assumed by humanity that guided their very creation. God created human beings specifically to carry out the divine will of creating a just society. (The Arabic word *islam* means "submission"—to the will of God.) The Qur'an then names a number of prophets, beginning with Adam and including many known to Jews and Christians, though not necessarily as prophets (Noah, Abraham, Moses, and Jesus, for example). It also includes others unknown to the earlier scriptural traditions, such as Shu'aib, Salih, and Hud. All the prophets have brought essentially the same message, although some communities have allowed their scriptures to be corrupted. The scripture revealed through Prophet Muhammad is considered the most complete. It provides the necessary correctives to misinterpretations of earlier messages, and the guidance required for effectively carrying out the will of God on earth.

But the Qur'an is not a law book. Of its 114 verses, only a few deal with specific legislation, such as those prohibiting female infanticide, prostitution, usury, and gambling; those imposing dietary restrictions (the prohibition of alcohol and pork); and those specifying family law on issues such as inheritance, dower, and arbitration in divorce. The majority of the Qur'an's verses deal with theological teachings, such as the oneness of God, and moral themes, establishing general standards for virtue and justice. What is more, they were revealed gradually, over some twenty-two years. Over that period, many of the themes developed, some made more specific, some exemplified by the Prophet's words and example.

Those words and examples, though not part of the Qur'an itself, are considered essential to full understanding of Scripture, since the Qur'an itself said repeatedly that Prophet Muhammad set the best example of how to follow its teachings. Collectively known as the Sunna ("way" or normative practice; also spelled Sunnah) of the Prophet, reports (*ahadith*; sing.: *hadith*) of these examples were originally transmitted orally from one generation to another. But by the second century after the Prophet's death in 632 C.E., scholars began to recognize the need to record these reports. They collected as many individual reports as possible, then carefully screened them for authenticity, organized, and codified them. By the third century after the Prophet (late ninth/early tenth century C.E.), there were six major collections of hadith reports for Sunni Muslims. (Shi'i or Shi'ite Muslims, a minority who differ with the Sunni Muslims on issues of community leadership, compiled other collections of hadith reports, and by the eleventh century C.E. had identified three major books of Sunna.) Two of the Sunni collections (those of ninth-century scholars Muhammad al-Bukhari and Muslim ibn Hajjaj al-Nisabur) were designated by the majority of scholars at the time as most authoritative.

The hadith collections, and especially those of al-Bukhari and Muslim, are the basis of commentaries purporting to amplify the meaning of Qur'anic verses (*tafsir*), and provide essential precedents in Islamic legislation (*fiqh*). Islamic law (collectively known as Shari'a; also spelled Shari'ah) is the basis of Islamic life—personal and collective. There are four major schools of Islamic law for Sunni Muslims, and another for Shi'i Muslims. Other, smaller groups of Muslims rely on other formulations of normative behavior. But all Muslims agree that the sources for knowledge of normative behavior are the Qur'an and the Sunna of the Prophet. They are, therefore, the sources used in the treatment of issues presented in this volume.

HINDUISM

The principal texts of Hinduism in which ethics in general, and the ethics of practical matters such as family life, work, and personal virtue, in particular, are covered are those that deal with *dharma,* meaning "duty" or "law." Some references to this topic already appear in the various texts collectively known as the Vedas (ca. 1200 B.C.E.–400 B.C.E.), especially in the philosophical and mystical treatises known as the Upanishads. The works that concentrate on dharma, however, are the somewhat later Dharmashastras and Dharmasutras, some of which have been collected and translated by Georg Buhler under the title *The Sacred Laws of the Aryas* (reprint ed., Delhi: Motilal Banarsidass, 1975). Among these dharma texts, the most important and comprehensive is the Manusmriti; this work has recently been translated by Wendy Doniger with Brian K. Smith as *The Laws of Manu* (Harmondsworth, Middlesex, England: Penguin Books, 1991). These texts on dharma have been regarded and used by Hindus for many centuries as the authoritative guidelines for personal and social duties of an ethical nature.

References to ethics may also be drawn from texts called the Puranas, encyclopedic and sectarian compilations composed during a long period between 200 C.E. and 1700 C.E. Another source for ethical instruction is two epics of the Hindu tradition, the Mahabharata and the Ramayana, both of them compiled between 300 B.C.E. and 300 C.E. The two epics serve as the foundations for Hindu culture and religion; their characters, stories, and plotlines are familiar to nearly everyone in India and are extremely important popular sources for ethical guidance.

Of especial importance is a text enfolded within the Mahabharata and preserved separately: the Bhagavad Gita. The Gita consists of a dialogue between a warrior named Arjuna and his charioteer, the Lord Krishna. In the course of the work, Krishna instructs Arjuna as to how to best perform his duty, or dharma, especially in circumstances where the right thing to do is not always obvious. The Gita has been translated into English many times, most recently by Barbara Stoler Miller as *The Bhagavad-Gita: Krishna's Counsel in Time of War* (New York, Bantam Books, 1986).

BUDDHISM

Buddhism begins with Gautama, the Awakened One (*buddha*), who lived and taught in India in about the fifth century before the common era; scholars frequently give 563–483 B.C.E. as the dates of his life, but they are not certain. Buddhism spread subsequently to many lands in Asia, from India to Sri Lanka and Southeast Asia, and from India to Central Asia and then to China, Korea, and Japan, always developing and adapting as it spread; more recently, it has been embraced and transformed in Europe and the Americas. In this process, its authoritative ideas, practices, experiences, and values have been multiplied in almost every way imaginable, and the modern historian sees Buddhist authoritative literature as a record of that grand process. The resulting diversity of Buddhist life has been so exuberant that we do well to speak of Buddhism in the plural—Buddhist traditions—for this helps us to remember that the basic premise of this series applies to Buddhism alone; the point can be made by altering just slightly the statement made by Jacob Neusner in the preface, "even where [different parts of a religion] appear to resemble one another, they turn out to be different" and thus we have to be careful against being misled by failing to recognize that "what looks alike . . . may upon closer examination prove quite different, and difference may well obscure the meaning of points of concurrence."

When approached with the yardstick of the relatively simple canons of authoritative literature in Islam, Judaism, and Christianity, Buddhists may appear to
accept an extraordinarily wide variety of texts as containing authoritative statements. All Buddhists do not accept the same texts, however, and there is no single canon on which all Buddhist religious systems build. In fact, there are very
few individual texts that can be found in every Buddhist tradition, not even those
statements that a modern historian would take as the record of the teaching of
Gautama Buddha, the founder of Buddhism. Moreover, the size of individual
canons accepted by particular traditions—whether these are defined on sectarian grounds (for example, Zen Buddhism) or cultural grounds (for example, Ti-
betan Buddhism)—can be huge in their own right, and we might think of them
more as a library than as a "canon" or "scripture." The Chinese Buddhist canon,
to take one impressive example, is almost one hundred thousand pages long. It
goes without saying that the contents of these many texts are varied, and frequently contradictory.

To give an account of the literature that has been authoritative for Buddhists
would be to give an account only of difference, and this would obscure some
important points of concurrence among Buddhists. We still need to generalize
about *Buddhism* out of the study of many *Buddhisms*. One generalization we
should keep in mind is that Buddhists have not seen their own history as simply
as the modern historian portrays it. Even as all Buddhists have acknowledged the
importance of Gautama Buddha, in their honor and devotion to him especially,
no Buddhists have seen the Truth that he taught as beginning with him as an individual. He taught Truth, to be sure, but he only rediscovered it. Truth has
been known and taught by others too. Consequently, the record of Gautama's
teachings is not the only place where one should expect statements of Truth.
There have been other awakened persons, other Buddhas, and there will be
more in the future; indeed, Truth is directly available to us now.

This observation is key for understanding where the contemporary Buddhist
and the academic student of religion both can look for authoritative statements
on the topics addressed by this series. We turn to *buddhavacana*—"Buddha-
speech"—but it is important to remember that this does not name the record of
the teachings of Gautama Buddha, nor was it ever only that in the eyes of Buddhists. The basic point we should keep in mind is best expressed in an old Buddhist aphorism: "what Buddha taught is well-said," but it is equally true to say
that "what is well-said Buddha taught."

Buddha-speech comes in a number of genres, some concerned with monastic life, others with philosophy, but for the purposes of this series the most important genre will be *sutra*. This is a generic name given to an account of an
occasion on which a Buddha taught. Most *sutras* are attributed to Gautama
Buddha, although a modern historian would be skeptical about any claims that
the *historical* Gautama Buddha actually taught some of the most influential ones,
such as the *Lotus Sutra* (Saddharmapundarika) and the *Sutra on the Land of Bliss*
(Sukhavativyuha), to name two texts that have been very important in East
Asian Buddhism.

Another generalization about Buddha-speech draws our attention to another
source of authoritative statements. Buddha-speech contains two kinds of sentences:

some that have obvious meanings that do not require interpretation or elaboration in order to be understood, and others, that do require their meaning "to be drawn out." The latter kind of sentence thus requires commentary for proper understanding, and the commentaries by learned or spiritually accomplished teachers on Buddha-speech are as authoritative as sources of valid and useful knowledge as Buddha-speech itself. Buddhist sectarian differences can stem from disagreements over what counts as Buddha-speech as well as from disagreements over how to understand a text or statement about which there is concurrence that it is Buddha-speech. In this series, we will turn then both to Buddha-speech and to commentaries to find authoritative statements that address the practical issues of everyday life taken up by each volume.